The Practical Handbook of

COMPUTERIZATION FOR DISTRIBUTION MANAGERS

First Edition

The Practical Handbook of

COMPUTERIZATION FOR DISTRIBUTION MANAGERS

Colin Barrett

Published by THE TRAFFIC SERVICE CORPORATION

Washington • New York • Chicago • Westport

Boston • Atlanta • Palo Alto

Actually, a good deal of what's included in the book never appeared in the magazine. I've added a lot of new material, written especially for this book. And I've also felt free to make editorial changes in the column material, both to reflect afterthoughts I may have had after the original was published and to correct errors or misleading comments I may have made.

Nor is everything printed in the magazine included here. Some of it dealt with particular events that, being now years in the past, are no longer of importance; in other cases time and technology have made what I wrote then obsolete for today.

In particular, I've excluded all reviews I wrote about particular transportation/distribution software packages; these necessarily reflect the programs only as they existed at the time when I wrote about them, and it would be unfair to the developers—who in many cases have subsequently made major changes in their programs—to republish them in more permanent form.

So that's what this book is all about. I hope you like it. If you do, I'll be happy to take the credit; after all, I wrote it.

If you don't—blame Dick; the whole thing was his idea.

A NOTE TO THE READER

"Begin at the beginning," the King of Hearts advises the White Rabbit in Lewis Carroll's classic, *Alice in Wonderland,* "and go on till you come to the end; then stop."

Perfectly sound (if humdrum) advice in reading a book as well as telling a story, I suppose; it's the way most books get read. But you may get more out of *this* one, especially if you don't know anything much about computers, if instead you read the last part first. Specifically, I suggest that you look over the appendices that discuss various aspects of the "nuts and bolts" of computers and computerization, in order to better be able to understand the real body of the book.

I don't pretend the appendices will offer you more than the most superficial grounding in some of the basic concepts and technology of computers. There are plenty of books that will do a lot more than that for you; but most of them are also very long and, unless you have an avid interest (or "need to know") in the field, very boring.

It's my view that you don't need more than a once-over-lightly about the technical side of computers to make effective use of them; and that's what the appendices are aimed at providing. So if you start there, instead of on page 1, you may be able to glean a better understanding of what I'm writing about in connection with computer applications in the transportation/physical distribution industry.

Because that's the whole point of this book. It isn't just another computer book; there are plenty of those already about, and they're written by people with a lot more expertise about computers than I. Rather, it's a book about transportation and distribution with a focus on how computers can help managers (and others in the industry) to do their jobs better.

I hope you find it of value; and the appendices may help you in that. And just so you don't have any qualms about peeking at the last pages first, I'll tell you in advance how it comes out: The butler didn't, in this case, do it; the programmer did.

DEDICATION

This one's for all those who've faithfully read my *Traffic World* computer column, and listened to me talk about computers, in gratitude for their patience with my admitted non-expertise.
And for Alexandra.

Table of Contents

Part 1: The Computer and the Transportation/Distribution Manager 1

1. The Computer as a Management Tool 3
What Computers Do Well 4

2. Computers as Information Providers 17
The Value of the Tool 18
Assembling Decisional "Parts" 19
Information and Transportation 20

3. The Computer and Time Management 23
"On the Road" 23
In the Office 25
"Undoable" Work 27
The Computer as a Time Manager 29

4. Distribution Modeling Techniques 31

5. Transportation Cost-Finding and the Computer 37
ICC Standards 38
Complexity of ICC Form Costing 39
Limitations of Costing Software 40

6. Computerization of Transportation Rates —A Viewpoint 45
The Tool Shapes the Handiwork 45
ZIP Rates & Co. 46
The Drawbacks 48
Consequences, and Alternatives 49
And Another Viewpoint 51

Part 2: The Computer and the Transportation User 57

7. The Manager and the Technician 59
Technicians and Managers 59
How the Computer Fits In 61
The Technician's Tool 62
The Manager's Need 64

8. Demands on the Computer User 67
Disillusionment at Home. 67
. . . and Sometimes in the Office 69
Whither the "Revolution"? 69
The Need for Skill 71
Learning How It Works 72
Of Power and Complexity 73
The Meaning of "User-Friendliness" 74
The Point of Diminishing Returns 76
The Consequences of Complexity 77

9. You Don't Have to Be a Programmer. 81
The Mystique of Expertise 81
Computerization Without Fear 83
A Better Way 84

10. Be Your Own Computer Expert 85
Expertise v. Results 86
Who's the "Expert"? 86
Some Simple Criteria 87
The Tale of the Artist's Pig 89

11. Keyboardphobia 91
The Roots of Keyboardphobia 91
The Dictates of Technology 93
The Limitations of Keyboard Alternatives 94
Some Keyboarding Aids 96
The Dvorak Keyboard 97

Part 3: The Computer in the Organizational Structure 99

12. Justifying Computerization to Higher Management 101
Why Computerize? 102
Approaches to Cost-Justification 103
Obstacles to Cost-Justification 104

13. "Selling" Computerization to Higher Management 107
Problems With a Demonstration 107
Doing It Right 110

14. MIS-Management and Mis-Management 113
A Tower of Babel 114
Microcomputers and Colinos 115
The Limits of MIS 116
Eliminating the Middleman 118

Part 4: The Start-Up Process 121

15. The Problems of Starting Up 123
The Computer Arrives 124
Mastering Your System 125
Data Input 127
Some Ideas for Easing the Transition 128
A Personal Lesson 131
A Semantic Misunderstanding 133

Part 5: Computer Security 135

16. The Failings of Security 137
The Fallacy of Passwording 137
A History of Break-Ins 139
Improving Security 140

17. Computers and Foreign Travel 145

Part 6: Computer Software in General 147

18. A Guide to Programming "Languages" 149

19. Word Processing **153**
Neatness Counts. 153
A Key Office Tool 155
What Word Processor? 158
Important Features 159
A Curious Addendum 161

20. Spreadsheets **163**

21. Data-Base Managers **169**

22. Free Software—How to Get It and Use It **175**

Part 7: Specialized-Applications Software **181**

23. Some Rules for Buying Software **183**

24. Shopping for Software—A Personal Approach **199**

25. The Meaning of "User-Friendliness" **203**
A "Do-able" Job 204
Screen Displays 204
Inputs and Errors 207
Other Features 209
How Feasible? 210

26. User Manuals and Their Problems **213**

27. Aftermarket Support for Software **215**

28. Things to Watch Out for With Software **219**
Operating Speed (or Lack Thereof) 219
Displays 220
Coded Input/Output 221
User Manuals 222
Confusing Commands 223
"Vaporware" 224

Part 8: Software Copying 227

29. About Piracy 229
What's Legal. 229
. . . and What's Not 230
An Easy Crime 232

30. The Importance of Backups 235
A Personal Story 236
The Lost Chapter 236
"UNERASE" & Co. 238
Learning From Experience 239
Care About Backups 240

Part 9: Some Lessons From Experience 243

31. Using a RAM Disk 245
Why a RAM Disk? 246
Eliminating the Mechanics 247
How to Use the RAM Disk 248
Getting a RAM Disk 250
Some Cautions 251

32. "Bugs" 253

33. Monochrome Screens and Their One Color 255

34. Modems and Telephone Lines 257

35. Planning for System Upgrades 259
The Un-Adaptability of Software 259
New Hardware Developments 261
Minimizing the Burden of Upgrading 263

Glossary 267

Appendix A: How Computers Work (and Other Details) .. 289

Appendix B: "Ports" and "Peripherals" 296
Appendix C: A Primer on Binary Math 299
Appendix D: Hex Codes—An Explanation 300
Appendix E: All About ASCII 302
Appendix F: Open and Closed 304
Appendix G: Computers and Numbers and Errors 309
Appendix H: EDI 311
Index 313

Part 1

THE COMPUTER AND THE TRANSPORTATION/DISTRIBUTION MANAGER

1

THE COMPUTER AS A MANAGEMENT TOOL

What can a computer do for you?

Provided you're not fussy about the time, effort or cost involved, just about anything you want it to do, up to and including (with the aid of robot-like servomechanisms) putting out the cat at night.

If, however, you *do* care about how much time, effort and money you invest (and what good business manager doesn't?), the list of *practical* applications narrows considerably. The machine can still do a great many tasks, but regarded in this light it's scarcely a panacea for every managerial problem. The day when those cartoon images of computers instead of people occupying managerial desks becomes a reality is still far into the future (if indeed it will ever arrive).

The computer's proper role (for the moment at least) is as a managerial tool, an aid to help the manager better do his job. And as with any other tool, the manager must be prepared to use it intelligently for tasks that will benefit him and/or his organization—not to apply it blindly to every activity in sight merely because it's "high-tech."

There are countless horror stories being told of companies whose profits plummeted, who even went completely under, because of ill-judged computerization. The computer performed as it was told; but it was given faulty instructions, or fed inadequate or incorrect data—or, not at all infrequently, simply proved less efficient and/or cost-effective than the "old-fashioned" manual system it replaced because it was assigned to the wrong job.

I don't mean to sound like Cassandra predicting gloom and ruin all around me (especially in a book dedicated to the pros, not the cons, of computerization); but I feel it's appropriate to start off this discussion of what computers can do with a big *don't*: Don't try to use computers to handle things that are going pretty much to your satisfaction now. You wouldn't apply your new hammer to a nail that's already been sunk home, even if you'd banged it in with the butt of a soft-drink bottle. By the same token, don't set your computer to doing jobs that are being done just fine right now.

As with everything else, if it ain't broke, don't fix it.

That should still leave you quite a range of potential computer applications—jobs that aren't being done efficiently or cost-effectively, jobs that threaten to outgrow (or already have outgrown) the present system of doing them, jobs that need to be done but aren't *being* done now because of the lack of available resources, and so on. It's to the problem areas (and every manager has them) that the computer should be dedicated—either to solve problems directly, or to free resources now consumed elsewhere to deal with them.

What Computers Do Well

Before getting into some of the specific transportation- and distribution-related functions computers can handle, let's take a glance at the general character of things computers can probably handle better than anything (or anybody) else:

- Its memory sets the proverbial elephant's in the shade. You need tell it something only once, and it will remember so long as its electricity keeps flowing (unless, that is, you tell it to forget, in which case it will do so quicker and more thoroughly than a drunk on a bender).
- It can perform repetitive tasks tirelessly and endlessly. Terms like boredom and fatigue, the twin enemies of human efficiency at

such tasks, are simply not in the computer's lexicon. Set it to work and it will keep going as long as you like, the last iteration no less speedy and accurate than the first.

- It can flawlessly handle any mathematical operation you set it to doing, giving you correct answers with incredible speed and total accuracy. Indeed, everything a computer does, it does by "number-crunching"; even familiar word-processing and other "verbal" applications are handled by translating everything into numbers and manipulating those numbers.

And it does all these things as fast as the electronic pulses that control it can scurry along its circuitry—which is to say, at right around the speed of light itself.

What the computer can*not* do is exercise judgment. It does what it's instructed to do, neither more nor less. If its instructions are wrong or incomplete, it nevertheless follows them slavishly, no matter how obvious the error may seem to human intelligence. This is the characteristic that leads to those maddening situations that are so much a part of the popular mythology of computers: chronically incorrect accounts, duns for balance-due bills of $0.00, etc., etc.

With these capabilities and limitations in mind, let's take a look at some of the computer applications of interest and value too transportation/distribution managers, as represented by available "state-of-the-art" software:

Accounting: One of the most commonplace uses of computers, in almost any business sector, is in bookkeeping. Software exists to handle receivables, payables, auditing and numerous other specific functions, some of it designed expressly for freight bills (from both the carrier's and the shipper's perspective).

Not only will such software keep your records for you, but it can also handle such ancillary tasks as cutting bills and checks, preparing them for mailing, or even electronically transmitting and/or receiving billing and payment information and authorization. (The Interstate Commerce Commission has already given its formal blessing to "paperless" billing, and the banking industry has developed electronically driven funds-transfer systems. As of this writing relatively few shippers and carriers participate in such systems, but their potential for reduction of administrative costs is evident.)

But *beware!* When you give a computer direct access to your treasury your security precautions should be as high as you maintain in safeguarding your actual cash, checks, etc. The computer itself won't, of course, steal or embezzle your money on its own initiative (what would it buy with the ill-gotten gains?), but it can be programmed to do so by larcenous individuals; and it can also make inadvertent mistakes due to programming or data-input errors.

Recent innovations in accounting-oriented programs aimed at transportation/distribution applications have combined them with rate storage/retrieval software *(see below)* in order to perform a freight-bill auditing operation. At their simplest level, such programs simply check for duplicate payments and review such arithmetic portions of the bill as rate extensions, etc. More complex programs, however, will also compare billed rates with those set forth in carrier tariffs, rate circulars, contracts, etc.

Rate storage and retrieval: In essence, such software reduces your tariff library to electronic coding and lets you access it selectively and more or less instantaneously. No more need to take the document down from the shelf and thumb through its pages; just punch in the key parameters (origin, destination, shipment weight, commodity identification, etc.), and the applicable rate or rates pop right up on your display screen or your printer.

Again, there are a number of ancillary functions the computer can also be programmed to perform in this connection. For carriers, such software can prepare tariffs; I have programming that does much of this work for those of my consulting clients for whom I file tariffs, and many rate bureaus and professional tariff publishing agents have gone further than I down this path. The ICC has even established standards by which carriers may file tariffs with it electronically, rather than on paper (although, ironically, budget constraints have thus far prevented the Commission from getting computer equipment capable of accepting such electronic filings, making it impossible to actually use these procedures).

From the shipper's perspective, the big advantage of rate computerization is the computer's potential to do the traffic manager's "shopping" automatically. Many rate storage/retrieval programs have the capability of automatically digging out *all* rates applicable to a given shipment, rating the shipment, then comparing the aggregate charges and displaying them selectively on a least-cost basis. They can even accommodate the increasingly varied rate structures carriers are publishing—commodity rates, class rates, discounts, mileage rates, etc.—and can deal, where applicable, with routing restrictions on any rates.

The drawback of this type of software is the massive amount of keypunching required to develop and maintain the computer files. A typical tariff page may contain literally scores of rates; and even the smallest working tariff library contains a *lot* of such pages, which are constantly being changed and/or replaced. A few years ago I estimated* that there are perhaps a trillion different rates maintained by railroads alone (that's a "1" followed by more zeroes than you care to count), and likely several times that many by motor carriers; and even these numbers are probably way low for today's deregulated, competitive transportation marketplace.

Some carriers and rate bureaus have sought to resolve this problem for their shippers by making rate information available in electronic form—either on disks that are distributed (free or at quite low cost) to shippers, or by means of electronic "on-line" services directly accessible by computer. By and large, however, there is little standardization of either data format or access

---

* *Paying the Freight Bill—A Management Approach,* by J. S. Traunig and Colin Barrett. Reston, VA: Colin Barrett, Transportation Consultant, 1979.

programming, so that each carrier's/bureau's rates must be accessed separately using different software, command sequences, etc.—at best a cumbersome problem.

Several commercial on-line providers maintain extensive electronic tariff libraries of multiple carriers, including, at the request of subscribers, "private" libraries of the tariff and/or contract rates negotiated by individual shippers. Again, this serves to eliminate the extensive keypunching that must be done by each user, and allows some spreading of the cost of that activity across the spectrum of the service's customer base. Even so, however, such services tend to be expensive enough that they are uneconomical to use for any but organizations with relatively large volumes of traffic. In addition, even the largest such data base can encompass only a tiny fraction of the total universe of transportation rates and charges, meaning that reliance on them sharply limits the shipper's range of choice.

Realistically, the problem of maintaining broad-based electronic tariff libraries probably can't be resolved until the basis of transportation ratemaking itself changes. Some carriers are already seeking to publish at least some rates in "algorithmic" form ("algorithm" is computerese for a mathematical equation). This avoids the difficulties involved in storing and retrieving large numbers of individual rates; rather, freight charges are calculated mathematically based on shipment parameters. As of this writing, however, algorithmic ratemaking had not proved very popular because of the difficulty of fine-tuning such rates to competitive marketplace conditions.

Ultimately, further technological advances may do much to ease the keypunch and data-base management difficulties of maintaining electronic tariff libraries. Some optical scanners are already capable of translating printed images into usable electronic data, and the technology in this area is receiving considerable attention. And the steadily increasing power of computer processors, coupled with improving techniques in software design, is making "real-time" applications feasible with ever-larger volumes of data.

Carrier costing: A variety of off-the-shelf software packages allow carriers to perform detailed costing of individual operations based on historic cost experience.

The earliest such programs relied on standardized costing approaches such as those of the ICC's Highway Form B, Rail Form A and the Uniform Rail Costing System (URCS). There are still a number of packages available that use these approaches; for rail operations they are still the only "generic" packages available (although individual railroads tend to have their own proprietary computerized costing systems).

For other modes, however, there are a number of programs that deviate from ICC-prescribed costing standards in an effort to put costing on a more real-world basis (the ICC standards, designed primarily to implement rate regulation, are in the eyes of many cost experts both outdated and inappropriate for operational use). These programs employ various cost-allocation formulae, which in many cases can be altered to at least some degree if the user wishes.

Cost information is obviously crucial to carriers' ratemaking and/or contracting decisions. But shippers, too, can often benefit from the availability of such information to support negotiations with carriers and/or regulatory rate litigation (cost data is, for example, the key element in market-dominance rail rate complaints under provisions of the Staggers Rail Act).

At the same time, as should be evident, no costing program can be better than the raw data fed into it ("garbage in, garbage out"). If you plan on using a computer for costing purposes, a great deal of attention must be dedicated to ensuring that the input accurately reflects, in as much detail as the program demands, the real-world costs being encountered; otherwise the results, although mathematically correct, will have little bearing on operational experience.

Industrial site location: Transportation and distribution factors obviously play important roles in a company's decision where it will locate a new factory, distribution center, warehouse, terminal, etc. But the process of evaluating those factors is far from simple, entailing weighted analyses of many disparate factors concerning traffic routings, lanes, commodities, shipment weights, etc.—making it ideally suited to the computer's power.

Necessarily, software that offers site-location assistance is input-heavy, requiring extensive research and keypunching of the results of that research. In light of the magnitude of corporate resources at stake in this kind of decision, however, and the time and effort that must in any event go into the making of the decision, this should not be regarded as a significant drawback, especially considering the computer's superior ability (over that of any manual approach) to weigh multiple factors.

A good software package of this type will also allow for the numerous *non*-transportation/distribution elements that must be considered in this kind of decision-making; it will also take into account the costs of real estate, construction, labor, local taxation and so forth. The programs allow comparison of different preselected locations, and some of the more sophisticated ones will even help determine the optimum geographic location based on specified (principally transportation-related) criteria.

Site-location programming is but one example of a generic breed of what is known as "analytical modeling" software. In essence, such programs help give management a blueprint of the consequences, pro and con, of particular decisions as the decision-making process goes along. A well-designed analytical model will in essence allow the manager to "try out" alternative decisions and measure them against one another.

There are, of course, many uses for such models; but one of the most critical (because of the scope of the commitment involved and the difficulty of shifting the decision once it's been made) is in the area of site location. I recall a time years ago when the organization I was then working for was planning to close one of its distribution centers and transfer that facility's inventory and its service area to another. My office was asked to conduct a full-scale review of the organization's distribution network, and we designed a computer program to help us in that endeavor. Our researches revealed that (a) the facility that was to have been closed was in fact the lowest-cost, most efficient one in the entire network, and (b) the facility to which the inventory and service area were to have been transferred was the *highest*-cost, *least* efficient of all the centers. Not surprisingly, the decision to make that change was hastily reconsidered in light of our findings.

Order processing and inventory management: Shippers can take advantage of software designed to process incoming orders and keep track of product inventory—or, at the other end of the production line, to track inventories of raw materials and determine reorder cycles.

This is especially valuable in implementing Japanese-style "kanban" (also known as "just-in-time") inventory maintenance policies, increasingly popular in today's business community. The drawback of such policies is that they expose the organization to significant risk in the event of even a relatively small-scale breakdown—inventory failures that can lead to lost orders, shutdown of production lines, etc. Computerizing the activity can, by eliminating much of the error-prone human element, significant reduce the likelihood of such failures.

Some of the more sophisticated packages in this area combine the order processing and/or inventory management functions with product storage detail, identifying the precise location (in a warehouse or other storage facility) of on-hand stocks. This can greatly simplify the put-away and order-picking activities within storage facilities.

Once again, heavy volumes of keypunch input will be required to drive such a program. In this case, however, the input process merely substitutes for the manual record-keeping that would otherwise be required, and in fact usually entails less clerical work than maintaining non-computerized records. In addition, new-technology aids such as light-wand devices to read product bar coding can also facilitate the periodic physical-inventory checks that must be conducted in any storage operation, making it both faster and more accurate.

Where product inventory is involved, such programs are often integrated with software packages to handle the routing, scheduling, rating, documentation, etc., of outbound shipments, as well as such activities as customer invoicing. For incoming raw-materials inventory, invoicing and payment subroutines can also be added.

Dispatching, routing and shipment consolidation: Software that optimizes the efficiency of motor carrier operations is available from a number of developers. Variants on the same theme enhance the capability of shippers to select shipment routings and/or accomplish cost-effective consolidation of small shipments.

At its most straightforward level, such software consists mostly of massive data bases in which, in essence, highway maps have been encoded in digital form. Some of these data bases are concerned with intercity operations, providing optimal routings between pairs of points (via, if needed, additional stop-off points)—or, alternatively, offering point-to-point routes and mileages based on the Household Goods Mileage Guide. Others are specific to individual locales, such as the metropolitan areas of large cities, and offer street-by-street modeling.

More sophisticated programs take such data bases (or algorithm-based approximations) and then provide routing/scheduling guidance based on user-defined service and cost objectives. For example, a carrier might input the weights and destinations of a group of small shipments for "peddle-run" delivery, and have the computer determine the most efficient sequence of stops. Likewise, the computer might accept details of a shipper's outbound traffic and advise where consolidation would reduce costs.

The efficacy of such programming depends in large part on the user's input, in which he describes the parameters for the dispatching, routing or consolidation function. This is a tedious and time-consuming process, requiring both extensive knowledge of traffic patterns and the exercise of sound managerial judgment in specifying the criteria the computer will employ; but if it's properly done, the software can often generate substantial benefits in terms of both economic and operating efficiency, especially where complex structures are involved.

This is an archtypal use of the computer's ability to remember and manipulate large volumes of information far better than can even the brightest and most adept of humans. An experienced dispatcher is accustomed to dealing with such questions, and usually does so with a skill that's astonishing to the uninitiated; but the computer's performance leaves even the dispatcher himself likewise agog at its ability to make optimum choices.

Equipment management: A number of vendors offer software that automatically schedules, and keeps records of, maintenance for carrier operating equipment. Maintenance schedules can either be standardized according to manufacturers' specifications, industry norms, etc., or can be customized to a particular carrier's desires.

For motor carriers, software is also available to handle the various use-tax activities, including in particular fuel tax recordkeeping and reporting. Software in this category can also set up depreciation schedules, devise equipment procurement criteria (based on operating parameters dictated by the user), handle licensing activities (including automatic preparation of paperwork), and so forth. And unit costing information—a key in determining when to replace older operating equipment—can also be generated by this type of programming.

Obviously, this type of program is more valuable for the carrier with a large operating fleet than the one with a small fleet. There's no clear rule of thumb based on fleet size; some firms can efficiently handle these functions manually for even fleets of several hundred units, while others struggle with just a few vehicles. The prospective user should base his decision mainly on a straightforward cost/benefit analysis, based on a comparison of the cost of doing the job manually vs. that of buying and using the computer system.

Documentation: Transportation is an extraordinarily paper-heavy industry. Each individual shipment must be documented by a bill of lading or the equivalent; each normally requires a separate freight bill. Then there are delivery receipts, cargo manifests, claims, waybills, tracing forms and countless other pieces of paper intended to document some portion of the transportation process and/or the shipper-carrier relationship.

Virtually all of these documents consist basically of forms

that are simply completed with specific information being repetitively inserted in the appropriate blanks—the kind of task at which the computer excels. And programming is available—some of it "stand-alone," more in conjunction with various other computerized activities such as rate-finding, routing, etc.—to handle all aspects of transportation documentation.

The obvious advantage of filling out these forms by computer, rather than manually, is the potential to retain the data for other purposes. It takes as much time to prepare, say, a bill of lading by hand as it does with the aid of a computer; but the hand-preparation is, by its nature, a one-time use of the data. If the form is prepared by computer, the data can at the same time be electronically retained for reporting purposes, use in other documents, etc., with no need for further human intervention.

In addition, computerization of required documents leads to the attractive possibility that such data can be electronically transmitted, dispensing with the physical paperwork altogether. The quest for paperless transactions, much discussed in the news media, has proved unexpectedly slow in materializing; although the technology is now in place for electronic interchange of information on quite a wide scale, managerial resistance to dispensing with the familiar paperwork has severely retarded progress. Nevertheless, some companies are already handling some types of transactions electronically, with little or no "hard-copy" (paper) exchange, and as computerization becomes more widespread it's almost certain that this trend will grow.

Other applications: The foregoing doesn't pretend to be a complete or comprehensive listing of the many ways in which computers can assist in the transportation/distribution managment process. I've just tried to explore a few of the more obvious, and more commonplace, ways in which computers can be, and are now being, used in this industry.

But it will be an unusual manager who, with diligent investigation, can't find additional and perhaps even more beneficial uses for computers in his own particular circumstances, to meet his own particular needs and those of his organization. There are countless areas in which an eidetic memory, the ability to deal with large masses of information without becoming overwhelmed, and a nonpareil mathematical capacity can prove useful—and these are the areas the manager should look at in considering possible uses for computers in his operation.

2

COMPUTERS AS INFORMATION PROVIDERS

A question from one individual, and a comment from another, set me off on a train of thought that I think warrants exploring.

The question was, "Can you tell me about how many companies are using microcomputers in their operations [carriers] or traffic departments [shippers]?"

I couldn't answer with precise numbers or percentages, and frankly doubt that anyone can; the transportation community is simply too vast and diversified to allow for the accumulation of the needed data. And because of the pace at which the business community is bringing microcomputers "on line," even if you dedicated the formidable resources to do a comprehensive (or even adequately representative) survey, it would take so long to complete that your first-collected data would no longer be reliable by the time you got to the end.

I can, however, say one thing pretty categorically in answer to that question: I expect there's a good deal less microcomputer usage in transportation than there would be if too many people didn't share the view of the second individual I mentioned, that "a computer won't let you do anything new or different; it just helps you work faster." It's understandable that a lot of folks believe this, especially given the unfocused marketing efforts of most hardware and software manufacturers; but it's simply not true.

The Value of the Tool

There's no realistic question that the computer is not an alternative to good management. It completely lacks judgment (except for any judgmental factors you might program into it) to make sound managerial decisions, and is useful only as a tool to help you, the manager, in the decision-making process.

At the same time, however, the root of any good managerial structure is the decision-making apparatus. Most often this will consist of just one individual at whose desk—though he may be surrounded by advisers and staff, and accountable to stockholders, boards of directors, bosses, etc.—the figurative buck stops. Occasionally, despite the well-known inefficiency of committee decision-making ("a camel is a horse designed by. . ."), it will be a group of several individuals who reach decisions collectively; but whether it's one person or many, the center of the decisional nexus will always be *human;* a computer, no more than a chimpanzee, cannot fill this role.

All roots depend, however, on the fertility of the soil in which they grow; and the nurturing loam in which decision-making is implanted is information. Of course, there do exist so-called managers who make their decisions more on whim and guesswork than hard data ("I have my opinion, don't bother me with facts"); but in general, the better the informational base the better the resulting decision.

And this is where the computer shines—at assembling, organizing, analyzing and, above all, *remembering* factual information. No human being, not even the *idiots savants* who occasionally win renown as freak "human calculators," can possibly match a modern microcomputer in these areas; the machine reigns supreme and unchallenged here.

By thus making available a depth and range of information hitherto unavailable, the computer opens up an entirely new realm of decisional opportunities to the manager. No longer need he hypothesize as to what may or may not be so; now he can *know,* and act accordingly.

Assembling Decisional 'Parts'

As students of the Renaissance Era know, Leonardo da Vinci designed a working helicopter in the 14th century. That is, it *would* have worked. But Leonardo's helicopter couldn't be built in his time because the parts for it couldn't be built; the underlying technology—of energy generation, metallurgy, precision machining, etc.—did not exist. It took more than five centuries for technological development to reach a level such that this 14th-century design could be translated into a working machine, which then took its place in the world as something new and altogether different from what had gone before.

Similarly, it has certainly been possible in the past for business managers to *envision* what they might be doing if they had adequate information. ("If we had some ham, we could have some ham and eggs, if we had some eggs.") But until the information technology was in place, they could no more do those things than Leonardo could produce a helicopter because they, too, lacked the "parts" required to translate their dreams into reality. It's the computer that has bridged this gap.

The importance of information in almost every area of human endeavor cannot be overstated. The late Arthur Hays Sulzberger, long-time publisher of the *New York Times,* noted: "A man's judgment cannot be better that the information on which he has based it. Give him the truth and he may still go wrong; but give him no news, or present him only with distorted and incomplete data, . . . and you destroy his whole reasoning processes and make him something less than a man."

Ask any group of historians what was the single most important invention of the past thousand years and you'll quickly get a consensus on movable type and the printing press. By making the written word, and the information it conveyed, accessible to all, this one invention gave rise to the Reformation; the political and nationalistic upheavals that are still, in some areas, going on; the Industrial Revolution; and, indeed, virtually everything that has gone into creation of our modern society.

Printing, however, made information available only in an essentially "raw" state, as any high-school student who's ever tried to research a term paper can tell you. You get what a book's author deems important, presented in the way he thinks best; and many sources must be combined to develop even an approximation of the full picture.

The computer carries this a quantum leap further forward, by taking this raw data and structuring and massaging it according to the specific needs of each individual who wants to use it. The effect is to make a much larger informational base usefully available to the decision-maker, allowing activities once beyond the range of realistic possibility.

Information and Transportation

To bring this home to our own industry, consider just a few of the areas in which this capability lets the transportation manager do altogether new things.

Take freight consolidation. Say a shipper has 100 small shipments a day available for consolidation, and wants the optimum configuration. The possibilities are all but infinite, represented by the mathematical term 100! (100 x 99 x 98 x . . .) and adding up to a fantastic 42 followed by *158* zeroes—a number so large no name has been coined for it. The traffic manager, of course, need not work with anything like this number of options; by judiciously applying geographic, weight, cube and other criteria he can probably reduce quickly down to a few hundred, or even a few dozen, realistic possibilities.

But from this point forward optimizing consolidation demands an option-by-option analysis. If you had a couple of weeks and were adept with a calculator you might eventually get the job done; but in the real world what you must do instead is to make your choices more or less arbitrarily, based on experience and estimates rather than hard facts.

The computer, on the other hand, provided you give it proper guidance in terms of decisional parameters, can sift through the whole range of choices in just seconds. In other words, optimum consolidation, until recently beyond reasonable contemplation, has now become not only thinkable but operationally do-able.

Likewise for pickup-and-delivery scheduling. You have 100 pickups and 100 deliveries for a particular workday, and 10 vehicles to do the work. In the past you had to set up your routes heuristically, as much by guesswork as anything else. Now the computer can not only optimize your runs, it can let you add and delete stops throughout the day while still maintaining the highest possible efficiency.

Shopping for the lowest total freight charges amid tariffs providing a welter of different line-haul rates and accessorial charges? Preparing freight bills based on similar multiplicities of rates and charges? Tracking goods through a warehouse, with FIFO, fixed reorder points, etc.? Costing out individual shipments across a large network of terminals and routings? The computer can do it, and more—and all on a usable, "real-time" basis. The human brain, realistically, simply can't.

I suppose, strictly speaking, you could argue that the computer makes these things possible by just "helping you work faster." But we're taking about so *much* faster that there's really no comparison with pre-computer times. It's like the difference between jet airplane transportation and transportation by covered wagon; after all, 150 years ago you could also eat one meal on the east coast and your next on the west—provided the weeks of fasting in between didn't kill you first.

As transportation managers become more aware of the immense opportunities opened up to them by the information-assembling abilities of the computer, it's going to be increasingly easy to answer the first individual's question. Indeed, not too many years from now I expect the answer will be simple indeed, because virtually *every* carrier and *every* shipper will be using microcomputers to perform a whole array of tasks heretofore thought of (if at all) only in idle dreams of "what if."

3

THE COMPUTER AND TIME MANAGEMENT

"Time management" is one of the most revered buzzwords of modern-day business consultants and educators.

The concept derives from the recognition that, unlike other, material, resources, time can't be replaced or stretched. If you run short of, say, money—or, for that matter, of most things that can be purchased with money—you can seek out more of it by such means as borrowing, attracting new investors, even (if you're really desperate) outright theft; alternatively, you can look for ways of making what you do have go further through economization.

But the clock ticks inexorably on, do what you will; it is the poet's "moving finger [that] writes and, having writ, moves on," indifferent to all we can do to stay its course or turn it back. The best anyone can do—*all* that anyone can do—is try to garner the maximum possible output from each increment of time.

That, of course, is the definition of time management—making the most out of the time available. And in that endeavor the microcomputer is perhaps the single most important tool ever devised.

'On the Road'

What brought this thought particularly to mind is the circumstances under which a good part of this chapter was written.

I was fighting an especially heavy travel schedule which kept me out of the office for more than a third of that particular month. But my office workload, too, was heavy; and publication deadlines stubbornly refused to go away simply because I was on the road.

In times past this might have pushed me into a heavy evening and weekend schedule during the periods when I was home. Not any more, though, now that I've got my handy-dandy three-pound, battery-powered portable computer; all I needed was a chair, a table (or my lap would do in a pinch) and reasonable reading light, and I was ready to make effective use of those idle hours that always seem so abundant during business travel.

As a result, substantial portions of not only this but several other of my writing commitments were written in airline airport-club rooms, on airplanes, in hotel rooms, even (on one occasion) in a hotel bar. By using this time, which would otherwise have been largely lost in terms of productivity, I was able to keep my office schedule reasonable when I was back in town.

To be sure, not everyone writes for a substantial part of his or her living, as I do; so the portable computer may not serve everyone's needs in this regard as fully as it does mine. But my experiences vividly illustrate how the computer can offer virtually everyone in the business world the opportunity to improve his or her time management.

The true portable computer—the kind you can carry in your briefcase and use just about anywhere, anytime, like mine—provides, of course, the most dramatic example of this potential. I use mine principally for word processing—the setting down, manipulation and (most important) preservation of written material. But there are countless other, equally valid uses for portable computers; quite literally, they can be your "traveling office."

Want to jot down notes as they occur to you? Pull out your portable, turn it on and you're ready to work. (I find when I pull mine out at business meetings, computer shows, ICC hearing sessions, etc., it does have the drawback of startling people, leading to a lot of time-wasting conversation; but it gets the job done excellently once the initial astonishment has worn off.) Do you need to work with numbers instead of letters? Most portables today have spreadsheet as well as word-processing software built in.

And if you short-sightedly neglected to bring with you the information you need, it need be no further away than the nearest phone. My portable, for example, has a built-in modem and communications software; with only a plug-in phone jack, I can access either my own or anybody else's office computer from wherever I happen to be. And I know I'm getting up-to-date, accurate information; I'm not dependent on correctly hearing and jotting down what somebody chooses to read to me over the phone, taking up both his/her and my time in the process.

People are mobile; but the accoutrements of their business activities often are not. The portable microcomputer provides the link that bridges this productivity-impairing gap.

In the Office

But that's far from the most important way in which the microcomputer can improve your time-management capacity; indeed, the only reason I started off with it was because of the circumstances that triggered this train of thought in my mind. For most of us, where the microcomputer really shines is in the office itself.

First, of course, there's information storage and retrieval. You need a particular piece of information. In pre-computer times a business manager might ask his secretary or assistant to dig the requisite information out of paper files or stacks, a request that very likely would be passed further down the chain of command until a bottom-of-the-totem-pole file clerk did the actual paper-shuffling. By the time the data got bucked back up the hierarchy, (1) probably about half an hour's worth of employee-time would have been consumed passing the request down, getting the information itself, and then passing it back up, and (2) enough time would have elapsed that the manager might have forgotten all about making the request, and would certainly have lost the idea that led him or her to want the information in the first place.

OK, maybe I'm exaggerating a little; certainly not every useful piece of information need be buried quite that deep. But much of it is (or at least, pre-computer, used to be); and even if it was nearby, locating it was an appreciable time-eater. Compare that to the ease, and *speed,* of touching a few computer keys and having the data you need almost instantaneously appear on the display screen before your eyes.

And any kind of repetitive operation—in which the transportation/distribution industry is especially rich—is vastly accelerated by using the computer. That holds true for anything from multiple copies of form letters to data storage/retrieval to arithmetical calculations; if you have to do more or less the same thing over and over again, the computer can do it with *far* less use of your own or your subordinates' time than any manual approach you can devise.

Correspondence, reports and other writing? I have a life-size recollection of how I used to handle this from my days (long years ago) as a government worker. I'd dictate, and my secretary would take it down in shorthand (or transcribe it from a dictaphone). Then he or she would have to type it up neatly, a process that alone could take some secretaries I had half an hour or so per page, with several wasted sheets of paper. Then I, or someone else who needed to sign off on the document, would turn up a mistake, an infelicitous phrase, etc., and it would be back to the typewriter—perhaps even two or three times before everything was finally letter-perfect.

I got rid of secretaries when I got a computer. Now I use word-processing software to type the letter myself, review it on the display screen (and can have anyone else do likewise, or even print "hard copy" drafts if I must), make changes without having to go through a complete retype—and spend a fraction of the man-hours that used to be required. Now, I'm pretty quick with the keyboard—100 words a minute or so—but even if I were in the hunt-and-peck category as a typist it would *still* be faster and more efficient, in terms of not only my own but others' time, to do my writing this way than the old, non-computerized manner.

The same holds true with other types of document preparation, such as (pertinent to transportation/distribution) bills of lading, trip records, claims/claim acknowledgements and the like. The computer can churn these out by the hundreds in the time it used to take, when the process was handled manually, to prepare just a handful of them.

And there's more. After-hours work—the "good time" used by many managers whose days are too full of the distractions of worktime activities—need no longer be conducted under the handicap of never having adequate information available because it's someone else's province and that someone else has left for the day. Properly equipped, you can even access computer-stored data at remote locations directly, 24 hours a day, seven days a week. And you can keep abreast of current developments as they occur, without having to wait for others to pass the information along to you, and without, too, having to worry about key employees disappearing because of illness, vacation, etc.

'Undoable' Work

So far I've only talked about "regular" work, the long-established office routine. But the computer also allows you to get involved in many new areas, areas that were previously beyond the realm of possibility because (a) the work would take too much time, too many man-hours, to perform with existing office resources, or (b) it was so complex and intricate as to be essentially impossible if done by manual means.

Tariff research is a good example. In the post-deregulatory era of the 1980's the proliferation of transportation tariffs—not to mention unregulated rate circulars, contract rate schedules, etc.—has been formidable. For any shipper to keep track of all (or even a substantial proportion) of his transportation rates today . . . for any carrier to keep abreast of the rate changes of his competitors . . . would, if the operation had to be performed manually using printed copies of tariffs, etc., require an unrealistically excessive commitment of office resources.

With the aid of the computer, though, and the various services and software available to assist in this task, the process is not only feasible, it's actually easier than it was back in the old, regulated days when but a fraction as many tariffs had to be checked.

Good record-keeping likewise has moved from impracticality to reality. Back a few years ago, you had to dedicate humongous numbers of man-hours to keeping your bill-of-lading, freight-bill, etc., records current, or you'd be out of luck if you needed to look up any past records. And even if you *did* take the trouble to maintain truly "clean" files, you could only retrieve your information on the same basis under which you'd filed it; that is, if your records were maintained by B/L pro number, identifying a shipment whose pro number you didn't know—you knew only, say, the consignee, the commodity, etc.—was impossible without laborious file-by-file searches.

Today you can put the information in permanent electronic storage with but a few keystrokes; and, once stored, any good software package will let you retrieve data selectively on *any* parameter, or combination of parameters, within seconds.

Freight consolidation—whether by shippers to reduce rates, or carriers to cut operating costs—need no longer be a matter of the skills and experience of a key employee (and woe betide you if he or she took sick or went on vacation). Now the computer can do it "by the numbers"—and do it, in addition, far more efficiently and less cost-intensively than even the most adroit human being.

Advance strategic planning? Transportation/distribution modeling to let you chart the consequences of alternative "what-if" scenarios? In the past such things were flatly impossible for all but the most sophisticated of transportation/traffic offices, and posed extreme difficulties even for those with the resources to do the job at all. By taking over much of the handling of such processes, and *all* of the so-called "dog work" that eats up both managerial and clerical time in such endeavors, the computer has put these important managerial tools within reach of even the smaller, unsophisticated shipper or carrier.

The Computer as a Time Manager

I could go on just about indefinitely, but I expect you get the idea: In making optimal use of your work time, you could ask for no more valuable assistant than the computer.

"The days of our years are threescore years and ten," one of the Bible's psalms reminds us. "So teach us to number our days," it continues, "that we may apply our hearts unto wisdom." And in modern times business consultants, advisers and educators have been telling us exactly the same thing (albeit in less flowery terms), at least so far as our working lives go.

Today the micro-computer—accessible, at minimal cost, to every business manager—at last provides us with a vehicle to let us comply with this Biblical/business-management mandate. Any manager without such a machine on his desk (or at least readily accessible) is, almost by definition, making much less than the best possible use of his time, in both his own and his employer's interests.

4

DISTRIBUTION MODELING TECHNIQUES

I'm extremely impressed with some of the innovative ideas that are being translated into useful transportation/distribution programming these days.

Up to now, most transportation/distribution software I've seen has focused on (1) speeding up and improving the accuracy of operations that were previously performed manually, and/or (2) substituting electronic for paper record-keeping. In other words, the idea was to take activities presently being performed within a company's organization and improve their efficiency.

Certainly the computer can do this very nicely, and very usefully; and I don't at all mean to disparage this type of programming. But even more important, in my opinion, is the computer's ability to let the manager perform tasks that simply can't otherwise be accomplished—things that are just too complex and involved to be done manually at all.

A columnist in one of the computer magazines recently wrote about his first experience with a computer. It seems he was trying to do some broad statistical analysis which involved laborious record-keeping and calculating. Once he shifted from a manual to an automated mode of handling this task, however, he found the job so vastly simplified that his horizons immediately expanded, and he realized he could perform a much more detailed analysis with (still) much less time and effort than his initial project would have required on a manual basis.

Thus it is with computers: They not only let you do what

you're already doing with vastly greater speed and efficiency, but they give you as well the opportunity to do new things of which you may not previously even have dreamt. And transportation/distribution software developers are at last beginning to tap into this idea, too.

The most significant exponents of this new generation of software, I think, are distribution modeling programs. They give the user a chance to build up a full model of a distribution system (either his present system or one that exists only as a concept), and then tinker with it as he sees fit, observing the results. In other words, trying out new ideas can be as simple as making a few changes in a computer data base, not laboriously putting the change actually into real-world effect (with possible negative economic consequences).

Realistically, this is something you just can't do any other way. I suppose it would be possible, given enough time and manpower, to handle the various mathematical calculations manually, even to draw out charts and graphs depicting the calculated result. But in a modern business office this much time and manpower just can't be found; office routine is too demanding to permit the luxury of this kind of project. The computer thus opens up the possibility of performing tasks which realistically are simply undoable without its aid—which is, in the final analysis, the real value of computerization in any business environment.

Because I think it's so important a use of computers in our industry, let me describe the modeling process in more detail:

Every kid (at least of my generation) knows all about scale models. Planes, ships, cars, railroad equipment and the like, I tried most of them at one time or another. I wasn't very good at it, mind you; most of the models I started remained in various stages of incompletion until my mother got sick of the mess and threw them out. But it seemed so inviting to take all those loose pieces of balsa wood and plastic and paper and somehow stick them together to make something that the memory of last month's failure never seemed to deter me from wanting to try yet again.

Computer modeling works about the same way. Instead of

balsa wood and so on you work with bits of information; instead of using razor knives and glue to assemble the parts into a coherent whole, you keyboard the data into your computer and let it take things from there. Like building a physical model, putting together a computer model takes a fair amount of time and effort and a good bit of attention to detail; but like the physical modeling process, too, you get in the end a product that is a great deal more than merely the sum of its parts.

But it's possible to carry this analogy too far. In the final analysis, physical scale models, however accurate you may try to build them, have their inherent limitations. To start with, physical forces don't always work quite the same on little objects as on big ones; then, too, you can miniaturize *things* such as planes, trains, etc., but you can't miniaturize the people that fly and drive and otherwise use them. So your physical model, however faithful to the original you try to build it, can't perfectly imitate the real-world performance of the original.

Provided you've input enough data, the computer model, on the other hand, can. In other words, you can use your computer model, once built, to play endless games of "what-if"; and the results you get will depict with uncanny accuracy what would happen if you did the same thing, made the same choices, in the real-world environment you're modeling.

And that, of course, is the value of the computer model in a business environment—to see what the results would be if you made choice A, choice B, choice C and so on, so that when you return to your real world you can make the right decisions first rattle out of the box.

A number of highly sophisticated software packages are available to apply computer modeling techniques to a company's transportation/distribution system. Step by step you build up in the computer's memory a picture of the system, real or imagined, that you want to examine. Then you can start making changes—adding a distribution center here, eliminating a plant there, including or deleting market areas, tinkering with traffic volumes, etc.—to study the consequences of various options you may want to consider in your future decision-making.

But there's another side, too, to computer modeling, which may even be its most important attribute. Remember, unlike physical modeling, all you actually do is gather up the various pieces (in the form of elements of data); it's the computer's job to actually assemble them. If you leave the machine alone to do that job as it sees fit, it will put them together in what it deems to be the optimal form (which, in the case of transportation/distribution modeling, is generally construed to mean most cost-effective). Comparing that optimized result with what actually exists in the real world can be both instructive and lead to substantial improvements in both the economy and efficiency of the real-world system.

Many years ago, when I first got into computers, the office I then headed was asked to do such a modeling job of a major distribution network ($100 million-plus in annual costs). At the time we had no off-the-shelf software on which to rely; we had to design our own modeling program from the ground up. Moreover, we were given just six weeks to get the job done; at the end of that time some key decisions had to be made, and the organization was relying on us to say just what those decisions should be.

With lots of overtime and co-opted help from other offices we got the job done. What we found illustrates clearly the important role this kind of modeling can play.

First, the organization had at the time 26 separate distribution centers. It was proposing to close one of them and transfer its activities to another. We found, ironically, that (1) the center targeted for closing was the single most cost-efficient of all (if you were going to reduce the entire system to but a single distribution center, this was the one you'd keep open); and (2) the center whose activities were to be expanded was the *least* cost-efficient of all (if you were going to close only one center, that's the one you'd pick).

In addition, we identified some $14 million in savings possible by simply realigning the system (*i.e.,* changing the centers assigned to service particular demand points), and another $5 million or so available through closing selected distribution centers and reallocating their activities among the remaining centers.

I'm both proud and sorry to say that the organization's distribution system is still being run on the basis of the results of this study—proud because it's always nice to leave behind you work of lasting value, but sorry because the computer industry has come a long way in the intervening 13 years and both hardware and software have greater capabilities today than we were able to apply then. But it does illustrate how powerful and valuable a tool computer modeling can be in making long-term managerial plans.

5

TRANSPORTATION COST-FINDING AND THE COMPUTER

What are the costs of producing a given unit of economic output?

For the producer himself this information is obviously of key importance in pricing, marketing and many other decision-making areas. His customers, too, may make good use of cost data as they negotiate purchase agreements with him.

Accuracy in such cost determinations, however, is in large part a state of mind in most economic sectors. There are many ways in which to figure costs and ascribe them to specific functions, virtually all of which produce sharply different results. Chances are that if 20 different cost analysts looked at the operation of even a moderately complex organization, they would come up with 20 different costs for any particular activity you cared to identify.

The problem, of course, is that there is no meaningful standardization of costing principles or procedures. Books are kept only in accordance with what are termed Generally Accepted Accounting Procedures (GAAP), which are far too loose and imprecise to be termed "standards" even by the most liberal of definitions. Within the limits of these extremely inspecific guidelines companies may calculate their costs according to the particular approach that strikes them as best; and even if all cost experts thought alike (as they most certainly do not), subtle distinctions in the circumstances of different organizations would alone dictate significant costing differences.

ICC Standards

In surface transportation, however, costing has historically been under considerably tighter control due to the regulatory oversight of the Interstate Commerce Commission. (Air and ocean carriers have had similar—albeit less comprehensive—controls imposed by, respectively, the now-defunct Civil Aeronautics Board and the still-extant Federal Maritime Commission.)

Back in the days when regulation was younger and everyone took it very seriously indeed, the ICC recognized that it could meaningfully exercise its rate regulatory functions only if it had some clear means of assessing and analyzing carrier costs. Leaving such matters to the discretion of carrier management was unworkable; the carriers would have an obvious economic incentive to adjust their books to maximize apparent costs on any given service, in order to generate apparent cost-justification for rate increases that, under other costing approaches, would be deemed unreasonable and therefore disallowed.

Accordingly, the Commission developed formulaic standards for both railroad and motor carrier costing. In addition, both for this and other regulatory reasons, it compelled carriers to submit to it detailed annual reports revealing both expenses and revenues, which had to be apportioned according to closely prescribed standards; and it devised its costing formulae so that all of the required data could be extracted directly from those annual reports.

Thus were born the historic standards of transportation costing, Rail Form A and Highway Form B.

Nobody I know suggests that either methodology has a corner on the accuracy market—especially today, when carrier operations are vastly different in many respects that when the costing parameters were established. Indeed, the ICC itself has acknowledged that Rail Form A is no longer altogether suited to today's railroad industry, and in the early 1980's developed a supposed replacement, the Uniform Rail Costing System, or URCS.*

But for all their acknowledge deficiencies, these costing systems have two salient virtues: (1) they have become over the years established and recognized industry standards, in an area where standardization is rare indeed; and (2) they are realistically usable for other than proprietary purposes, since they're based on data that is even today, to at least some degree, publicly available through carriers' reporting.

Thus, even though the Commission is today pretty well out of the rate-regulation business, most industry cost experts see significant advantages in continuing to rely on these familiar approaches.

Complexity of ICC Form Costing

As must inevitably be the case with any standard striving for both accuracy and acceptability in an area as complex and diversified as costing, the ICC methodologies are complicated. We're talking *complicated* here, as in requiring literally months (or more) of training, plus hours or even days to manually complete a single calculation.

Obviously, in times past this effectively meant that these methodologies were realistically inaccessible to the average transportation manager. It was simply too expensive—in time and expertise if the job was done in-house, in money if the service were purchased from outside professionals—to get the job done in most cases.

The advent of the microcomputer has changed this picture dramatically. Today one can purchase a machine capable of performing the entire costing operation for less than $1,000; for

*URCS did not receive the warmest of receptions from the industry when it was introduced, and in fact, as of this writing, had not yet been officially adopted by the Commission. Nor is URCS itself truly "modern" in concept; some of the calculations it employs are based on studies conducted as long ago as 1949.

another few hundred one can then acquire software to instruct both the user (through detailed on-screen menus and user manuals) and, of course, the machine itself in how to do the calculations. Some services even make available data files for various carriers, or (if the carrier data isn't available—only a relative handful of motor carriers submit full annual reports to the Commission) regional-average data, to eliminate the need for the user to keypunch the raw numbers needed as data inputs.

It used to cost more than that just to have an outside expert cost out a single movement.

Limitations of Costing Software

Programs I've seen in this area go out of their way to be as "user-friendly" as possible. Developers recognize that the average user is not likely to be well-versed in the intricacies of ICC form costing, and strive to make their programs usable by even the non-expert. Some boast that even the rankest novice at costing can go through the menus, follow instructions, and come out with the same result an expert would get.

Actually, that's a considerable overstatement. For one thing, the ICC's methodologies involve a certain number of "judgment calls" in computing either rail or motor carrier costs. For example, the user must decide whether system- or regional-average data should be employed, or more specific information be substituted—and, if the latter, *what* specific information, from what source. There are many other imponderables of a similar nature. The programs I've seen deal with these questions in various ways—some better and/or easier to work with than others—but it is in the nature of the computer itself that no pre-programmed decisions can substitute satisfactorily for sound managerial judgment.

A further constraint is that it's always hard for an expert in any discipline to put himself or herself in the position of one who knows nothing about the subject. Costing software is, of course, written by true experts in costing; and their efforts to make menu and user-manual instructions comprehensible to the true tyro are not always 100% successful.

So if you buy one of these packages, expect to spend considerable time learning to operate it properly. You won't have to become a full-fledged costing expert; but neither will you be able to run the programs and get valid, usable results without studying the user manual fairly intensively, and perhaps getting some further guidance as well in particular areas.

Moreover, don't expect, even once you master the programming you've purchased, that you'll get "perfect" results. The various judgmental decisions I mentioned earlier make any discussion of perfection moot when it comes to costing, even with the ICC format as guidance.

I recall witnessing one demonstration of an URCS program by its developer, presented to traffic officials of a shipper organization based on data they provided. The developer duly keyed in the numbers and showed the result to the officials, only to be told that his program must be wrong; they had had the same work done by a recognized cost expert, they said, whose computed costs were 50% again as high. During the ensuing half hour the developer made a variety of seemingly small adjustments in his calculations, which made the computed costs jump up and down as if they were on a pogo stick, and finally shrugged and said he'd done all he could. Only then did the shipper officials reveal they'd actually had the costing work done by *two* experts, one of whose figures were, as they said, 50% higher than those calculated by the software—while the other's were 50% *lower.*

Nevertheless, even with these limitations, the costing software available for microcomputers offers vastly superior access to basic cost information than has previously been available—or than is now available in other economic sectors. Used with full recognition of those limitations, it can provide extremely valuable guidance to both shippers and carriers as they make the pricing, marketing, purchasing, negotiating, etc., decisions to which cost information can be so critical.

At the same time, I do think it's worth emphasizing that ICC costing formulae do not, in my opinion, provide truly realistic estimates of real-world costs. They were designed for regulatory purposes, and were never intended by their designers to be used for operational purposes.

But the problem with costing software that doesn't follow the ICC pattern is that it must, therefore, follow some *other* pattern—to wit, that of its developer. And if you're going to use this type of costing software, you're necessarily going to be dependent on the approach taken by the developer.

Not long after the first part of this chapter was published in my *Traffic World* column I had a letter from an individual who asserted flatly that there are no good motor carrier costing systems generally available, and saw a nefarious reason for that. The large motor carriers and the rate bureaus, he said, have conspired to discourage development of—even to suppress—such systems, in order to place smaller carriers at a competitive disadvantage.

Especially since this writer is a consultant who has his own computerized costing program (for use solely by his clients), and moreover, he told me, is currently seeking to sell that program for a very large sum, I was at first inclined to dismiss his views as self-serving, paranoiac, or both. But a little research indicated that his perception is shared by a number of others in the industry. Thus, the subject is perhaps worth airing here.

For me, however, the conspiracy theory of history holds little attraction. Admittedly it's a popular one in some quarters. Older readers will recall how both World Wars, and other, lesser international conflicts of that era, were often ascribed to the plottings of "international munitions manufacturers" who supposedly encouraged warfare to promote a market for their wares. Economic recessions are said to be encouraged by anti-labor interests who want to cut wages and get rid of unions. Detroit has frequently been accused of suppressing inventions that would vastly improve auto technology because they might hurt car sales. And there are incessant whispers of super-durable fabrics, electric storage batteries, rubber for car tires, etc., etc., being hidden away by greedy manufacturers allegedly fearful of losing their replacement markets.

Well, maybe. Before I believe such things, however, I want a lot more solid proof than ever seems to be forthcoming. If a U.S. President can't keep his efforts to thwart criminal prosecution of subordinates secret from a couple of (then) cub reporters, it's going to take a lot to persuade me that much larger conspiracies can go on for decades without clear evidence ever materializing.

So I discard the notion that any shortage of motor (or other) carrier costing systems has a conspiratorial genesis. Certainly large carriers and rate bureaus, who have their own proprietary costing systems, have not in times past strongly encouraged development of such systems for their competitors; whyever would they? But that's a long way from saying that the large carriers and bureaus have actively impeded development of broadly available costing software; and, without clear-cut proof, it's a distance I will not personally traverse.

Furthermore, the fact is that there do exist costing programs available to anyone who wants to buy them, some at readily affordable prices. I've seen demonstrations of a number of such systems, some of which I find quite impressive. If the big carriers and/or rate bureaus did indeed seek to block costing development, they have been, ultimately, singularly unsuccessful in that endeavor.

But I want to restate the word of warning I offered earlier: There are some wide differences in costing principles even among the best experts in this field, and they are, not unexpectedly, reflected in the available software.

What, at root, is a cost? The layman's attitude that it's simply how much money you spend is, in the specialized milieu of the financial analyst, ludicrously simplistic. For example, such things as depreciation reserves, loss-and-damage outlays, etc., represent future and/or contingency costs whose present values are therefore unknown and must be estimated. There are many different ways in which to allocate administrative and other overhead expenses to various traffic segments. The cost of debt and equity capital is another area of debate; and some even feel that profit should be regarded as an identifiable cost element. And so on and so forth.

Given these conceptual variances, it goes almost without saying that no two approaches will produce exactly the same results. And the differences are not small in many cases.

In other words, when you adopt particular costing software you also necessarily adopt the underlying costing approach of its developer; and you can only expect results consistent with that approach, which may differ radically from those that would obtain under another set of assumptions and choices.

6

COMPUTERIZATION OF TRANSPORTATION RATES—A VIEWPOINT

A consulting job, some conversations with various motor carrier and shipper executives, and a discussion in one of the computer magazines I read conspired to get me thinking some fairly heterodox thoughts about rate computerization.

The more I see of what's being done in this area, the more I'm persuaded that the industry is positioning the cart at the wrong end of the horse.

The way I look at it, the computer is simply a glorified, high-powered filing system for rate information. As such, its proper place is, to me, at the very tail end of the ratemaking process—*after* all other steps in the process have been completed.

But what I keep seeing, increasingly, is the mountain being dragged kicking and screaming to Mohammed—that is, the ratemaking process being adapted (perhaps "perverted" is a better word) to the capabilities of present-day computer technology, rather than the other way around.

The Tool Shapes the Handiwork

I've seen this sort of thing happen before, in other areas; it seems to be a chronic by-product of our modern age of specialization.

In times past the tool was always crafted to fit the job for the simple reason that the craftsman—in the modern business world, the operations manager—was his own toolmaker. That is, since tools were devised by the same individuals who would work with them, in response to specific needs, it was axiomatic that the tool would seek to fulfill the need, not dictate it. Moreover, the pace of progress was sociologically much slower; no-one was in a great rush to adopt the new simply because it *was* new. Thus, one way and another, there was less pressure to change one's way of doing things simply to comport with the capabilities of new tools.

Today there's a vast separation between the craftsman and the toolmaker—one so large that the latter often doesn't have the faintest notion of what use (if any) the former may make of his new creation. Those early "hackers" who cobbled together the prototype microcomputers, for instance, didn't have any idea at all how their machines would come to be used; they just built them, more for the sake of doing it than anything else. And today's business computer users, for the most part, similarly haven't a clue how the machines themselves work or what their capabilities are.

At the same time, the pace of progress has intensified to the point where there's great pressure to bring new technology "on-line" quickly, whether or not its uses or values are fully understood. No-one dares lag behind. For example, we keep hearing in the news media of the urgent need for universal "computer literacy"—even though few (if any) of its proponents seem able even to define it clearly, much less explain why they lust for it so.

The natural result is that, instead of having tools to do pre-defined tasks, we're increasingly—in the transportation industry especially—adapting the tasks to fit the tools that happen to come along. Not only does that distort the tasks themselves, but it's also, at least in the case of rate computerization, altogether unnecessary.

ZIP Rates & Co.

Let me be specific: What I'm talking about is exemplified by such things as ZIP-Code-based ratemaking in the motor carrier sector.

Although I've had some arguments from motor carriers on this point, I continue to believe the three-digit ZIP class rates are excessively broad in scope. Some of these three-digit ZIP areas encompass literally tens of thousands of square miles of terrain—and we're not always talking about low-population areas. For example, Miami and Key West, FL, with over 150 miles of two-lane highway separating them, fall into the same grouping in most three-digit ZIP scales. Even where relatively long-haul movements are concerned—say, 1,000 miles and over—you can get serious distortions from such groupings.

Then why three-digit ZIP scales at all? Well, assuming you fix rates for, say, 15 separate classes of traffic, you wind up with a nice tidy matrix of 776 (the number of grouped three-digit ZIPs) by 776 by 15. Now, computer programmers are quite content thinking in terms of matrices—they fit neatly with both computer hardware and programming language limitations. And that, I think, is the primary reason these scales were devised in the first place: to make ratemaking "computer compatible."

As this is written, carriers are increasingly abandoning the three-digit scales for new, more geographically detailed scales based on *five*-digit ZIPs. These do away with my objections to the three-digit-based scales; but are they really an improvement over the old scales that used rate-basis numbers? I really see only one significant distinction: the ZIP-based scales are more easily computerized. Once again, ratemaking is being adapted to the computer—at the cost of a great deal of time and effort in redesigning rate scales—rather than the reverse.

Furthermore, there's an increasing tendency to base non-class rates—not only exceptions rates and ratings, but also commodity and other specifically tailored rates, even contractual rates—on these computer-compatible scales. That is, instead of a particular rate being stated in dollars and cents, it's expressed as such-and-such a percentage of the rate between the same ZIPs for a given class (*e.g.,* 60 per cent of the Class 70 rate). These are the so-called "discount" rates that have become so popular.

Again, this comports with what's easiest for the computer programmers. As with matrices, programmers understand and are comfortable with algorithms (what the rest of us call mathematical equations). A rate expressed in its own dollars-and-cents terms is an irritant to the programmer, another individual input; a rate expressed as a percentage of another, already-input one is an algorithmic rate, with which programmers much prefer to work. And thus, again, the task is being adapted to the tool.

The Drawbacks

But what's fundamentally wrong with that? This is the attitude I encountered in both the consulting job I mentioned and in my talks with carriers and shippers. Indeed, on several occasions I've been told that computerization is serving to accelerate rate simplification, itself long viewed as a highly desirable objective.

To me, the problem lies in the fact that, while the computer goads the industry toward such tidy solutions as matrix and algorithmic rates, the real world in which those rates are supposed to work is anything *but* tidy. In other words, as rates become more responsive to the dictates of the computer, they become less so to the exigencies of the marketplace.

Take a simplistic illustration: If each rate is established separately, independently, any changes in it—increases to account for inflation, reductions for competitive purposes, etc.—must be dealt with the same way. That comports with the reality that individual market segments operate more or less independently of one another; one is dealing, that is, with the marketplace the way it really is.

On the other hand, if rates are expressed as functions of other rates (such as percentages of class-rate scales), changes tend to occur in bulk lots. That is, virtually any change, even if intended to respond only to conditions in a particular market segment, tends to be propagated throughout the rate structure—all increases are general increases, all reductions are general reductions, etc. No longer does changing a particular rate require an affirmative act; now such an act is needed *not* to change it.

But the diversified marketplace, unlike the unitary computer, is not so readily susceptible to this kind of "batch processing." In the computer-inspired drive for rate simplification we're overlooking the fact that tariff complexity didn't come about merely by chance; it was a direct response to the dictates of market forces. Thus, what we're winding up with is a lot of marketplace square pegs forced into the uniformly round holes that represent our perception of what the computer offers.

Consequences, and Alternatives

If you follow this notion out to its logical extension, computerization is inevitably going to lead to some serious marketplace distortions. Shippers' procurement practices, and carriers' marketing strategies, will be mandated not by intelligent managerial decision-making, but rather merely by the technical constraints of the *non*-intelligent tool which is supposedly intended as a decision-making aid.

Frankly, I think this is a pretty unlikely result in most cases. Perhaps I'm overrating the intelligence of transportation managers, but I think most of them are too smart to blindly follow the path of making rates computer-compatible in the face of hard evidence of adverse consequences in the marketplace.

But in that case, if you go along with the thinking that rates must be simplified to matrix and algorithmic forms in order to work properly on the computer, you then come to the conclusion that, if rates *can't* be thus simplified without doing real-world damage, Q.E.D. they aren't susceptible to computerization at all. And that's just not true.

This is where the computer magazine I mentioned came into my thinking. The issue in question dealt with new, more powerful and (especially) more readily accessible data storage technology that is coming into use—especially laser-based storage media that are replacing slower mechanical disk and tape drives.

What I gleaned from this was that the technology is either already in place, or very shortly will be, to deal with computerization of transportation tariffs *as they are,* without any need to make concessions or changes to accommodate rates to the computer. In other words, contrary to what many people seem to think, we *can* adapt the tool to the task rather than the other way around.

The supposed "need" for tariff simplification to make rates computer-compatible has always stemmed from constraints of the input/output process. A computer has no limitations at all as to the type of data it can store; and it's not beyond the skills of a competent programmer to develop routines to access data stored in a multiplicity of forms. The problem lies, then, mainly in the time required for the computer itself to retrieve and manipulate large and variegated data bases.

But the new data-storage technology largely alleviates this problem, by making it possible for the computer to store and retrieve data *much* faster. Essentially this eliminates (or at least minimizes) the advantage of matrices and algorithms against storage of multiple data elements; the computer can no longer calculate a rate significantly faster than it can fetch that rate out of data storage.

And the second nominal advantage of matrix or algorithmic rates—the reduction in the number of rates that must be separately input—is also falling before the onslaught of advancing computer technology. It's obviously easier, quicker and more accurate to have the computer calculate rates from matrices or algorithms than to keypunch each individual rate manually. But new optical-scanner technology, just coming into practicable use as this is written, lets computer users accomplish the input process *without* keypunching.

In other words, we don't have to adapt ratemaking to computers in order to make it computer-compatible. The computer tail doesn't have to wag the ratemaking dog; with a very tiny amount of patience, and a good deal of attention to the rapid-fire developments in computer technology, will let us use computerization to do the job we *really* want it to do. It can, at last, be a true adjunct to managerial decision-making about rates rather than a determinant of the ratemaking decisions managers are permitted to make.

And Another Viewpoint

After the foregoing was published in my *Traffic World* column, I had a letter in response to my comments from a friend, Philip E. Hendren, director of operations for the Rocky Mountain Motor Tariff Bureau. Phil and the bureau are pretty deeply involved in rate computerization, and he offered another viewpoint that I think warrants attention.

Here's what he wrote me.

"To us, the most interesting aspects of your article dealt with '. . . the ratemaking process being adapted (perhaps "perverted" is a better word) to the capabilities of present-day computer technology, rather than the other way around.'

"Perhaps we find the referenced comments most striking because we believe them to need extension in the case of adaptations necessary to perform the ratemaking process in the computer.

"If your reference to the adaptation ('perversion') of the ratemaking process to present-day computer technology was intended to convey the fact that the ratemaking process had to change in order to be usable in computers, we wholeheartedly agree. The data necessary to perform the ratemaking process five years ago on a nationwide basis . . . the time necessary to find that data and perform rate calculations . . . and the decisions required in that complicated process . . . were beyond the capabilities of computers. The published formats were too varied and complex, the number of exceptions unbelievably high, and their application required judgment, a purely human capability.

"So if computers were to be used for the drudgery portion of the ratemaking process and relieve the human being to make better use of the capability for judgment, many changes had to take place in the ratemaking process. No computer, then or now, could handle all the data the way it was previously published. Many changes have been made, and more will be. It's the only way, since we cannot teach the computer to think.

"You also wrote, in reference to the five-digit ZIP Code rate scales: ' . . . [T]he ZIP-based scales are more easily computerized. Once again, ratemaking is being adapted to the computer—at the cost of a great deal of time in redesigning rate scales—rather than the reverse.' Here we believe your comments are in need of some correction.

"There seems to be an inference in your article that if the five-digit ZIP Code was usable by the computer, were not other grouping codes just as usable? You are correct. The computer could not care less whether it's working with a ZIP Code or a Standard Point Location Code (SPLC) or longitude/latitude or any other alpha, numeric, or alphanumeric code that might be devised.

"The reasons for use of the five-digit ZIP Codes for point grouping are these: (1) It provides a very reasonable grouping of points from a cost-of-operations standpoint, and (2) *everybody knows it!* No-one has to look it up; it's on the bill of lading, the letter from the customer, the order form, the invoice, every piece of business paper. There's no need to go to a code book and look up the code.

"The creators of computerized rate systems must accommodate the opinions of the users, since if the users don't like certain systems they won't buy them and won't use them; the creators must then change the systems or forego the potential market. Rather than just bending the ratemaking process to fit the computer, we believe the shippers and receivers of the nation (sometimes through the rate bureaus, sometimes not) are truly working toward a more useful, usable and understandable system which will fit even microcomputers.

"The matrix of five-digit ZIP Code grouping with formulaic rate structures is of reasonable size while permitting an infinite adjustment of the matrix through the discounting process. The use of five-digit ZIPs is logical; it's the best-known code there is. The use of formulaic rate structures is logical. Should there not be a recognized relationship between classes; was that not the original intent of the Classification, and is the same not rational for weight-break levels?"

Phil's comments reflect the views of one of the major "players" in the ratemaking process. The Rocky Mountain organization has the broadest purview of all the rate bureaus, since its ICC-approved "territory" encompasses the entire continental U.S.; it makes transcontinental rates, whereas other bureaus are regional in geographic scope.*

But I don't altogether agree with some of the tacit theses that underlie what he's saying.

First, let's dispose of the incorrect notion that it's *possible* to have a rate structure, no matter how "complicated," that's "beyond the capabilities of computers." You can certainly go "beyond the capabilities" of this or that *particular* computer, due to the limitations of operating systems, memory sizes, disk- or tape-storage devices, etc.; but if you just move up the line to the next model, or the one above that, you get right past the problem. And I'm not talking about main-frames or even minis; today's higher-powered microcomputers, with RAM (Random-Access Memory) expansions and high-capacity data-storage media, are quite powerful enough to handle any rate structure I've ever seen, bar none.

As for decisions requiring "human judgment," there are, of necessity, none—zero, nil, *nada*—involved in *using* (as distinct from designing) a rate structure. There can't be; if there were, the structure wouldn't be susceptible to objective interpretation and application, as it legally must be. Remember, under regulatory law tariff ambiguities are always construed in the shipper's

*I'm simplifying; the geographic split of bureau responsibilities is actually quite a bit more complicated than this, due to ICC-prescribed territorial distinctions. Each bureau has more or less exclusive jurisdiction in its own assigned territory (although there's a little competition in some areas), so that Rocky Mountain, though it makes rates on *some* traffic to and from points in all 48 contiguous states, is forbidden to compete with the regional bureaus on *other* (generally shorter-haul) traffic moving to and from the same states. If you want a full exegesis on the territorial divisions, maps are provided in *The Official Directory of Industrial and Commercial Traffic Executives* (the so-called "Blue Book") which is produced in annual editions, the current edition of which is available from the publisher of this book. Some bureaus have asked the ICC to remove the territorial restraints so all can compete in making rates on all traffic; but other bureaus have opposed it, and the Commission has decided not to take any action for the present.

favor; and even if you leave regulation out of the picture (as it may well be in the not-very-distant future), the same fundamental principle applies to the common-law construction of price lists, rate circulars, etc., if buyer-seller disputes arise.

In other words, the rate structure has to be complete, and clearly defined and constrained, *within itself,* so that each rate applies to particular traffic according to inflexible, predefined standards. And those standards, no matter how complicated, can be programmed into a computer if you're willing to put in the time and effort required.

As for ZIP Codes, sure they're convenient for the user. That's not my point. What I'm saying is that you can quite easily use a cross-referencing approach to relate them to other types of groupings; there's no need to redesign the entire rate structure itself to put it on a ZIP basis.

My quarrel with such redesigns, and with "formulaic" rates (I prefer "algorithmic," which means the same thing in more computer-oriented lingo—rates fixed by mathematical equations/formulae/algorithms) is that they subordinate ratemaking substance to form. That is, marketplace considerations, which in my view should be the primary driver of the ratemaking process, wind up taking a back seat to the supposed dictates of what does and what doesn't "fit" computerization.

Today's motor carrier industry is perhaps the most intensively competitive environment of all major economic sectors. There were, as of when I wrote this, some 35,000 carriers out there (according to ICC figures) battling one another for traffic, not to mention the other modes (in particular, rail piggyback and freight forwarders) that are also active in the fray. And by and large that competition is strictly price-oriented; service differentials, although critical in some market segments, by and large play a very secondary role.

So a sound market-responsive rate structure is going to need continual fine-tuning, often on a commodity-by-commodity, point-by-point, weight bracket-by-weight bracket basis. And if, in an effort to make your rates "computer compatible," you design a rate structure that can't accommodate such narrow distinctions, you cripple your competitive capabilities.

To illustrate, let's say conditions in a particular market segment dictate an adjustment (increase, reduction, whatever) that doesn't fit neatly into the algorithmic structure your computerized system is designed to accommodate. That is, if you stick to the algorithms you're going to have to spread that adjustment to other traffic as well, where it's contra-indicated by the exigencies of the competitive market.

OK, you have two choices: (1) You can make the adjustment algorithmically, in which case you're simultaneously changing *other* rates that may hurt your competitive position; or (2) you can make it specifically, in which case you're "off the computer" in that market segment—the computer system you're using can't reflect the particular rate you've changed, which is apt to confuse both your customers and your own rate staff (both of which have come to rely on your computerized system).

Neither, obviously, is a very satisfactory answer. But this kind of Hobson's choice, repeated many times in many ways (the example I've offered just skims the surface of the potential problems), is precisely what overattention to the "computerizability" of rates produces—when you twist and distort the rate structure to fit the computer.

Isn't it preferable to build the computer system to accommodate *all* the rate variables the marketplace requires—to adapt the tool to the job, not the reverse?

I, too, can use regression-analysis and other mathematical techniques to translate just about any rate structure you care to name into an algorithmic one. And I'll come pretty close; the algorithm will produce rates no more than a few percentage points up or down from the originals, which is statistically pretty good indeed.

But what if those few percentage points happen to be of key competitive importance in this or that particular market segment? Bear in mind that an individual with one foot on a hot stove and the other in a bucket of ice is, on a statistical average, comfortable.

It may be "logical," as Phil says, to build rates algorithmically. But the marketplace itself *isn't* "logical" in this sense; it's driven not by statistical averages, but rather by its own situational dialectics which aren't reducible to simple (or even complex) universally applicable algorithms. The goal of rate computerization should be to make it easier, not harder, for carriers to respond directly and specifically to marketplace conditions; and any computer system that doesn't meet this key criterion, no matter how greatly it simplifies the programmer's task, is in the long term a handicap rather than a help, in my view.

Part 2

THE COMPUTER AND THE TRANSPORTATION USER

7

THE MANAGER AND THE TECHNICIAN

A dinner conversation during a transportation/distribution computer show got me thinking about the nature of computers and of the people who like working with them—and those who don't.

I was dining with two individuals involved in developing transportation/distribution software—one in programming, the other as a conceptualist ("idea man") and marketer. During the course of the evening we made the interesting discovery that all three of us are professional "loners" in our working habits—we all work in basically one-man offices isolated from routine contact with others, and strongly prefer that type of environment.

And we found ourselves in agreement that the computer is a far more congenial tool to men and women who share our particular turn of mind than to those—considerably the majority—who are more "people-oriented" by inclination.

Technicians and Managers

I tend to divide the working world into two broad categories—individuals who are by nature "technicians," and those whose innate bent is as "managers." The distinction, as I think of it, has nothing to do with professional qualifications or attainments; rather, it's concerned with personal characteristics and predilections.

The technician, in my definition, is one whose primary interest lies in the technical side of his work. He's more comfortable with the true-or-false verities of problem-solving than with the uncertainties and intangibles of what the psychologists call "interpersonal relations." He works best alone, tends to focus single-mindedly on one task at a time for long stretches, and finds the interruptions and diversions of the typical office environment unpleasantly and counter-productively distracting.

The manager focuses more attention to the "people" side of his job. He may not always be gregarious or friendly; but to him the office interplay among supervisors, subordinates and colleagues—whether congenial or not—is not a distraction but an important stimulus. His energy and productivity are highest when he has the opportunity to exchange ideas and information with others.

Few individuals can be consigned wholly to either category; most of us are blends of the two, in varying proportions. (That's just as well, since the "pure" technician tends to be an uncommunicative iconoclast whose results are of at best uncertain real-world value, the "pure" manager a social butterfly who generally doesn't produce much in the way of results at all.) But humankind is a socially oriented species; most people have more of the manager in them than they do of the technician.

And society generally rewards the successful manager much better than it does his technician counterpart. To be sure, there is the occasional exception to this rule—the Nobel Prize-winning scientist, the world-renowned surgeon, the best-selling author, etc. Short of this acme of brilliance, however, it is the managerially oriented individual who will normally attain the greatest success in terms of recognition, power and money. That, in all likelihood, is why so many individuals who start their working lives as technicians gradually shift over into the managerial arena, while there's virtually no traffic in the opposite direction.

Personally, I agree with society's judgment; I, too, think management is the higher calling. Managerial skills act as a multiplier of an individual's ability to achieve his goals, by letting him enlist the skills of others to achieve them; the technician has only his own mind, voice, hands, etc., on which he can call. Just as

"God is usually on the side of the big battalions," so (all other things being equal) the individual with the most resources at his disposal—that is, the manager—will usually be in a position to accomplish the most.

How the Computer Fits In

But the skills and mind-set of the manager are wholly unsuited to the discipline of computer operation.

Pre-1980 or so, that wasn't important. Computers were great unwieldy things (main-frames or, at least, large minis) requiring exotic skills and long training to use. They were closeted away from the rest of the business under the jurisdiction of a carefully segregated Management Information Systems (MIS) Department, and the closest most managers ever came to them was an occasional visit to the MIS quarters to hand down directives and requests.

This sort of structure had its problems, often major ones *(see Chapter 14).* Communications between management and MIS personnel tended to be spotty and imperfect, often producing some poor (or even downright disastrous) results; and costs tended to run high. But it had the benefit of letting the manager stick to his last—managing—while the MIS technicians took care of computer operations.

The advent of the micro ("personal") computer wrought a dramatic change. It brought the power and potential of computerization right to the manager's desk, with no need for the costly and cumbersome MIS "interface"—but only at the price of the manager's having to learn at least the rudiments of computer operations himself.

This is where the manager/technician dichotomy suddenly has become significant. The simple truth is that there are no computer operating systems, and precious little software, truly geared for the managerial frame of mind. You have only two basic choices, and neither one is comfortable for the average business manager.

Most computer systems require a pretty hefty dollop of "technicianism" to use effectively. The widely used CP/M and MS-DOS operating systems more or less challenge users to plumb their depths without offering much help or sympathy for the uninitiated; the newer multi-user systems such as UNIX and Pick tend to be even more overbearing. And most software follows the same pattern.

Occasionally you'll find an operating system (that of Apple's Macintosh is a prime example) or applications program that is intended to be especially "user-friendly" even for the novice user. Almost without exception these are offensively patronizing. The average manager may not be happy having to learn all manner of technical details to use his computer, but neither does he want his intelligence insulted by being required to move little arrows around a display screen filled with cutesy sketches of waste-baskets, file cabinets, etc.

Somewhere (at least so one would think) there must be a happy medium that will neither require the manager to become extensively "computer-literate" nor treat him like a dyslexic child. So far, however, progress down this path has been slow and uncertain; and the result has been considerable disaffection for micro-computers among business managers.

The Technician's Tool

The computer, of course, is the ultimate business technician's tool. Not only does it offer a magnificent challenge to his problem-solving mentality, it lets him do his work in the solitude he prefers.

Furthermore, used with a modem and telephone, it gives our antisocial technician access to all those stimulating "outside" ideas and information managerially oriented people find so valuable, yet shields him from the social distractions and pressures of face-to-face, or even voice-to-voice, interpersonal contacts. For some of us, that's the best of all possible worlds; I spend most of my workdays somewhat like a hermit—me, a computer and a phone—and my productivity is several times what it used to be when I was in a more "normal" office environment.

It's of course by individuals with that sort of mind-set that computer operating systems and software are written. They spend hours and days on end thinking and writing and even talking to themselves in computer code, zeroing in on the task at hand with their problem-solving mode turned up to full gain. And then they've reached their goal—they've solved whatever problem they set out to solve—and emerge from their home-made cocoons with finished product proudly in hand.

Assuming they've done their work well (not every technician is necessarily a good one, just as there are good and bad managers), the results will be fairly easily understandable and usable—to another technician. But to the manager-type individual, accustomed to doing business in a world of people rather than one of things, those same results will usually range somewhere between difficult and downright incomprehensible.

Yet for the most part it's the manager, not the technician, whose need the developer's product was intended to fill. Having found himself, during the course of his programming, up to his neck in proverbial alligators, the developer has simply lost sight of the fact that his original objective was to drain the swamp; his product, that is, doesn't entirely comport with his initial intention.

(Even when developers *don't* lose sight of their prospective customers, things may not be much better. Computer programmers tend to regard anyone not sharing their peculiar skills as verging on complete idiocy; so in an effort to produce software usable by what *they* conceive to be the managerial mind, they gear everything down to the Mickey Mouse (pun intended) level of the Macintosh & company.)

If people were computers, the problem would be easy to resolve; just insert a "technician" circuit board in the manager's head (developers might include one with every software package), and presto! the communications gap is bridged. Since the human mind isn't nearly this susceptible to quick-fix adjustments, however, another approach is necessary.

The Manager's Need

Realistically speaking, it's the manager, far more than the technician, who needs the advantages afforded by the microcomputer.

That "multiplier factor" I mentioned earlier in talking about managers is a sword with two edges. Not only does his ability to work through others, rather than just as one individual, enhance his potential to implement his decisions, it also helps him spread his *mistakes* far and wide. Information is, of course, the best protector against such mistakes; and the computer is the premier information-provider of the day.

Delegating computer responsibilities is no real answer, as the era of MIS Departments showed. The manager is simply substituting the problem of communicating with his own computer people for that of communicating with the software directly. At best such an approach dissipates the value of the microcomputer in allowing managers direct access to the information they need; at worst it leads to a Babel of misunderstandings out of which disasters tend to emerge.

No, the modern manager, to be an effective manager, is going to have to use the computer (at least to some degree) himself. So either he's going to have to become much more technician-minded in order to use the type of programming that's currently available—which is likely to entail concomitant sacrifices in his dedication to those crucial "people skills"—or the technicians are going to have to change their product to accommodate him.

As is obvious from the way I wrote this, my vote is for the latter. Just from a logical standpoint, it's clearly easier to reeducate one individual (the software developer) than hundreds or thousands of them (his customers). And in plain economic terms, it's likewise obvious that people are more readily induced to buy something they like and can work with than something they don't and can't. In other words, if software developers want to sell their wares, let them tailor those wares to the needs and mentalities of their customers, and not expect their customers to do the changing.

From here on, that is to say, it's up to the technicians who write and produce the software to broaden their markets by making their products more readily accessible to the non-technically oriented manager. That was the consensus my two dinner companions and I reached.

If microcomputers are important to managers, they should be usable *by* managers. And in transportation/distribution—especially with deregulation having already proceeded as far as it has, and with more in the offing—there's no question that computers can be one of the most important tools as managers in that economic sector try to cope with the new complexities of the industry of which they're a part.

8

DEMANDS ON THE COMPUTER USER

Does the so-called "computer revolution" portend truly meaningful changes in our society? Are computers really important to our future?

From one standpoint, I think the implications of the computer have been considerably exaggerated. Now that the initial euphoria has faded a bit, it's evident that the once-vaunted notion of a computer in every home, office and classroom, and every person "computer literate," is an idea whose time has not yet come, and probably never will.

From another, however, the revolution is indeed living up to its promise. Computers can and do perform wondrous feats that are of genuine value and significance, and are making some extremely beneficial contributions, especially in business environments. It all depends on how you approach computers and what you want them to do.

Disillusionment in the Home. . .

When the microcomputer first came along in the late 1970's, it was seen in large part as something for use in the home. Now, if you're a computer manufacturer that's certainly an attractive market at which to aim; after all, there are over 240 million people in this country and just about *all* of them have homes.

That way, unfortunately, lies the kind of marketing disaster that such as Coleco, Texas Instruments and even IBM (with it's unlamented PCjr) encountered. Because the problem is: Of what real use is a computer in the average home?

Sure, you can use it to balance your checkbook, figure your taxes, keep track of your recipes, prepare your shopping lists, etc. You can also use an elephant gun to kill mosquitoes if you like.

You can use it for work you bring home from the office. But how many people are really eager to bring home work from the office if they can avoid it? Indeed, a home computer's a definite liability in this regard; if the boss knows you don't have the right equipment at home, he can't insist that you work when you'd rather be watching reruns of "Gilligan's Island."

Your kids can use it for their schoolwork. Now that's at least a rational home use for the computer; my own 13-year-old daughter already uses one for that purpose. But I got along nicely without one in my schooldays, as did probably every reader of this column; although useful for the purpose, the computer is definitely a non-essential for most types of scholastic endeavors, and a costly one into the bargain.

Or you can use it to play games. But the games get tedious and repetitious after a while; most of us can watch Pac-Man gobble up only so many of those little blobs before we're ready to exile him and his electronic kinfolk permanently to the silicon chips from which they came. Like the hula hoop and the Rubik's Cube (remember them?), video games seem to pretty much have had their day.

The truth is, computers for home use were really not much more than an upscale fad. For a while there was a certain social cachet to talking about your Apple, your Trash-80 (the impolite name by which Tandy's Radio Shack TRS-80 machines came to be known), etc., at cocktail parties and the like. But times change, and the computer is no longer "in"; talk about computers at cocktail parties today and you'll quickly find yourself branded a bore (or worse).

As most people by now have realized, the fact is that there are precious few home applications that demand more than the most rudimentary computer power (if even that). And without such applications, the computer's main virtue in the home is that it's a cute toy—and $1,000 and up is a lot to spend for cute.

. . . and Sometimes in the Office

Not a few business offices have likewise become disillusioned with computers, albeit for different reasons. When microcomputers first came along—particularly after IBM's now-classic PC came on the market—they seemed like a "must" for every office. After all, weren't all the news media talking about the new "Age of the Computer," with machines taking over all the drudgery; wasn't the computer *Time* magazine's "man of the year," and all that?

But once you actually bought a computer for your office, it often turned out that (1) it wasn't very easy to use, and (2) nobody had a very clear idea of what it was supposed to do. So it sat there and didn't do much of anything except give the junior clerks a little lunch-hour recreation. If they were really bright, ambitious junior clerks maybe they figured out how to put it to some serious work for the company (and stopped being junior clerks); but mostly they didn't, and it was just another $2,000 or $3,000 or $4,000 or maybe even more down the tubes.

Or, worse yet, the machine *did* get put to work—and chewed the work it was supposed to be doing into corned-beef hash. After all, breathes there a man with brain so bright he never bollixed up a computer application? If the company was lucky, all the foul-up did was waste about an employee-week for it; if it wasn't, the price could go all the way up to bankrupting the firm. And all along that spectrum, the only sound heard (once all the cursing was done) was the boss' vow that never again would he let one of *those* blankety-blank things anywhere near his work.

Whither the 'Revolution'?

So by these standards, the much-talked-about computer revolution has indeed proved to be a bit of a dud. And yet . . . .

The problem with the computer applications I've been describing is the machine lacks clearly defined uses in these situations. At home, or in the wrong type of office environment, it's a fish out of water, and little more valuable. Like any machine, it's nothing but a tool; and if you haven't an appropriate use for this particular tool, it's not much good to you.

But if you have that use—and you're willing to take the time and effort to learn to use your tool properly—then nothing else will do. And this is where the computer revolution has truly lived up to all its promise, and more.

For every home and office where the computer's been discarded or stashed in the back room, there's another whose denizens wouldn't be without it, and can't imagine how they got along before it arrived. These are the places where the job the computer was to do was clearly defined at the outset, the computer was chosen with the doing of that job in mind, and the necessary energies were dedicated to bringing it "on line" to actually get the job done.

And a great many of these places are offices where transportation business is transacted.

As much as any other economic sector, and more than most, transportation is particularly needful of the capabilities a computer offers. The industry is replete with the myriad bits and pieces of detailed information on which computers thrive; and it's oriented heavily toward the number-crunching at which the machines excel. Potentially, the computer brings a capability to the transportation industry that traffic managers of the past could only dream about—just at a time when, with the information explosion occasioned by deregulation, the industry most needs that capability.

But there remains the question of whether the potential can be fully exploited. In this there are two components—the willingness of the user to develop the requisite skill and competence to make the machine live up to its capabilities, and the software that drives the machine. Defective performance in both areas still makes computers a sometime thing for the transportation industry today, despite the clear need for its power.

The Need for Skill

When most people think about buying and using a computer, their minds skip light-heartedly over the big intermediate step—learning to use the machine after it's been purchased. And when reality strikes them, it can be a pretty unpleasant feeling.

Perhaps someday we'll have computers no more difficult to operate than, say, a TV set. Turn them on and they're all ready to go to work, with the learning process being little more complicated than finding an empty desk or table, a wall socket and the on-off switch. Some off-the-beaten-track types of machines have already made considerable strides in that direction.

But these machines are not exactly the ideal for transportation applications, simply because they *are* off the beaten track and won't run the bulk of the software that's currently in use. And the machines that can do the truly useful things transportation-oriented users need done tend to have a much steeper learning curve.

Plug in almost any business-oriented microcomputer, turn it on and, after it's gone through a few internal gyrations it will have this to say on its display screen: "A>". That's all, just "A>" (or occasionally "C>", which isn't much better). The novice user can be forgiven if at this point his reaction is something like, "Now what?" But if he actually types that in, the machine will chide him with "Bad command or file name," and then go back to that stolid "A>" or "C>".

To get past the "A>" to where you can do some serious work you've got to spend quite a lot of time and effort mastering the intricacies of both the machine and its operating system. You've got to learn about such things as formatting disks, copying them, making and accessing directories, creating files, reproducing them, backing them up, deleting them, etc., etc. You must, in sum, be prepared to do some rudimentary "hacking" on your new machine, because if you don't you won't be able to use it.

And you've only just started—because the machine still isn't capable of doing much of anything productive for you. To get it to do useful things you have to put in some applications software—and that entails a whole new learning experience.

Even the simplest and most user-friendly of software requires a good deal of learning before you'll be able to operate it efficiently; and the rule of thumb is, the more powerful the software the more learning it requires. The tip-off is when your slim, trim floppy disk comes with a user manual about the size of an encyclopedia volume, *all* of which you're expected to read and understand before you go to work. The floppy-disk copies of all the software I use regularly occupy an inch or two of space on my shelves. The user manuals for those same programs take up several *feet* of shelf space. And I don't use an extraordinary number of programs—only a dozen or so on anything like a regular basis.

If you're dealing with the big general-purpose software packages aimed at the mass market, the developer will have at least tried to simplify the process of using it. You'll have on-screen menus, help messages and the like available to you while you're working with it; and the user manual, formidable though it may be in size, will at least be written in something approximating understandable English.

If you're dealing with more specialized applications programs, though, you may not have these advantages. On-screen information is likely to be less complete and/or less clear (if, indeed, anything is available on-screen at all); and user manuals may be poorly written, confusing and, often, woefully incomplete or even flat-out inaccurate. And whether good or bad, clear or unclear, you've still got to wade through the material and come out with a fair understanding of your software before you can make it work for you.

Learning How It Works

A book I once read whimsically described the workings of the four-cycle internal combustion engine (intake, compression, ignition and exhaust) as "suck, squeeze, pop, phooey."

That's a perfectly adequate description for anyone who doesn't plan on monkeying around under the hood of his car. In fact, you don't even need to know *that* much to operate the car; all you really need to know is how to manipulate two foot-pedals, the gearshift and the steering wheel.

Similarly, you can take high-quality photos with today's auto-load, auto-focus, auto-just about everything cameras merely by pointing and clicking. A two-year-old can manipulate the knobs and/or pushbuttons that control the modern TV set. Even flying a plane has been reduced to pretty much by-the-numbers fiddling with an ever-diminishing number of switches and controls.

But if you're going to operate a computer—any kind of computer at all—you're going to have to learn more than you perhaps care to know about how it works.

Of Power and Complexity

The reason lies in the versatility of the computer, which is at once its strength and its Achilles' heel. Unlike the car, the camera, the television, the plane, and, indeed, most other so-called "modern conveniences" of technology, the computer is not designed to do one job, but many—nearly as many, in fact, as its operator has wit and imagination to devise for it.

But this means the operator must have, in addition, enough expertise to properly superintend its performance of those assignments. Perhaps in the distant future, when the now-infant concept of artificial intelligence has achieved fruition, there will be computers that can direct their own activities; but for now even the largest and most powerful of computers is wholly dependent on the instructions of its human operator, and can do nothing whatever beyond what it's directed to do.

Indeed, unless artificial intelligence somehow manages to outstrip its human prototype, this is a situation that may never entirely change. The entire concept of supervisory management, so central to almost any activity or organization in which two or more people participate, is founded on the reality that productivity depends less on how individuals perform their particular tasks than on how those diverse tasks are dovetailed into a coherent, goal-oriented whole.

And it's true in human management, just as in the operation of technological gizmos, that the higher the level of the activity involved, the more expertise and skill is required to elicit satisfactory results. A pool of clerks, a crew of laborers, etc., can be efficiently supervised by an individual with only rudimentary managerial ability; a group of skilled professionals, on the other hand, requires far more able and creative management to do its work effectively.

The computer being the most powerful technological aid yet devised, it thus necessarily requires a lot greater expertise to use properly than do more "simple" contrivances.

The Meaning of 'User-Friendliness'

This need for operational expertise is somewhat obscured by the frequent, not to say ubiquitous, promotional and advertising references to the "user-friendliness" of this or that computer, peripheral, software, etc.

User-friendliness has, however, very little (if anything) to do with how much you have to know about the products involved. Rather, it is concerned with the so-called "learning curve" of the operator—especially with the degree of preliminary knowledge he must acquire before he can begin seeking useful output from his system.

The earliest computers were programmed by means of toggle switches. If you wanted to use such a machine, you had first to acquaint yourself with the logic of its structure—what the computer interpreted each "bit" of information, at each "address" in its processing memory, to mean. Then you had to learn how to express both bits and addresses in the octal or hexidecimal numeric system the computer used. Then you had to be able to translate that math into the binary notation which comported with the toggle switches you'd be using for your input procedure.

Only then were you in a position to devise the task you wanted the computer to do and translate that task into symbols that would instruct the computer to do it.

Needless to say, this greatly restricted useful access to the computer's power; only the *cognoscenti* who had dedicated themselves to mastery of disciplines involved could tap its potential. The ordinary applications-oriented user—the business manager, for example—simply couldn't afford the time and energy necessary (and probably also didn't have the personal proclivity) for all this technical learning. (You can compare this to the earliest days of the automobile, the TV, the camera, the airplane, etc., when the operator also had to be a knowledgeable mechanic to make the thing work.)

Two early developments still stand as the most important achievements in genuine user-friendliness. First came the operating system—memory-resident programming that took over the job of directing input to the proper address in the computer's processor. Second, more visibly, the computer was attached to a typewriter-like keyboard so you could input using ordinary alphanumeric characters, and to a video display so you could see your input (and get output) on a "real-time" basis; and programming was developed to translate for both. No longer did the user need to know that the letter "A" was binary 00100001, and that this coding had to be directed to address 4FH, for example; now the machine could do its own translating. And thus was the now-legendary original Apple and its many more sophisticated successors—and, indeed, the entire concept of computer accessibility to the uninitiated (those, that is, not indoctrinated in the more arcane of its mysteries)—born.

Since then there have been many more advances in user-friendliness, designed to further ease the non-expert user's efforts to work with computers. Today's epitome is probably Apple's Macintosh, with its cheerful on-screen icons and cursor-directing mouse to supplant the blind "prompts" and sometimes-obscure program commands that were previously required (and still are for most other systems) to invoke routine functions. And software developers are increasingly carrying such notions forward to likewise simplify their own input/output processes.

But even with these simplifications, if you don't know your way pretty thoroughly around your computer system—hardware and software alike—you're going to have considerable difficulty getting it to do anything terribly useful. And you're also going to be altogether helpless if the slightest thing goes awry—as it inevitably will, if for no other reason than that (a) computers are slavishly obedient to, and dependent on, what their human operators tell them, and (b) those human operators, being human, can be expected to make mistakes.

The Point of Diminishing Returns

With most other technological marvels of our modern world, as I've already mentioned, the point has been reached that little or no expertise is required to operate them. With computers, however, it appears that, short of a true breakthrough in artificial intelligence, user-friendliness has pretty much (in the Rodgers-and-Hammerstein phrase) "gone about as fur as it can go"—and it's still well short of doing away with the requirement for extensive user expertise.

Not that there's no prospect of further developments; I'm not so foolish as to suggest that the present generation of computer hardware and software can't be improved upon, nor that (as a former U.S. Patent Office director said 80-plus years ago, in recommending abolishment of that organization) "everything that can be invented, already has been." But it's become evident that the law of diminishing returns has set in—that each further advance toward greater user-friendliness produces an ever-dwindling benefit to the computer user.

In fact, the current trend of developments in computers is in the opposite direction—toward, rather than away from, operational complexity. Each new machine, each new software package, offers its users more power—*viz.*, a wider range of options—than its predecessors. But to invoke that added power, an ever-broadening lexicon of commands must be learned and applied. In other words, the more the machine is capable of doing, the more difficult the user's task of defining which particular thing it wants the machine to do *now* and telling it to do that and not something else; and no amount of sprinkled-on-top user-friendliness can overcome this problem without at the same time restricting performance.

It's like training an animal; in the process, the trainer must also train himself to give the proper commands in the way the animal has learned to understand them. Tell your dog to "heel" and he walks obediently at your side; tell him to "walk alongside me," and he looks at you curiously and then goes his own way.

In this sense the computer is no smarter than your dog; it, too, will give you a curious glance (usually in the form of a display-screen question mark or some other version of, in effect, "Say what?") if you fail to command it in the proper way. But your dog, with a mind of his own, will go ahead and do what *he* feels like doing if he doesn't understand your wishes; the computer, lacking any sort of "mind" (it hasn't the intellect of an average oyster), simply won't do anything at all in those circumstances, entering a state of somnolescence from which nothing but the proper instruction codes can rouse it.

Thus, today's computers are actually *more,* not less, complicated to use than were their toggle-switch ancestors. The user-friendliness of the operating system, keyboard, display screen, icons, mouse, *et al.,* has been more than offset by the ever-widening range of options and complexities that the vast increases in computing power have introduced. You need very *different* training and knowledge to operate today's computers than you did to run the machines of yesteryear; but you also need, in aggregate, *more* such training and knowledge today than in the past.

The Consequences of Complexity

All this is bound to be bad news for the business user (or would-be user) of computers. He's looking to improve his office's productivity through the machine, but he invariably finds that his new computer actually *reduces* productivity, by being itself extremely demanding of the very time and energy it was ostensibly intended to save.

This can be highly frustrating. I remember telling a friend in exasperation, shortly after I got my first microcomputer a few years back, that "I'm not sure the computer revolution is for me." I had work to do, and the machine was eating up so much of my time in the learning process that the work wasn't getting done; moreover, its early output tended to be somewhat spotty (to say the least) because I hadn't yet mastered it. On several occasions I seriously thought about returning the machine and going back to my old, tried-and-true style of working.

Looking back on it, I expect the adjustment was probably easier for me than for most business managers. I'd had considerable previous experience on computers (main-frames), and, being mathematically inclined by nature, had something of an affinity for the machines; so my learning curve was quite a bit steeper than normal. I also had a friend who was something of a computer hobbyist, and was willing to help me over some of the rough spots. Moreover, as a consultant I was accustomed to spending blocks of time on research and study rather than using all my working hours to generate tangible output; so the process of learning something new was a familiar part of my business day, not a deviation from my routine.

Even so, I was nonplused by the sheer amount of time and effort required for what I initially scorned as the mere "mechanics" of computerization. It was only after I resigned myself to dedicating hours on end to learning my way around the "nuts and bolts" of both my machine and the software I was using that I began to make real progress. And I've found this experience has repeated itself with total consistency every time I've changed machines, have added peripherals (modem, printer, etc.), have brought in new software, or have in any other way changed the configuration of my office system.

All the same, I can't imagine now having to run my business without the aid of a computer. It's said about countless things that "you get out of it what you put into it"; but with computers I've found that's a vast understatement. The time and effort I've put into learning my system, considerable though it's been, has been repaid manyfold by the improvement in my productivity the system has made possible. And I think almost any business user of computers will enjoy the same happy experience in the long term.

But the price of achieving that result is investing the time and effort required to truly learn some pretty complex, and perhaps uncongenial, things. By comparison with the normal experiences one has with other products of modern technology—the car, the camera, the TV set, even the airplane—that's a high price. Then again, the computer, with its immense power and flexibility, offers a proportionately high payback.

9

YOU DON'T HAVE TO BE A PROGRAMMER...

You don't have to know anything about programming to use a computer.

Sure, it helps if you do. It gives you the flexibility to write your own programs to do the jobs you particularly want done, or to modify purchased software to better suit your own needs and wants. It lets you, in other words, tailor your computer's performance precisely to the rest of your operation.

But it's not necessary—any more than it's necessary to speak French in order to tour France, or Japanese to visit Japan. You can get along in the world of computers, often very nicely indeed, without any ability at all to write a program.

Unfortunately, too few business managers realize this. They shy away from computers, and the advantages computers can offer them, because they don't know anything about programming, are uninterested in (or even fearful of) trying to learn, and believe the computer will be of little or no benefit to them without that knowledge. That's untrue; but it's a difficult untruth from which to dissuade many people.

The Mystique of Expertise

Those who do know how to write programs are often pretty insufferable about possessing that knowledge. In particular, they tend to adopt a disdainful view of computer users who lack the skill—and, because they do speak from the vantage of superior knowledge, have a fair amount of success in selling the notion that the non-programmer is an altogether unworthy creature of some lesser species.

It's a familiar scenario, repeated endlessly in a wide range of both social and professional settings—a kind of pseudo-intellectual one-upmanship. Person A knows something that Person B doesn't, and can't resist rubbing it in; Person B, though he'd rather die than admit it, is secretly envious of Person A's accomplishment, and comes to believe it elevates Person A to a somehow higher plane of existence (which is just the attitude Person A was trying to inspire in the first place).

Of course, in these days of social and economic specialization it's hard to find *anybody* who doesn't know *something* most other people don't; even a ditch-digger can boast of exceptional prowess with picks and shovels. For the most part people accept such distinctions with equanimity, feeling that their own unshared skills at least offset, if they don't actually outweigh, the other fellow's.

In a few areas, however, a sort of social *cachet* has come to be associated with certain types of specialized knowledge. Generally such status is conferred on those whose specialties are (1) fairly intricate and difficult to learn, and (2) reasonably important in the daily run of life, so that the average person has at least occasional recourse to consult a practitioner of the specialty. Lawyers enjoy, on that basis, a somewhat exalted standing, for example; so, to a greater degree, do doctors.

And with the rapid growth of computerization both at home and in the office, computer programmers are fast taking on similar airs. More and more people need, and are making use of, computer software, but only they—this cliquish caste of experts—know how to write it.

The trouble with this is that, like the trade guilds of yore, practitioners of these well-regarded specialties tend to gather unto themselves, for their own exclusive use, the tools of their respective trades. Lawyers regard lawbooks as their particular province; scalpels, stethoscopes, even simple tongue depressors are viewed by doctors as their own; and because of the high regard in which these specialties are generally held, the "lay" public meekly accepts these attitudes (even to the point of approving laws that confirm the exclusive purview of such specialties).

By the same token, programmers are making a move to lay claim to computers, and are having considerable success "selling" that notion to others. Many people are coming to feel that, if they don't know (or intend to learn) how to program, they have no business owning or using a computer at all.

Computerization Without Fear

A greater piece of rubbish would be hard to find. It ignores the fact that both the computer *and* its software are intended to serve its users, not the other way around.

There are indeed a few prerequisites to using a computer, but programming expertise isn't among them. All that's needed is that (1) you have a job a computer can help you do, or do better, and (2) you develop the necessary skills to use the computer effectively *for that purpose.* Anything beyond this is for hobbyists, "hackers" and the like, but has little to do with serious computer usage.

I know how to program, some. To be sure, my knowledge is pretty limited; I can program only in one language (BASIC), and I'm a long way from truly expert even in that one. But I'm good enough at it that I can get the job done when it's necessary to do it.

Mostly, however, it isn't necessary; whole months go by when I don't write a line of computer code. Yet I use my computer almost daily, often for long hours, as the mainstay of my consulting business.

What I do, of course, is use programming others have written—a word processor, a spreadsheet, a data-base manager, a communications package, etc. I suppose that, given enough time and effort, I could produce passable versions of each of these, but why should I? My business is consulting, not programming; why dedicate days, weeks, months to produce software that would almost surely be inferior to what I can buy off the shelf with the fruits of a fraction as much labor in my own particular vineyard?

Yes, such software needs to be learned, just as do programming languages. But there's a vast qualitative difference in the learning processes. I was preparing finished documents within an hour after I first "booted up" my word processor; my spreadsheet was generating valuable results within 15 minutes of my first acquaintance with it; and so on. By contrast, it took me literally weeks to become proficient enough in BASIC that I could do anything very useful with it.

A Better Way

In sum, you can get a job done on a computer by being a programming expert. You can get it done a lot faster, more easily and more efficiently by relying instead on what those who are already experts in that area have done.

And the availability of off-the-shelf software to do almost any job you might have in mind is increasing daily by leaps and bounds. There are countless program developers out there, ranging from "moonlight" basement operators to IBM itself, striving to produce packages that meet your needs. I don't say every possible niche is already filled with good, usable software; there'll always be specialty-type applications for which the marketplace doesn't afford programming. But you can go an awfully long way with computers despite a complete lack of programming skills.

So learn to program if you want to; it probably will help you, some, in the long run. But don't by any means feel you're cut off from the world of computers if you don't have such knowledge. As any good manager knows, it's quite possible to benefit from the specialized labors of others without knowing how to do their jobs yourself; and nowhere does this hold more true than with computers.

10

BE YOUR OWN COMPUTER EXPERT

"Why are you writing about computers?" I was asked a short time after I'd started doing so. In a disdainful tone my questioner, a self-acknowledged programming expert obviously irritated at my presumption in invading his field, continued, "What are your qualifications?"

Well, they're nothing to boast about, I'm afraid. In fact, what you read in this book is pretty well the sum total of what I know about computers, at least as of the time it's written. And I know enough to realize that, about as quickly as I learn something new in this fast-paced industry, some smart aleck about half my age (or less) is going to come along with a new development that makes my hard-won knowledge as obsolete as spats and moustache wax.

A computer expert, in other words, I most assuredly am not. But then, I'm not at all sure that doesn't give me an advantage over my expert acquaintance in some respects.

You see, I'm not at all sure one *needs* to know a lot about computers in order to either evaluate or use them in particular applications. If a little knowledge is, as the proverb has it, a dangerous thing, a lot of knowledge has a tendency to get in your way when your primary interest lies in end results. And to the computer user—as distinct from the designer or manufacturer—the point is, after all, how well the job to which the computer is assigned gets done, not the process by which the getting-done is accomplished.

Expertise v. Results

I'm not trying to tout my own credentials to write or talk about computers (both of which I do, as an author, educator and consultant, fairly frequently). What I really want to stress is *your* credentials to evaluate and work with systems in your own job—you, the (like me) non-computer expert who wouldn't recognize a bit or a byte if you tripped over one.

And whyever should you? If you're reading this book it's because you have a serious professional concern with transportation and distribution, not with computers. You may know something about computers, you may even have become interested enough to make them something of an avocation . . . or you may not know enough to be able to beat your teen-ager at computer games (I can't). It really doesn't matter a great deal.

Because to the business professional, whether in transportation or any other field, the computer is nothing more than a tool, a means of getting work done. If it's an effective tool for a given purpose, then it's clearly the one to use—just as a screwdriver is preferable to a nail file if you have a screw to drive. But you needn't know how the screwdriver is cast and assembled to be able to use it—you merely need to know enough to pick it up, insert it in the appropriate slot and turn.

Indeed, were it not for the utility of the computer *as* a tool, all the real computer experts would be pounding the pavement and collecting unemployment compensation. Computers don't exist merely because a few electronic whizzes thought it would be really neat to build them; they exist because there's a genuine need for what they can do. And their value in any given set of circumstances lies solely in how well they fulfill that need.

Who's the 'Expert'?

It's only human nature that every field, no matter how humble, breeds its own experts; even habitues of the city dump will boast of their prowess as "garbologists." Being both "high-tech" and relatively new, though, the computer industry breeds more such experts than most.

And because of the newness and complexity of their field, those knowledgeable about computers are able to capitalize fully on what I call the intimidation factor. They arrogantly parade their expertise before us non-experts in the expectation that we will duly cower before them in our assigned role as inferiors; and too often we oblige them.

Do you think well of a particular piece of hardware or software? Tell your views to a computer expert and you'll receive a pitying stare and a detailed explanation (most of which you probably won't even understand) of just why your choice is the silliest thing he ever heard. Never mind that the hardware or software does the job you want done wonderfully; never mind, too, that the next expert you meet down the road will, with equal confidence, refute the first one on virtually every point. Your expert's notion is that he, and he alone, is qualified to hold an opinion; you, in your abysmal ignorance, are not, and must defer to his.

If you let yourself be bullied by this kind of rubbish you'll never get anything done. What you ultimately must do is to focus on what you, in your capacity as user, need the computer to do, and relegate everything else, quite properly, to the ashcan.

Now, I'm not suggesting you should totally disregard the experts; they have their role, and sometimes a very important one, as advisers. But the final decision on what hardware or software you should buy is not theirs, it's yours; and it's a responsibility you must not shirk simply because others lay claim to greater expertise about the workings of the tool than your own.

Some Simple Criteria

Most good managers learn this lesson early in their careers (otherwise they're unlikely to rise high enough to become managers). They acknowledge that others may know more than they about particular facets of their jobs; but they recognize, too, that it's their role to synthesize all of these nuggets of knowledge into a coherent whole in order to best achieve the end result toward which they're aiming.

The problem is that, when confronted with a brand new, and highly complicated area with which they're largely or completely unfamiliar, managers can easily lose track of this. As a result they can get sidetracked into quagmires of technicality, the effect of which is almost inevitably either (1) complete paralysis of the decision-making process, or (2) decisions being made for the wrong reasons.

The only things a manager *really* needs to know about computers before deciding to buy (or not to buy) a particular system are the answers to three simple questions:

(1) Can the hardware or software do the job I want done? (Of course, that means you must first define what it is you want done—not always the easiest of tasks, but certainly within the competence of an effective manager; indeed, the ability to come up with such definitions is one of the prerequisites of business management.

(2) What will this approach cost by comparison with the benefits it offers? (That includes, of course, not only acquisition and installation costs but also the ancillary outlays involved in training, operational time and resources, etc.)

(3) What is the similar cost/benefit comparison for alternative products and approaches?

With accurate, well-researched answers to these three questions you have all the knowledge you need to be your own computer expert, insofar as your utilization of the machines is concerned. And you have all the ammunition you need to fend off the assaults of those who, on the basis of their own expertise in computers (real or pretended), scorn your choice.

In sum, bear uppermost in mind that the function of a tool is to suit to craftsman—not, even in the high-tech world of computers, the other way around.

The Tale of the Artist's Pig

There's an apocryphal story of a famous artist who was called upon to help select paintings to be hung in a wealthy patron's home. Artist and patron disagreed profoundly over the selections.

"You know *nothing* of art," stormed the artist in outrage.

"I may not know much about art," replied the patron, "but I know what I like."

"M'sieu!" the artist said scornfully. "My pig knows that much."

The story is usually told, of course, to deprecate the patron's supposed lack of taste and his philistine unwillingness to follow the guidance of an expert who *did* have good taste.

On the other hand, I'll bet the artist's pig never had to stare at pictures on the wall of its sty that *it* didn't like.

11

KEYBOARDPHOBIA

If you're a steeplejack by trade, acrophobia is bound to be a pretty crippling ailment for you. If you're a coal miner, claustrophobia will surely cause you trouble. If you're a farmer, beware of agoraphobia.

And if you're a professional manager in this age of computers, "keyboardphobia" is apt to prove just as inhibiting both to your ability to do your job and to your career prospects.

Acrophobia, of course, is an aversion to heights; claustrophobia is an aversion to enclosed places; agoraphobia is an aversion to open spaces. And you've probably figured out that keyboardphobia is an aversion to the keyboard of a typewriter, data terminal, personal computer, etc.

Most phobias, however, are based on uncontrollable fear; sufferers experience reactions ranging from sweaty palms to outright panic when exposed to their pet aversions. Keyboardphobia, by contrast, seems to stem mostly from what you might unkindly call a terminal case of vanity on the part of the patient.

The Roots of Keyboardphobia

For most managers, keyboardphobia begins with their first managerial-trainee jobs. Now, there are three ways in which you distinguish management trainees from secretarial/clerical employees. One is that the secretaries and clerks (the good ones, that is) have a good deal more knowledge and expertise than the management trainees. The second is that the secretaries and clerks are doing productive work, whereas the management trainees (at least during the early stages of their training) aren't.

Neither of these distinctions, of course, is much of an ego-builder for the average management trainee. Sure, he knows his long-term career prospects are a lot brighter than those of the secretaries and clerks; he can at least hope to progress quite far in the organizational hierarchy, while the secretaries/clerks will probably remain just that all their working lives. But that lies in the future; the trainee wants something *now* to set himself above all those legions of secretaries and clerks.

Which brings us to the third distinction, the only one outwardly visible to at least the casual observer: The secretary/clerk is probably adept at using office equipment, especially the typewriter, and the management trainee usually isn't. Indeed, this distinction is often deemed so important that I've known management trainees who, after having painstakingly learned how to type so they could do their college papers, were at equal pains to conceal this ability once they stepped out into the business world. They feared that if their skill became known they might be shunted off their hoped-for "fast track" into dead-end secretarial and clerical jobs.

Now, that may seem a little silly to you; but, like many truisms, it contains a solid kernel of truth. I've also known managers who've made important personnel judgments based on just such petty criteria. What's more, individuals who are known to be able to type may be pressed into service doing just that on an emergency basis (with "emergencies" happening all too frequently), depriving them of training time and opportunities their less digitally skilled peers (and competitors for advancement) receive.

So at the lowest echelons the lesson is quickly learned that secretaries and clerks type, and their bosses—and those who aspire to be bosses—don't. It's a lesson many individuals carry carefully up the corporate ladder with them. Indeed, the closer to the top you get, the more entrenched the attitude becomes; in those frequent pictures of corporate chief executives at their desks that you see in such as *Fortune, Business Week* and other publications, is there *ever* a typewriter in view?*

The Dictates of Technology

Today's computer technology, however, has relegated such an attitude decisively to the past. The computer has in the past few years become an important managerial tool (perhaps the single most important such tool in many offices); and the keyboard is the principal means by which that tool may be used.

What would you think of an executive who refused to touch a telephone, but instead required subordinates to make and receive all calls? Or one who didn't know how to read, insisting that underlings read everything aloud to him? I suppose there are rare individuals who can surmount such handicaps, but in most cases such an executive would be out of a job in short order—replaced, very likely, by the individual who had been doing his phoning or reading for him.

By the same token, if today's executive shies away from the keyboard of his data terminal or personal computer, he'll be *de facto* delegating a significant portion of his job to the assistants, secretaries, clerks, etc., on whom he relies to handle this function. Inevitably, those assistants/secretaries/clerks are going to wind up knowing more about the organization and its vital decision-making apparatus than does the boss himself—a situation that's neither good managerial practice nor conducive to the manager's own potential for career advancement.

I do all my own typing—everything from the manuscript for this book to the reports and regulatory pleadings I prepare as a consultant down to the most routine of correspondence. I long

---

*In fact, I know of at least one company president who, although he is one of the exceptions and actually uses a typewriter himself, insists that it be removed from view before any photographs are taken. He's concerned that a picture that showed the machine might diminish his status in the eyes of subordinates and (particularly) his peers.

ago wearied of secretaries and clerks who can't spell or punctuate; and besides, at 100 words a minute I find typing a lot faster and more efficient than dictating to a type machine or a stenographer. (I could also mention some real horror stories from the days when I tried dictation, such as the new secretary who, after a full morning of taking shorthand, decided at noon that she didn't like her job and left without notice—and without transcribing any of her notes, either.)

Now, I'm not suggesting that anyone else need go nearly this far. It takes a *lot* of practice to hone really good typing skills (I've had 25 years as a writer), and the manager who didn't do it when young has better uses for his or her time and energies now. Routine word processing, keypunching large volumes of data input, etc., are in most cases best handled at lower levels; the traditional roles of the secretary and clerk still have a place in the modern era.

But the effective manager of today definitely needs at least a nodding acquaintance with the layout of the standard keyboard—and a willingness to use the keyboard without fearing any diminished status. Those who let vanity stand in their way ("I'm not a secretary, and typing is a secretary's job!") are going to find themselves at an increasing, and increasingly crippling, disadvantage as the already powerful role of computers in business continues to expand.

The Limitations of Keyboard Alternatives

If you're one of the anti-keyboard legion, by now you may be thinking smugly to yourself that there are today plenty of alternatives for communicating with a computer. There's the "mouse" device popularized by Apple with its Lisa and Macintosh machines; there's Hewlett-Packard's "touch-screen," sensitized to register the touch of a finger; and there are various other approaches, such as the "light pen," to using a computer *sans* keyboard.

Trouble is, they simply aren't adequate substitutes.

These gadgets do have their uses. The big selling point of the

Macintosh, for example, is its superb (though monochrome) graphics capabilities. And you really can't take full advantage of the Macgraphics without the Macmouse. I've seen some highly complex software packages that make creative use of the touch-screen. And the light-pen and other such systems also have their value in particular applications.

But—catering to the manager who still obsessively clings to the notion that keyboarding is beneath his or her dignity—those who produce these machines are trying to sell the idea that the gadgetry can take the place of the keyboard. And that's arrant nonsense.

If you want to tell me the gadgets are useful as *part* of your means of using a computer, I can go along. (I don't share even that view; I set the cat to catch mice, and touch-screens don't seem to thrill to *my* touch. But not everyone need be cut from the same mold; and I confess that a quarter century of typing has left me with a few prejudices of my own.)

To suggest that these things can serve adequately as your *only* means of communicating with a computer is like saying you can do business using nothing but sign language. Sure, the arched eyebrow, the pointed finger and the expressive shrug can speak volumes in the right circumstances; but you're hamstrung if you can't verbalize—just as you are if you rely on mice, touch-screens & Co. as the exclusive means by which you "talk" to your computer.

At best, such devices let you give a few simple commands. But they offer only as much flexibility and power as the machines' designers and/or the software's developers have chosen to build in. If you want to stray even a millimeter off the path these individuals—who are certainly not privy to your own needs and applications—have paved for you, you'll have to get your fingers dirty on the keyboard. And what are you going to do if you need to drop in a few fresh bits of data, for which none of the gadgets are usable at all?

We're beginning to see the rudiments of voice-recognition technology in the computer industry; a few machines now on the market can recognize a limited number of spoken commands (if properly programmed and rehearsed, the latter something the user must take the time and effort to do himself), and can also give limited "spoken" responses. In 10 or 20 or 30 years, when this technology has developed to a level such as you say in the science-fiction movies *2001* and *2010, perhaps* we can again relegate the keyboard back to the desks of secretaries and clerks (or even dispense with it altogether).

Meantime, however, I stand by my premise: Keyboardphobia is an expression of vanity the efficient, advancement-minded manager can no longer afford in the age of computers.

Some Keyboarding Aids

But don't be dismayed if you're unskilled at using the keyboard. Once you overcome your initial resistance to putting your fingers on it at all, you'll find the computer can help you quite a lot.

I'm referring to the various programs, such as ProKey and SmartKey, the allow you to pre-program frequently used keystroke combinations for automatic iteration. If you're in the hunt-and-peck category as a typist—or even if you're not, but have some frequently used multi-keystroke inputs (as I, in common with most heavy computer users, do)—you might benefit from this type of software.

These software packages let you pre-program any single keystroke to stand for just about as much input as you care to standardize. Hit the designated key and all the pre-programmed material is automatically input, just as if you'd typed it manually. You can include text, numbers or command sequences for other software, as you choose.

Obviously, much use of this software would soon deprive you of the standard use of your keyboard; so you're allowed to designate any one normal key—one you don't use often, such as the tilde or square-bracket key—as a "supershift." Hit any other key normally and you'll get the regular result; the "h" key will print out "h," and so forth. But hit the supershift first and *then* hit the other key, and you'll get whatever keystroke sequence you've programmed.

Nor are you limited to just one set of keystroke definitions; you can develop several alternate sets for use in connection with different applications programs, and save them into separate data files. Then, depending on what you happen to be doing with your computer at the moment, you can call the one you want into service with a quick command (and change your definition file with another command or two whenever you need).

I recommend these programs heartily; especially if you're not well versed in the use of a keyboard (and even if you are), they can save you a *lot* of time, effort and grief during your sessions with the computer.

The Dvorak Keyboard

Another feature of most of the programs of this nature that I've seen is that they let you redefine your keyboard into the so-called Dvorak configuration. Now, that requires a bit of explaining, so bear with me.

When typewriters were first introduced a century or so ago, there was, of course, no such thing as a "standard" keyboard. Different manufacturers arranged the keys differently, and typists had to learn a new layout each time they changed makes. (Needless to say, changing makes was mightily discouraged by this situation.)

Most of these various layouts were, not unreasonably, designed for what their respective manufacturers considered to be maximum typing efficiency. After all, the idea of the typewriter was to make writing faster, so why not make it as fast as possible, right?

Trouble was, the manufacturers underestimated human dexterity; these efficient keyboards tended to produce over-efficient typists. Even today, if a really skilled typist gets rolling on, say, an IBM Selectric, the machine can't keep up; sooner or later it has the mechanical equivalent of a nervous breakdown and starts printing out hyphens ("-") instead of what was actually typed. And back in the early era of strictly mechanical typewriters, rapid typing produced jammed keys with dismal regularity. To avoid this problem, manufacturers soon learned to make their keyboard layouts *less* efficient for the typist.

Thus, the layout that ultimately became the standard—known as the Qwerty layout, after the leftmost six keys on the top row of letters—was purposely *in*efficient. It made you stretch after the most frequently used letters, clumped common letter combinations together so they'd have to be struck by the same finger, etc. And despite technological advances in electronic typewriters (and now, of course, computers), the Qwerty keyboard remains unchanged.

Over the years various individuals have come up with alternative keyboard layouts which, at least theoretically, allow greater typing efficiency. Most of these have perished unsung; but one that has attained some (albeit small) following is the Dvorak layout. It places most of the more frequently used letters on the touch-typist's "home" row of keys, and separates common diphthongs and other letter combinations so they can be struck by separate fingers (and hence more rapidly).

In theory, at least (and various scientific studies have been done on the question), the Dvorak layout is inherently more efficient than Qwerty, and should permit significantly faster typing. In practice, though, the results don't fully bear this out; in speed/accuracy tests, expert Dvorak typists show up little, if any, better than their Qwerty counterparts. Nevertheless, the mystique of the Dvorak keyboard persists, to the point where all of the good keyboard-customizing software I've seen lets you reconfigure your computer keyboard to the Dvorak layout with a single command.

Personally, I doubt if a changeover is worthwhile unless you're starting out with a keyboard almost from scratch. If you are, though, you might want to consider it, especially since you can shift the layout back and forth (for others who might prefer Qwerty) any time you want to. But if you do elect this option, I'd suggest you also invest in some inexpensive "caps" for the keys listing the new key definitions (since the baked-on lettering identifies them according to their Qwerty meanings), at least until you've thoroughly memorized each key location.

Part 3

THE COMPUTER IN THE ORGANIZATIONAL STRUCTURE

12

JUSTIFYING COMPUTERIZATION TO HIGHER MANAGEMENT

"Do you realize how much harder you're making it for us to sell computerization to top management?" asked the plaintive voice on the phone.

The call came a few months after I started writing my regular "Computer Software for Transportation" column in *Traffic World* magazine. Since that was just the opposite of what I and *Traffic World* were trying to achieve with the column, I asked why my caller—a traffic manager for a middle-to-large-size shipper) felt that way. What it finally came down to was cost justification—a topic I stress heavily both in the column and in my other writings and talks about computerization, and one with which my caller was having difficulties.

"My boss keeps wanting to know how much money we can save by buying this or that computer, this or that software package," he told me. "I really can't answer that. I can make some guesses about what we can save, but they're just guesses; without the experience of using the system it's impossible to say just how much savings there may be.

"And there may be no savings at all, at least not directly. I have a very small staff, and there are some things we just don't have the time and manpower to get done. The computer would let us do them, but how can I say what the dollar results of that will be?"

Why Computerize?

OK, then, let's talk a little about cost-justification as it relates to computerization of the transportation and/or distribution function.

The reason many managers want to computerize is not far removed from what Sir Edmund Hillary said when asked why he climbed Mount Everest—"Because it's there." The computer, they feel (correctly), is the wave of the future, and they simply want to climb aboard before they get left behind.

But these managers miss the whole point of *why* the computer is the wave of the future. Unlike Hillary, a business organization is not engaged in a sport or a hobby; it's seeking a place in the world of economics and, unless it makes a profit, it won't find one. In that environment very little, not even the "high tech" so beloved of today's news media, is its own justification; virtually everything exists for, and is valued in terms of, its contribution to that fundamental goal of profitability.

In other words, the computer in the business world is a solution to a problem. If you don't have, or can't define, the problem—or if there's a better alternative answer to the problem you do have—then you don't need a computer, no matter how passionately you may love the little boxes.

Charging ahead blindly into computerization can be disastrous from a business standpoint. Make the wrong decisions about hardware and/or software and the *best* thing that can happen is that the system will prove useless to you, generating reams of information no-one cares about. If you're less fortunate, carelessly chosen systems can disrupt your operations no end while proving bottomless pits for added outlays. (A pleasure boat, someone once wrote, is a hole in the water into which you pour money; a computer system that isn't compatible with your operation is the electronic equivalent of that boat.)

As was much publicized at the time, computer problems—specifically, two systems that couldn't be made to work effectively together—contributed mightily to the old Penn Central Railroad's collapse; and there are countless similar stories of unwise computerization precipitating other companies into financial trouble, even bankruptcy. Unless you're a confirmed masochist, you certainly don't want a computer system that's going to impair, not improve, your profitability.

So when my caller's boss demands that he cost-justify his proposed acquisition of particular hardware or software, he's actually asking how that hardware or software will contribute to this key organizational objective. And without a clear-cut, supported-by-hard-evidence answer, I think he's absolutely justified in saying no.

Approaches to Cost-Justification

I sympathize with my caller's difficulty in meeting his boss' cost-justification demands. But I also think his problem is, with a little effort and initiative, a solvable one.

The answer lies in the oft-neglected discipline of strategic planning—determining (a) where you are right now (in terms of what your company, department, office, etc., is doing and how well it's doing it); (b) where you want to be (in the same terms); and (c) what benefits you expect to derive from bridging the gap between a and b. Only after you've done this exercise is it time to look at ways and means of accomplishing that, of which computerization is one.

This is a function foreign to many transportation/distribution managers, whose expertise and background lie more in the technical side of their jobs than in business management techniques. But that technical orientation can be a strength in the process of strategic planning, in that it provides the manager with a good grasp of both his present operations and his future needs.

I spoke with this particular individual for perhaps half an hour, during the course of which it became evident that he was very much on top of how he and his staff were spending their time at the moment. Equally, he seemed to have a clear picture of what he felt his office *should* be doing—*could* be doing but for the lack of adequate resources. His problem lay in breaking down the gap between those two things into documented (or documentable) dollars and cents.

There are basically three ways of answering that problem:

(1) By example: "We tried out this sophisticated routing system in thus-and-such experimental situation, and cut our freight bill by X dollars. That projects out to cost savings of X-times-Y dollars if we use this system on a permanent basis at all our shipping locations."

(2) By past experience: "Review of our freight bills for this past time period shows we incurred single-shipment pickup charges aggregating so-and-so much, which could have been avoided if we had used optimal freight consolidation. By allowing us to perform that consolidation, this system can be expected to save at least that amount on a continuing basis."

(3) By inference: "Our present equipment maintenance costs are X percent above what we would expect by established comparisons. We can't ascribe this to any differences in equipment type, age, etc. Thus, a more sophisticated records system should let us meet or beat the compared standard."

Obstacles to Cost-Justification

All these approaches are somewhat threatening to the manager, in that they entail admitting that his operation is currently functioning at a less-than-optimum level. In the back of his mind, at least, he must be wondering whether his boss(es) will accept his reasons for this shortfall and give him the resources he says he needs to correct it—or will instead simply blame him for not getting his job done.

I don't dispute the reality of this concern. But at the same time, if the manager won't acknowledge that there's any room for improvement in the way things are going now, how can he expect top management to back him in *seeking* improvement?

An additional obstacle is present in the fact that analysis of past operations, experimentation with new systems, research into what others may be achieving in given areas (and the report-writing to back things up) all require substantial time and not a little effort, which may be hard to come by in a busy working environment. One irony of the strategic planning process is that the busier you are the more you generally need it—but, of course, the less time and other resources you have to devote to it.

But computerization, too, is a time-consuming and effortful process. No matter how much systems are touted as "user-friendly" and "turnkey," a *lot* more is required that simply installing the system and switching it on. Depending on the application, it may be necessary to pre-input masses of data before you can make any use of it at all. And employees will also have to be trained in, and gain experience with, the new system. The hard fact is that if you don't have time to study and evaluate a computer system carefully before you buy it, you also don't have time to bring it into service once you *do* buy it.

In sum, I'm afraid I continue to feel that pre-justification, on cost and/or other terms, is a critical part of the process of computerizing any business function. I certainly don't mean to make it harder for my caller, or anyone else, to persuade his (or her) boss of the need for computerization; and I hope some of these suggestions will make that job a little easier.

At the same time, I don't want to paint an unrealistically rosy picture of computerization, leading you happily into decisions you'll later have cause to regret. As with any business decision, deciding to buy and use a computer requires careful cost/benefit analysis *before* corporate resources are committed.

13

'SELLING' COMPUTERIZATION IN YOUR ORGANIZATION

You have a micro-computer (or at least access to one). You have software you want to drive it.

Now: How do you "sell" your planned system to others—your top management, subordinates who will be expected to operate it, customers to whom you're trying to market, etc.?

Sooner or later every manager with any significant involvement in computers is going to have to face this problem; he or she will need to educate others in the discipline of computer applications. And my experience—from both sides of the fence (that is, both as presenter and as audience)—is that it's far from an easy problem to solve.

At various computer trade shows I've been highly critical of exhibitors and others who displayed transportation/physical distribution software to me. I've felt they did, generally, a pretty poor job of it, more often confusing rather than educating me. But I subsequently had occasion, on behalf of a client, to participate in making such a presentation myself; and I've developed a good deal more sympathy for those who undertake this difficult (though *not*, I want to emphasize, impossible) job.

Problems With a Demonstration

The occasion was the annual meeting of the transportation personnel of a major corporation (which shall, for reasons that will shortly become evident, remain nameless). The company was just getting into micro-computer usage for transportation functions, and its staff officials wanted to use that meeting to start indoctrinating line managers in the new area. Because the staff people, too, were somewhat unfamiliar with micro applications, I was brought in to help out.

Against my advice they decided on a "show-and-tell" type of presentation—one where attendees at the meeting would be able to view the display and listen to an oral presentation, but would not actually get their hands on a machine. I could understand their reasons; they expected more than 60 people at the meeting, and couldn't provide enough computers to offer them hands-on experience. But I did warn them that show-and-tell was apt, in my experience, to prove troublesome.

Just *how* troublesome, though, I didn't fully anticipate.

At first all went smoothly. I arrived at the meeting site (a hotel) the afternoon before the meeting with three software packages I planned to display. They were packages chosen for (a) their low cost, (b) their simplicity of operation, and (c) their usefulness in terms of my client's particular needs. The client provided an IBM-XT, with which I had a reasonable acquaintance, and I knew the software pretty thoroughly; with only a slight hitch or two, easily solved, I got all three programs loaded and running smoothly.

Because of the size of the gathering it was planned to use a projection-type display (like the big-screen TV's many bars use for sports events). Right on schedule, about 5 p.m., the hotel's audio-visual people arrived to hook up the display to the computer—and the real trouble started.

The blasted thing simply wouldn't work. One of the problems of present-day micro-computer technology is that almost *nothing* is standard in the way of hook-ups. Sure, plugs fit into sockets just fine; but beyond this point differences in wiring, in electronic input-output parameters, and in the equipment itself makes connecting almost anything to almost anything else a catch-as-catch-can, trial-and-error affair at best. In this case, no-one—not I, not the A-V people, not the client's MIS staff, and not several outside experts who were consulted over the phone—could persuade the projector unit to accept the computer's display.

This particular XT had only monochrome output; it wasn't equipped with the add-on circuitboard needed to display color. The A-V people said they'd had no problem in the past hooking up to XT's with color boards, so at 8 p.m. the A-V supervisor, a top staff member of the client and I hustled out to buy a color board at a nearby retail store.

We got the board, slipped it into the machine and, sure enough, we could now project the display onto the screen—so long as the computer would let us. But all the software we had was, of course, geared to a monochrome display; and every time we started to run a program the machine obstinately insisted on routing its display output through the old monochrome board, and shutting down the color board. So we were back to square one, $200 poorer (the price of the useless color board) and still with no display except the 12-inch monitor.

The hotel's A-V chief did the very best he could for us. He stayed up, literally, all night installing a video camera focused tightly on that 12-inch monitor. The camera (unlike the XT) *could* be hooked up to the projector, giving us an image of sorts—but one that was understandably so fuzzy as to be all but unreadable.

Nor was this the end of our problems. An XT normally "boots up" (starts operating, when you turn it on) using information stored on its built-in hard-disk drive, which its memory designates as "Drive C." Somehow, in adding the color board, we altered the memory circuits so it was now thinking of the hard-disk as "Drive D" (although the machine otherwise worked according to specifications).

An inconsequential difference in nomenclature, you might think; except that one of my software packages demanded that data files be stored on Drive C. Since the computer now didn't think it *had* a Drive C, it couldn't find the data files and the program wouldn't work—which I didn't discover until I was in the middle of my presentation the next morning. (I can only plead fatigue, since I was up pretty late myself working on the display problem the night before, but it was a couple of hours before I realized how to fix the problem—a simple one-line command—and by then my presentation was finished.)

The upshot was that those attending the meeting got only a blurry glimpse of several programs (one of which wouldn't run) and an impression that the computer is indeed a formidable beast which even the "experts" can't always tame. They were supposed to come away with a feeling of comfortableness and excited interest about computers; instead, as one of the attendees told me privately, "you scared the devil out of us" with all the problems that, unfortunately, were so vividly on view.

Doing It Right

In retrospect, I can see several steps my client and I should have taken that could have transformed this semi-disaster into the really effective presentation we'd hoped for. We did quite a lot right; but, as with so many things, it only takes one mistake to glitch up the whole operation, and we made more than one.

We started off well. The software was well targeted to the audience—right in tune with their needs, and neither so simplistic as to bore them nor so complicated and/or cumbersome as to confuse them. Both the client's people and I were familiar with the hardware we were using, and I was well prepared to both operate and discuss the software. We gave ourselves plenty of time to get the software up and running on the machine we were planning to use—on site, so the bumps and thumps of moving the machine couldn't foul us up.

(I mention these things because I've seen others run into serious problems on all of these counts. The software isn't appropriate to the audience; the individual demonstrating it fumbles around with the hardware and/or software; the program(s) won't work on the machine at hand; travel has damaged the computer; etc. Instead of demonstrating their programs, such individuals wind up showing off only their own ineptitude.)

Here's where we went wrong:

First, the show-and-tell approach. I should have fought harder about this; the more I see of it, the less effective I think it is. Watching somebody else operate a computer is not one of the most exciting, nor one of the most instructive, events in anyone's life; you have to actually get your hands on the keyboard before you really start getting tuned in to how things work.

The ideal, of course, is to have one computer available for each participant in the demonstration. Failing that, participants should be divided into the smallest possible groups, with each group having access to a machine. I know it's not always easy to locate enough computers, especially when you're talking about groups as large as 60 people; but machines can be rented or borrowed with a little effort and/or expense, and I think it's critical to a successful demonstration. Even if all had gone smoothly at my client's meeting, I think the no-touch approach would have really hurt the presentation's effectiveness.

Second, time. Computer hardware and software should be demonstrated in a relaxed, low-key atmosphere in which the participants are encouraged to take their time in the learning process. In this instance we simply tried to cram too much into too limited a time period; I had only two hours in which to demonstrate my three programs, and the client's staff people had two or three others they showed. Things went zip-zip-zip past the audience so rapidly they had little opportunity to see in detail, step by step, just how everything functioned. As a result, they were left with the impression of a learning process much more complicated and difficult than is actually required for any of the programs they saw.

Third, display quality. Giving eyestrain to those viewing your demonstration because of dim or fuzzy displays is a sure kiss of death. You want to give them clearly readable numbers and letters, not blurs and blobs they can only decipher with an all-out effort (if at all).

This is another thing I have against projection displays; it's extremely hard to get them clear and bright enough for easy reading. I've seen quite a number of such displays, but only one that was really "clean." In that case the developer used a high-quality projector and a special curved screen (the type you see with the most expensive projection TV's), and got genuinely high-resolution images. Every other one I've seen had serious focus problems; moreover, in most cases there's a very unsatisfactory choice of either having the projected image "washed out" by ambient lighting or forcing participants to sit in semi-darkness. If you *must* use a show-and-tell approach, either spent the money to get top-quality projection equipment or settle for big (26-inch) monitors.

Fourth, hook-ups. I can't blame my client for this one; I've had enough experience with hook-up problems to know better, and should have insisted that the client set this up well in advance. If you're going to link *anything* to anything else at all—monitors, disk drives, projection screens, modems, whatever—check it out *well* in advance to be sure everything's fully compatible and/or make any needed adjustments or changes in equipment.

Fifth, *don't* make last-minute changes. I still don't quite know how adding the color board caused the computer to change its designation of the hard disk; but I do know, from personal experience, that just about *any* change—in hardware or software—can have unexpected and unwanted side-effects. Computers can be extraordinarily delicate and temperamental; and it's foolish to give them any encouragement.

Remember, your objective in demonstrating anything—any product or any service—is to give participants a clear picture of its operation and its capabilities. You want to make it as easy as possible for them to get that picture, not force them to work hard merely to see what you're demonstrating or understand what you're saying.

And this holds doubly true for anything to do with computers. There are those who truly love and understand computers; but the majority of people are at best uneasy with them. If your demonstration becomes complicated or recognizable problems crop up in the middle of it, it's apt to have the opposite effect from that you intended—turning people off, not enthusing them. Lead your "demonstratees" gently into the waters of computerization one step at a time; don't simply dump them in the deep end, sink or swim, unless you're prepared to have most of them do the former.

14

MIS-MANAGEMENT AND MIS-MANAGEMENT

Perhaps it was just one of those unintentionally funny misprints. Or perhaps some anonymous typesetter had a waspish sense of humor.

Either way, the heading of a display classified ad in the *Wall Street Journal* a few years back read (honest) "Corporate Mis-Management Wanted." The job offered a hefty salary, which provoked a few titters when I showed it around the office where I was working at the time. We all agreed that *we'd* be willing to mis-manage a corporation for a *lot* less than what this job would pay.

What was really wanted, of course, was someone to handle corporate "MIS-Management"—the carelessly omitted capital letters standing for "Management Information Systems," which is the accepted jargon for computers. In other words, the would-be employer wanted somebody to manage its computer activities—which presumably were intended to avert, not cause, mis-management.

As I get more experience in the strengths, and the weaknesses, of computerization, though, I increasingly wonder whether (as with most humor) this misprint didn't contain a kernel of truth. Too often, I find, MIS-management really does cause, or at least becomes equatable with, mis-management.

A Tower of Babel

I don't mean to denigrate those individuals whose working lives are devoted to computerization. There are exceptions, of course (aren't there always?), but on the whole I find them an unusually competent and dedicated lot—at least as much so, all in all, as those employed in any other sector of corporate life. As a rule they're pretty good at what they do, and get the results at which they're aiming with a high ratio of success.

The problem doesn't lie with them; it lies, rather, with organizational structures that set computers and their operations apart from the corporate activities they're designed to serve. What tends to happen is what happens any time you divorce the craftsman from his tools (and what is the computer, ultimately, except a managerial tool?)—poor performance and second-rate results.

You're probably familiar with the parlor game in which one person starts by whispering into his neighbor's ear a phrase that's then passed on, by whispers, to another person, then another, and so on. When the last person is whispered to in turn, he repeats out loud what he heard—which usually bears little resemblance to what the originator began with.

Now imagine the same game played by individuals who all speak different languages. The results would certainly be hilarious; but it's a kind of hilarity that gets lost when the setting is not a parlor game, but a serious business environment with real-world dollars, investments, jobs, etc., at stake.

Yet that's exactly what the concept of a separate MIS structure entails. The manager who wants a particular computer-related job done must somehow convey his wishes—derived and expressed, naturally, in the argot of his own profession—to individuals whose chief expertise, background and, of course, terminology is in the wholly alien domain of computerdom. The wonder, to paraphrase Dr. Sam. Johnson's remark about dogs trained to walk on their hind legs, is not that it is done badly; the wonder is that it can be done at all.

Back in the days when computers were costly and forbidding

machines out of which performance could be coaxed (if at all) only by the gentlest and most expert of hands, there was no choice but to do things in this cumbersome, problem-ridden manner. Today, though, with computers readily and inexpensively available for every executive's desktop, and with "computer literacy" so accessible that even elementary-school children learn it, this separatist approach is no longer necessary—and it's certainly not desirable, as anyone who's had to wrestle with the problems of communicating managerial needs to the wizards of an MIS department will testify.

Microcomputers and Colinos

Nevertheless, I find that most companies large enough to have MIS staffs persist in assigning lead responsibility for *all* computer activities—including micro ("personal") computers—to those staffs. Often, indeed, the only micro-computers in the company will be physically located in the MIS Department, which therefore controls job prioritization, scheduling, etc. Even where individual managers are given their own microcomputers, procurement of hardware and software, training and other support activities and the like remain under MIS control.

Well, runs the familiar argument, and why not? After all, *somebody's* got to be in charge, and aren't the MIS personnel best suited to the job? A computer is a computer is a computer, isn't it, no matter how big or small—so doesn't it make sense to assign microcomputer responsibility to those who already have a computer background?

No, I don't think it does, for several reasons.

Suppose I walked into your office and told you I had a product called a colino that would improve managerial productivity and efficiency by vast measures. Moreover, colinos can readily be operated by non-expert personnel without extensive training; even children who still write their ages with one digit can use them effectively.

Would you really hire specialists to operate your colinos? Or would you let (or require, if necessary) the line managers whose job performance they're intended to enhance take responsibility for learning and using their own tools?

But substitute the word "microcomputer" for "colino" and you create a psychological barrier to rational thinking. Back in the bad old days when computers were huge, enormously expensive, complex beyond belief, and often riddled with "bugs," companies created a kind of high priesthood of computers, whose arcane lore alone could unlock the secrets of these mystical machines. (In this they were, of course, strongly encouraged by the computer specialists themselves, who, as commonly happens, tended to jealously guard both their expertise and their organizational purview.) In such a milieu it became reflexive to assign responsibility for anything bearing the name "computer" to these entrenched experts.

Thus, companies have done with the microcomputer precisely what no reasonable person would do with the eponymous colino—placed an extra, unnecessary organizational tier between it and the managers who need it. A mere word has served to place a barrier between the manager and his ability to make effective use of a key tool of his job.

The Limits of MIS

Not only do the "experts" constitute an unneeded and problematic link between line manager and computer, but they often have little real expertise to contribute. Indeed, it's not unusual to find MIS involvement, however well-meaning, hindering rather than helping in microcomputer applications.

The thing is, microcomputers are a very different breed from their larger cousins, the main-frames and minis. Oh, sure, almost all computers work on the same basic electronic principles, and all are based on the same underlying logical structure. But the micro and, particularly, its software are geared to very different applications from larger systems, and require quite a different approach by those who use them.

Part of the difference, of course, lies in the operating systems used by micros—MP/M, the various CP/M's, and, particularly, MS-DOS and its offspring, PC-DOS. They're certainly not more complicated than the operating systems of mainframes or minis (quite the contrary, in fact); but they *are* different from those systems. Experience with larger computers, in other words, while certainly helpful in learning the micro systems, can't be directly carried over as a substitute for that learning process.

And MIS departments often don't learn the micro systems very thoroughly. First, since micro operating systems and software are purposefully kept fairly simple, the learning process doesn't offer much intellectual stimulation or challenge to individuals accustomed to much more sophisticated and complex machines. Second, MIS activities tend to become compartmentalized, creating, in effect, specialties within the specialty; and micros, which don't fit well within any of these narrow areas of specialization, often consequently get short shrift.

Moreover, corporate MIS operations are geared to big jobs—extensive projects requiring manipulation of vast amounts of data and lots of programming. Micro applications, by contrast, tend to be smaller in scale and involve heavy utilization of prepackaged software. MIS experts, on the whole, have a difficult time making that adjustment.

Here's what I mean: On one occasion I had a phone call from a consultant who was using a standard spreadsheet package to make percentage changes in rate tables but was finding it cumbersome for a particular type of rate table. He'd engaged a friend—an MIS specialist—to help him, but the friend had advised him that (a) the spreadsheet use couldn't be appreciably simplified, and (b) it would require many hours, and cost a lot of money, to develop customized programming to do the job.

Nonsense. It took me ninety minutes by the clock—including several interruptions—to write a program that would do exactly what my caller wanted done. It's far from a perfect solution; my program's output has to be massaged through the spreadsheet to produce an acceptable-looking table. But it does get the job done, and I saw no reason to spend hours on end reinventing the wheel when I could use standard off-the-shelf software to do all but this one particular aspect.

Does that make me smarter or more computer-wise than my caller's friend, the MIS professional? Of course not; it simply means I'm mentally oriented to the micro-computer environment, and he, like most MIS experts, has an entirely different perception of computers and their uses.

If jobs must be explained in detail to others, sent out to another office to do, scheduled onto equipment costing hundreds of thousands of dollars (or more), with output taking hours or days to generate, it's only sensible to go through all this trouble and delay just for the "biggies"—and to establish centralized organizational screening processes to weed out unneeded or trivial projects. And it's only sensible, too, to program the entire project to run as a single entity, without the need for managerial intervention or supervision at intermediate stages; otherwise the operation becomes tedious, time-consuming and all but unmanageable. Such is the milieu of the main-frame and, often, the mini as well.

But if the computer sits right on the manager's desk, to be used by him at his own convenience, matters are quite otherwise. Now it makes perfect sense to use the machine for even the smallest of jobs, for individual tasks instead of whole projects. By making possible direct manager-computer dialogue, by permitting managers to see their projects through step-by-step, making decisions as they go, the micro-computer has opened up a whole new world of computerization. And it's a world with which MIS professionals, trained in the more exotic discipline of the larger machines, largely lack familiarity.

Eliminating the Middleman

I admit that, notwithstanding all I've said, there are some valid arguments for some degree of MIS involvement in microcomputers. It provides a focus of centralized control that allows standardization of a company's computer hardware, software, etc. Related to this, it provides a managerial nexus for the much-talked-about networking of multiple microcomputers. And it affords computer-using managers an in-house source of technical support when they have problems they can't solve.

But these arguments tend to be overstated. Standardization of hardware and software is often unimportant, since even the most incompatible of micros can readily "talk to" (*i.e.,* interchange data with) one another using ASCII coding (the *lingua franca* in which all micros are conversant), relatively inexpensive modems, and either telephone lines or "hard-wire" connectors. As for any economic benefits of standardization, forget it; discounting is so deep in the competition-rich retail market that only the very largest-volume purchases command any further price cuts at all.

Networking, too, is often of overrated value. Data-sharing among microcomputers can be accommodated by much simpler means (ASCII transmissions, shared hard-disk drives, etc.); and with resident computer memories growing as fast as they are, the need to pool the computing power of microcomputers through networking is dwindling rapidly.

As for in-house technical support—well, I've already discussed the lack of microcomputer expertise in the average MIS operation. For most micro hardware and software, it's better to rely on developers or vendors. Or, better yet, hunt up one of the ubiquitous "hacker" clubs. Hackers often don't know much (if anything) about the main-frames and minis, but a good one can make a micro sit up on its hind legs and beg. And most of them will help out just for the fun of it or, at worst, at very modest fees.

Finally, even if one or more of these arguments is really valid in your particular circumstances, it's still no reason to put microcomputer activities lock, stock and barrel in the MIS department. Especially where the machines themselves are physically lodged on MIS premises, kept under lock and key and accessible only to "authorized" (*i.e.,* MIS) users, the advantage of the micro has been all but negated.

One of the recurrent themes of modern business management is to eliminate the middleman whenever possible—to deal, as much as you can, principal-to-principal. Certainly the middleman qualifies as a clear undesirable if he contributes little or nothing to the end product. And the key advantage of today's low-cost, easy-to-learn microcomputer is its potential to get the MIS middleman out of the manager-computer relationship without impairing—perhaps even enhancing—the end product.

In the modern workplace there's no valid reason why the computer-using manager can't be his own MIS expert—at least within the parameters of his use of the machines in his own job. Companies that substitute reliance on separate MIS support operations and staffs for training line managers to handle their own computer applications are simply perpetuating an organizational sort of apartheid, with all its inherent problems and opportunities for error, that technology has rendered obsolete.

Part 4

THE START-UP PROCESS

15

THE PROBLEMS OF STARTING UP

What should you expect when a computer first makes its appearance in your office?

Reduced productivity and increased inefficiency, probably by a very wide margin—that's what.

No, I haven't inadvertently reversed my terms—and no, too, I'm not trying to turn you off computers. But I do want to warn you that the benefits computerization offers are not easily realized in most cases, and that until you're in a position to realize them the computer will be worse than useless to you; it will be a positive handicap as you seek to keep your office running effectively.

The industry's promotional literature, and the writings of enthusiasts, paint a picture of sharp contrasts. It's like those tawdry "before-and-after" ads you see for cosmetic aids: Here we are shown an office of weary drudges, struggling to keep abreast of an ever-growing overload of paperwork; there we see the same office now happy, relaxed and a nonpareil of efficiency because of the advent of a computer. But this sequence of pictures skips briskly over the key period of transition between the two scenes—a period so traumatic that some operations never emerge from it.

And it's that transition—which will last for weeks at the very least and which will to a greater or lesser extent be repeated every time you add new increments of hardware or software—that I'm discussing here, with a view toward how you, as manager, can live with and minimize its stresses.

The Computer Arrives

Typically, the office and its denizens will be woefully underprepared for the computer when it first shows up.

The manager may *think* he's prepared. He may have studied the machine carefully, had demonstrations of its capabilities, even attended (or had his subordinates attend) training classes. He may have a clear idea of the job(s) he wants the computer to take over, at least to start with.

But unless he's extraordinarily astute *and* versed in the ways of computers, he, too, will have a rosy before-and-after view of how the computer will affect his operation, with no really clear plan for getting from before to after. And even those systems touted as "turnkey" interpose a number of obstacles in his path.

Right off the bat you face the need to make a stack of cable connections. Although it has a singular name, a computer is not just one integrated piece of equipment; it's comprised of several separate units, each of which comes in its own carton and all of which must be linked together with various types of wiring. At the least there's the computer itself, the keyboard, the monitor and the printer; and you may also have separately housed disk (or tape) drives, a modem, a plotter, and perhaps even more. (All the descriptions I'm giving you here deal with a microcomputer, or "personal" computer; if you're getting anything bigger, the problems can be so formidable you don't even want to know about them.)

The whole process is something akin to the way a lot of parents wind up spending Christmas Eve night, plugging together all those toys that you buy with "some assembly required." You get to bed at 3 a.m. with skinned knuckles and severely frayed tempers.

Your user manual will undoubtedly describe the process of making these connections as "simple." But as any experience with Christmas toys may have shown you (the same word also shows up a *lot* in their instruction sheets), that's an ominous adjective indeed. Unless you're *very* lucky, you can expect to spend a good bit of time just getting the various devices hooked together properly so they can communicate with one another.

To give you an idea, my first microcomputer and printer were both very popular, commonplace models. Yet when I wired them up the computer obstinately refused to drive the printer, and neither the manufacturers of either unit nor my dealer could help me solve the problem. It ultimately took me about 20 hours of mainly trial-and-error to make the proper adjustments (which turned out to involve both rewiring and some software manipulation) just so I could get a printout.

Then there are a host of other details that must be attended to—things like programming your function keys, formatting disks, adjusting your monitor, "installing" your software and the like. By now you're probably several hours into the whole process, and you still haven't got the computer to actually *do* anything; all you've managed thus far is to make it *ready* to start doing whatever it is you want it to do.

Mastering Your System

OK, you've got this far. (That assumes, of course, there were no production or shipping glitches that have left you with a defective unit; quality control in the computer industry leaves quite a bit to be desired, and the machines are notoriously vulnerable to the bumps and thumps of the transportation process.) Now you have the unenviable task of figuring out how to use your new system.

Start with your operating system. If it's MS- (or PC-) DOS, as it probably is (that's the system most business microcomputers use), you'll have to learn the in's and out's of "tree"-structured directories and how to shift around among the various branches and twigs. With any operating system you'll have to sort out at least a few basic utility commands and programs, which you'll need on a regular basis. And you'll find your machine isn't much help to you as you do all this; it simply displays that infamous, uncommunicative "A>" (or, in some cases, "C>") prompt while it's waiting for you to tell it what to do.

Haven't lost hope yet? Good; now you're ready for the truly tough job: mastering the word processor, spreadsheet, data-base manager, dedicated purpose programming—whatever applications software you've acquired.

If I tell you that colleges offer full-semester courses merely in the operation of the most commonly used applications software, does that give you an idea of what's in store?

The appellation "user-friendly" that's so often applied to computer software is the computer version of "simple"—doubled and squared. At best it has to be taken with a grain of salt; at worst it's an out-and-out untruth. To be sure, some programs are easier to learn and use than others; but I don't find anything very "friendly" about programming that obliges me to strike *precisely* the right keys, in *precisely* the right sequence, before it will follow my commands—and that figuratively spits in my eye if I make even the tiniest of mistakes.

There are two basic types of software you can expect to encounter. The first, and easiest to learn and use, is "menu-driven." These work about like the storybook Chinese restaurant; choose one from column A and two from column B, as it were. You do it merely by designating your selection by pressing the specified function key, numeral, etc., and the machine then presumably does your bidding. Unfortunately, columns A and B—and usually C, D, E and F as well—are on different screens, which you have the thumb your way through tediously to get to the option you happen to want. Moreover, in many cases the screens have something else in common with that Chinese menu: they tend to be written in a language (in this case, computerese) which you probably don't understand. It's going to take you a while to learn to use the program with anything approaching facility.

The other type of software, called "command-driven," is even more complicated. You don't register your choice from menu displays; you have to hit particular command sequences that make liberal use of the "CONTROL" and "ALTERNATE" keys (as well as the special function keys). Usually there are numerous command options, entailing multiple keystrokes, through which you may or may not be guided by judiciously placed "help" screens which again tend to be laced with a heavy infusion of jargon. Again, attaining any significant proficiency is an effortful, time-consuming process.

And as a general rule, the more the software will do for you, the more effort and time you have to put into learning to use it.

Data Input

Even now, your computer isn't fully "on line" in your application. Indeed, in many applications you've barely begun. The software merely instructs the hardware how to deal with the information you give it; but you still have to give it that information.

This is where the biggest problem comes in terms of office productivity and efficiency. As a rule, computer applications in the transportation/distribution industry demand formidable amounts of start-up data—lists of transportation routings, basic cost information, customer identifiers, rates, etc., etc. And, again, the general rule is that the more you want the computer to do, the more data you must feed it. Furthermore, you must doublecheck every keystroke attentively ("garbage in, garbage out") for accuracy and completeness.

It's a lot like training a brand-new employee. Unlike a human worker, the computer won't ever forget what you tell it; but the machine offsets this virtue by demanding that you specifically input, keystroke by keystroke, reams of information a human would normally absorb serendipitously while already doing productive work. Until it has a *complete* store of information, most software won't function at all, since the computer is incapable of making even the most obvious of assumptions in order to fill in the gaps in what it "knows."

Meantime, of course, time is obviously not standing still for your office; day-to-day operational requirements are still as pressing as ever. If the workload was heavy before the computer arrived, the demands of learning and loading data into the system will obviously have aggravated rather than eased the problem—possibly to a degree you simply can't afford.

The manager who's short on patience and/or unprepared for these start-up problems may never get beyond them. I've seen a number of cases where managers have brought in computers full of high hope and then, a few weeks or months later, dejectedly had them removed with the fervent wish that they "never see the gosh-dratted fooling misbegotten pile of natural fertilizer again" (well, words to that effect, anyhow).

With computers, however, it truly is darkest before the dawn. If the manager can somehow endure the inevitable start-up traumas, they will ultimately pass and the computer begin to fulfill its role as the productivity-enhancer it was intended to be. After all, think of the problems that beset the managers of yore when the typewriter (for example) was just coming on the scene—the glowing glimpses of improved productivity clearly in view, the despair waiting for secretaries and clerks to learn to use the machines while current productivity plummeted. And think, too, of the probable fate of the manager unwise enough to give up halfway through the process and return his people to writing everything out in longhand.

Some Ideas for Easing the Transition

No matter how thoroughly you prepare, no matter how diligently you work, it's impossible to escape these transitional problems. That's fact, and there's nothing you can do about it.

But it *is* possible to ease them, and, particularly, to minimize the short-term damage they do to office productivity. Here are some steps you should consider in bringing that new computer into your operation:

• Get advance training. At least one individual in your operation, preferably more than one, should be "computer-literate" and versed in the particular system you're acquiring *before* you get it. And that doesn't mean you; as the manager, your job is to manage the people under you, and you can't do both that and spend hours on end in front of the computer as well. You need to learn it—but your time is later, when your responsibilities of managing this difficult transition period have abated.

(A violation of this principle led to my first exposure to computers 15 years ago. The chief of the office in which I was then working, who knew computers from a previous job, brought one in for another section of his operation; but for weeks the thing sat idle because the boss had no time to work with it (or train others), and nobody in that section knew a blame thing about computers or had the time or inclination to learn. One of my subordinates and I got to fooling around with the machine during lunchtime, after hours, etc., and ultimately taught ourselves enough to put it to work; but the section to which it was nominally assigned never did get any use out of it.)

• Get training in any software packages you're buying. Many vendors offer some assistance in getting you off the ground with the programming (especially where more expensive packages are involved); and in other cases you'll find help at computer schools, local community colleges and the like. Take full advantage of such training if you can get free, and give serious consideration to paying extra for it if you can't; it can save you countless hours of trial-and-error learning and can help you utilize the software's full spectrum of features. (No, perusing the user manual(s) is *not* an adequate substitute. Even a good user manual inevitably leaves a lot to be desired in walking you through the program. And most user manuals *aren't* very good; again and again I encounter user manuals that are so loaded with jargon as to make them incomprehensible, are incomplete, and/or are even downright inaccurate. Study the user manual carefully, of course; but get training, too.)

• Define your objectives of computerizing fully, in advance—and limit them. If you don't know *precisely* what you're going to use the computer for, you're not ready to get one. Sure, you may ultimately figure out some uses for it (I'd be astonished if you couldn't), but luck and ingenuity are no substitute for careful planning; among other things, relying on them can stretch out your start-up woes considerably. At the same time, don't try to do everything at once if you have several planned uses; you'll keep stumbling over your own shorts. A sound approach is to pick out one relatively easy-to-implement application as a starter, even if it's not your top priority, and get it operational before you try anything else. This reduces the time lag between acquisition and useful operation, and the experience (and the psychological boost) you gain from your first successful application will stand you in good stead as you proceed to others.

- Pick a slow time to bring the computer in—the summer months, the Christmas holiday period, sometime when the normal workload is least pressing and you can best afford some disruption. (But watch out for vacation schedules, which also tend to coincide with such periods.)

- Plan for the problems and delays you'll surely encounter in getting your hardware and software fully "up" in your operation—and educate your boss(es) to expect and make their own allowances for them. Take your worst-case expectations of the time and effort required, double them, double them again, and regard the results as your *most optimistic* forecast; and even then you may be underestimating. It can be very discouraging if you expect quick results and base your planning on that expectation—and doubly so if you've "sold" your superiors on buying a computer with unrealistically rosy expectations of how rapidly and easily it will improve your efficiency.

- Seek out help when you run into difficulties; don't struggle on valiantly trying to solve problems you don't understand. A classic illustration (this actually happened) is the company that spent nearly six months trying to get a particular program to run before calling in the experts—who then took five minutes to recognize that the problem was a faulty disk drive that, moreover, was *now* out of warranty.

- Schedule temporary help, overtime, etc., if you have a lot of start-up data to input. You want to get the machine up and running, reaping the benefits of efficiency and productivity for which you acquired the system, as quickly as possible, not wait for weeks while you try to sandwich data-input sessions in between your day-to-day activities.

• Finally, be patient, and take reverses in stride. One of the first major computer projects I handled was a survey for my then-employer that demanded a full week's worth of data input. When I finally ran the program everything seemed dandy—until, belatedly, it became apparent that my results simply weren't possible. But by that time I'd already scrapped my original raw data, and couldn't recover it; the only thing to do was re-input everything and start all over. Discouraging in the extreme—but we ultimately did come up with good results, which would have been pragmatically unobtainable without the computer's help. (And I learned, too, *never* to erase data until I was completely done with the whole project, if even then.) If you stick with it, the machine really will help you in the end.

A Personal Lesson

Here's an illustration, from personal experience, of just how difficult and problematic it can be to bring new computer hardware and software on-line.

For several years I published my own monthly *Barrett Transportation Newsletter.* Finally, with the mechanics of the publishing process becoming excessively time-consuming, I reached an agreement for the Traffic Service Corp., publisher of this book, to take over as publisher of the *Newsletter,* which I continue to write. Part of that agreement was that I would transmit the *Newsletter* contents each month directly from my computer to Traffic Service's, using a modem and telephone lines.

Well, I had never used a modem before, but my computer had the proper hardware to accommodate one and I figured it should be no great problem. So I went out and bought one.

The first thing I discovered was that you can't just hook up a modem to your computer and start phoning up other computers; you need the proper software to "drive" it (*i.e.,* interpret what your computer tells the modem to transmit). And that software is strictly model-specific; it has to be adapted for precisely the computer you have. Since the Osborne I I was then using was made by a company that was by that time out of business, finding the software gave me fits; but finally I was able to locate a couple of programs, both of which had their pros and cons for different types of modem communications.

Then there was the problem of physically hooking up computer and modem. This is done through a standardized plug-and-socket arrangement known in computer vernacular as a "Serial RS232 port." Almost every computer has such a socket, with 25 tiny holes into which 25 tiny pins of the modem's (or, alternatively, a printer's) male plug fit.

I say "standardized" because plug and socket fit snugly. The *wiring* of RS232 plugs and sockets, however, is anything but standard. Pin No. 20 of my modem, for example, is supposed to connect with hole No. 6 in my computer, and so forth. If you plug the modem in without first doing this cross-wiring the system figuratively spits in your eye. (Don't ask me why fittings are standardized but wiring isn't; it's just another illustration of the rather discombobulated state of the, after all, pretty new microcomputer industry.)

Anyhow, I needed a short piece of linking cable to make these cross-connections; and I needed to know just which pins and holes to cross-wire, since this varies significantly from one machine to another. A computer-consultant friend well-versed in these things helped me out here.

All ready to go now, right? Well, sort of. I could link up with such computer services as The Source okay. But my inexperience showed through when I tried to hook into Traffic Service's system. It took me and Stephen R. Hunter, Traffic Service's production vice president, over three hours of, more or less, trial and error before we could satisfactorily send information from my computer to the company's. (Fortunately Steve and I are long-time friends, which probably kept us from shouting at one another in the frustration of repeated failures.)

All things considered, I estimate that, conservatively speaking, it ate up four full workdays of my time just to get this done—and I followed all the advice I offered above about how to minimize problems. Well, all the advice except the part about *expecting* problems; but maybe I'll learn not to make *that* mistake again.

A Semantic Misunderstanding

One thing that caused me a lot of trouble in establishing the Barrett-Traffic Service link was a misunderstanding of terminology. The trouble arose—and I suspect this type of problem isn't very unusual—because of the unfortunate fact that the specialized terminologies of different disciplines often overlap confusingly.

My communications software allowed me to turn something called a "copy buffer" on and off by hitting a key that acts as a toggle switch. Now, a "buffer" is a segregated corner of the computer's memory that serves as a staging area for information being transmitted or received; I knew that much. And as a long-time writer I also knew perfectly well that "copy" is the manuscript I prepare for books, magazine articles, etc. (as in "Haven't you written your copy for the computer book yet?").

Since I was transmitting "copy," it was obvious to me that the copy buffer should be switched on; and so I did. But communications kept being garbled; the beginning of each transmission was cluttered up with messages that *Traffic Service's* computer was sending *me,* even though *I* was the one supposed to be doing the transmitting.

It wasn't until Steve Hunter commented that my transmissions seemed to be copying everything his computer said that the penny dropped for me; I toggled the copy buffer off, and the final bug was out of our communications. My deathless prose may be "copy" to me, but it's just another data file to my computer and is handled by my *file* buffer; the copy buffer is for, literally, copying information my computer receives, and has to be off to prevent me from echoing the other computer's transmissions right back to it.

Part 5

COMPUTER SECURITY

16

THE FAILINGS OF SECURITY

"We have really good security for our system," the sales representative told me. "We've even had people try to break our security, and they couldn't."

I'll call her Mary, because I don't want to single out either her or her company for unfair criticism; they're no worse in this regard than most I've seen, and better than many. But I've got some news for Mary, and for her bosses, and for anybody else who claims his or her computer system is "really secure."

No, it's not.

The fact is that there's truly no such thing as a genuinely secure computer system, just as there's no such thing as a pick-proof lock. Oh, there are steps you can take to improve security, to make the system harder to break into and/or misuse. But the system that's truly proof against a determined "hacker" who wants to get in (a) has not yet been devised, and (b) probably never will be.

The Fallacy of Passwording

Most people, when they talk of computer security, have in mind some sort of passwording approach which limits access to the system (or key features of the system) to those who know the proper password(s).

I won't waste time discussing the more obvious failings of systems of this type, such as having the display screen "echo" the password (so anyone standing nearby can read it), allowing users to write down their passwords on slips of paper they leave in plain sight or "hide" in their unlocked desk drawers, etc. Let's stick to cases where there's at least some effort to take security seriously.

Mary's software was one such; it allowed users to authorize payments of money, which tends to get considerable security attention. Her firm had actually employed a two-tier version of the password approach, requiring users to input both a "User ID" code *and* a password, both of which were kept secret.

Let me describe just how easily even a relatively untalented hacker could get into that system. (The people who had supposedly tested her system's security clearly lacked the hacker mentality.)

First, the display screen that asks users to input the ID/password combination indicates how many characters each of these codes contains. That makes the job a lot simpler, because it lets a would-be invader know from the start how many combinations should be tried. In this case the screen made clear that the ID consisted of three characters, and the password of five or six.

Let's take the user-ID part first. Assume the ID is made up of three letters of the alphabet, which is at least a good starting point. The following is a nine-line BASIC-language program to let you try, in sequence, every such three-letter combination:

```
FOR N = 1 TO 26
A$ = CHR$(N + 64)
FOR I = 1 TO 26
A$ = LEFT$(A$,1) + CHR$(I + 64)
FOR J = 1 TO 26
PRINT LEFT$(A$,2) + CHR$(J + 64)
NEXT J
NEXT I
NEXT N
```

Try it if you don't believe me; call up your version of BASIC, key it in, and tell it to "RUN." Starting with "AAA" and going right through "ZZZ," you'll see all the possible three-letter combinations march up your display screen like little soldiers.

There are 17,576 possible such combinations, which seems like an awful lot; it would be prohibitively tedious and time-consuming to try all of them manually. But the computer program I wrote took less than 30 seconds to run through every combination. All I'd have to do is make a few changes in the program to channel its output as a response to the "User ID" query, and to quit when the software accepted one of the three-letter codes, and I'm halfway into the system already. (No, I won't spell out what those changes are; I'm certainly not trying to encourage security breaches here.)

A similar type of program will get me past the "password" protection. Because the password's a little longer, it would take more time to run the program—a bit under six hours for a five-letter password, a bit under six *days* for a six-letter one. And the time would be further extended if characters other than alphabetic letters (numbers, punctuation marks, graphic symbols, etc.) were used.

But I probably wouldn't have to run all the way through the program; there's a fifty-fifty chance I'd hit the correct combination before I was halfway through. And in any event, what's a few hours or days of sitting and waiting (the computer programming, after all, is doing all the work) when there are hundreds of thousands, even millions of dollars waiting to be stolen at the end?

A History of Break-Ins

And the approach I've described is pretty crude, akin to blasting a safe door open with dynamite. A really adept hacker could program his way past the kind of security Mary's system uses in much more adroit, and faster, ways.

If you think I'm exaggerating, I invite your attention to a tome called *Hackers,* by one Steven Levy.* Levy discusses one college student who regarded other people's passwords (securing

*New York, NY: Doubleday & Co., 1984, hardback; New York, NY: Dell Publishing Co., Inc., 1985, paperback.

their private files on the system he was using) as a personal affront; for sheer sport he'd find his way into those files and leave messages for the proprietary users suggesting that they dispense with passwords altogether. After a time, Levy says, many of the users simply gave up trying to keep this individual out of their files.

And what about the newspaper and magazine pieces you occasionally read about teen-agers who use their unsophisticated home machines to break into the supposedly secure files of banks, credit bureaus, government agencies, etc.? What about, for that matter, the movie "WarGames," in which a youngster gets into the key Defense Department system and nearly (inadvertently) precipitates a nuclear war? Yes, "WarGames" was fiction; but it was inspired by all those real-life cases in which hackers have proved again and again how insecure computer security really is.

So far we've talked only about the "outsider"—the truly unauthorized intruder. In fact, most instances of computer misuse are at the hands of authorized users of the system, individuals who legitimately have access and then abuse their positions of trust to steal, depredate and otherwise do things on the system they're not supposed to.

As I've noted, you can read quite a lot about such computer misuses in the newspapers; and the hard truth, I'm told, is that all these reported incidents are no more than the tip of the iceberg. In countless more cases the perpetrator(s) was (were) never identified with legal certainty; and in yet others (even those where sums of money were actually stolen) the victims refused to prosecute, so as not to reveal to the world at large how porous their security really was (and/or is).

And then, of course, there are surely numerous cases where break-ins, thefts, etc., have gone entirely undetected.

Improving Security

OK, I've said a lot about what's wrong with computer security, and why electronic systems like the password approach aren't effective. Now: How can you improve your computer security?

The first step is to get serious about your electronic approach. Mary's system, for example, let me continue to put in wrong user ID's and passwords indefinitely without doing anything except chiding me for my mistakes. Certainly it would be tougher to use the kind of trial-and-error programming I've described if the system "crashed"—perhaps locking up the keyboard and requiring a manual reset—if I entered the wrong ID/password two or three times in succession (leaving enough leeway for human keyboarding errors, but not enough for repetitive break-in attempts).

The same thing can be done with phone-access systems; the computer can break the connection if the required log-in procedure (ID's, passwords, etc.) isn't performed correctly, requiring a re-dial. Some highly sensitive and sophisticated systems are even tied into phone lines so they can tell where incoming calls originate; repetitive wrong-ID calls from the same phone set off the electronic equivalent of a burglar alarm.

In addition, it shouldn't be too easy for users once in the system to change their ID's, passwords, etc. Mary's system let me specify a new password without even knowing the old one. In addition to their obvious potential to invalidate password-entry requirements, such password-changing routines can sometimes offer expert hackers a "back door" into the system; the movie "WarGames" revolved around a back-door approach of this nature (although not, in that case, a password routine).

Even thus enhanced, electronic security systems should not be given full responsibility for protecting the computer from break-ins. Good old physical security—locked doors and the like—should also be used. Indeed, some computers—the IBM-AT and most of its clones, for example—come with a built-in key-lock, which should be used if security is at all an issue.

Especially should this approach be taken with systems that allow the user to make calls on the corporate treasury, by preparing payment authorizations, cutting checks, etc. The computer itself should be locked; it should be in a locked room (at least after normal working hours); and disks containing the software should themselves be separately locked up in places more secure than a desk drawer. You protect your money itself in such fashions; and a computer that can be used to get at that money is just as sensitive.

For phone-accessed systems, a friend of mine has developed the simplest, but hardest-to-crack, approach you could reasonably ask for: His policy is that the computer is never left hooked up to its phone link unless authorized phone use is actually being made of it. When you dial in you get a human being on the other end of the line, to whom you must immediately identify yourself orally with an ID and a password; only then do both of you switch over to your computers.

But all of these security precautions, of all types, must be backed up by close human attention. My friend's manual-connect policy, for example, is often sabotaged by his staff's laxness about disconnecting the machine after a hang-up; the next user, thus, can call directly in to the computer. People are notoriously careless about keeping their ID's, passwords and the like secret (most reported break-ins happen because somebody got sloppy about protecting that information). Keys are left casually lying about, lock combinations are written down and left around or poorly concealed; etc.

And finally, there should be close oversight—both electronic and human—of any computer system that has, even potentially, access to money or otherwise invites marauders. The kind of security precautions I've been describing will naturally be useless if the thief is someone with authorized access to the system.

Faked purchase orders, invoices, payment authorizations and the like are among the easiest ways to use the computer for stealing. Or a more expert thief can even write some invisible "parasite" programs to both channel funds illicitly and conceal what's been done; one bank official embezzled shocking sums by the simple expedient of programming the computer to deduct a penny from every deposit and credit it to his personal account.

There are two ways to detect such problems, both of which should be used. The first is to include undocumented alarm routines in the software that alert you to surreptitious efforts to interfere with its authorized operation. The second is to conduct periodic human audits of what the computer is doing—on a non-scheduled, non-announced basis—to make sure the computer's records are reconciled with the "real-world" situation they're supposed to represent. And in both approaches, *any* discrepancy, no matter how seemingly trivial, should be rigorously followed up; it may herald far deeper *non*-trivial problems.

And if, despite all your efforts, somebody does break into or otherwise misuse your system—*prosecute!* That doesn't mean the inquisitive teen-ager who gets into your system as a prank should be sent to jail, or even have his computer confiscated (as frequently happens); the punishment should obviously fit the crime, and in such cases a mere judicial talking-to might be enough to have fully adequate impact. But *no* such misuse should be ignored in the mistaken belief that you are thereby enhancing your company's or your computer system's reputation for invulnerability; anyone who knows enough about computers to pose a serious security threat will simply laugh at any such notion. And obviously serious crimes, such as the theft or embezzlement of money, should be rigorously prosecuted, just as they would be if the theft came about through non-computer means.

There's no such thing as total security, in computer systems any more than anywhere else in life. But if you treat your computer system with appropriate respect, and recognize how its misuse can damage you and your company, there *is* a lot you can do to cut the risk to an irreducible minimum. Unless you're one who truly believes the old saw about "who steals my purse steals trash"—an attitude of which few business organizations can afford to partake—I'd strongly suggest you give some serious consideration to how secure your computer system *really* is.

17

COMPUTERS AND FOREIGN TRAVEL

Planning to take a microcomputer abroad—or buy one there? Watch out for Customs.

Some foreign-made computers, especially the "bargain" machines, are legal contraband in this country; they are wholesale rip-offs of U.S. brands which infringe American patents, copyrights and/or trademarks. It's illegal to import them; if you try, Customs will seize them without compensation to you.

The International Trade Commission, in the U.S. Commerce Department, tries to maintain a list of such contraband machines, and you can get one from them. But it may not be 100% complete as of the time you return to the U.S., so you could get stuck anyway.

Be particularly wary of abnormally "good deals" on brand-name machines, such as Apple or IBM, that you may be offered while abroad. A few foreign pirates aren't content with copying the machines circuit-by-circuit; they copy the appearance and manufacturer's logo as well. Such "forgeries," of course, are also illegal—and they're likely not to function anything like so well as the real thing even if you can get them past Customs.

If you do buy a legally importable computer abroad, Customs has a rip-off of its own in store for you. You can bring up to $400 worth of foreign purchases back duty-free. The next $1,000 worth is dutiable at a flat rate of 10%—*even if the regular duty is lower than 10%!* For computers, the standard duty is 4½%—meaning that Customs is requiring you to pay more than twice that rate for $1,000 of the computer's value.

To get around this, try being careful how you list what you're bringing back on the Customs forms. If you have other purchases on which import duties are higher (liquor, perfume, etc.), let your $400 and $1,000 limitations apply to them instead of the computer. Then you'll only pay the 4½% duty on your computer import.

As for taking computers abroad for use while you're there, you may need an export license unless you own the machine personally (if, for example, your employer is the owner). Licenses are available through the Exporters' Services section of the Commerce Department. Some types of sophisticated computers are restricted (you may have read about Commerce refusing to let the chess-playing computer be shipped to an international event), but there's no problem for most standard business microcomputers.

Whether the computer is yours or the company's, make sure you register it with Customs when you leave. Otherwise when you try to bring it back they may presume you bought it abroad, and make you pay import duty unless you can prove otherwise.

Part 6

COMPUTER SOFTWARE IN GENERAL

18

A GUIDE TO PROGRAMMING 'LANGUAGES'

If you do any programming at all, chances are you do it using some version, or "dialect," of BASIC.

BASIC (the name is an acronym for Beginners' All-purpose Symbolic Instruction Code) was developed during the 1960's at Dartmouth College. It was designed to incorporate most of the features of the two then-popular computing languages—COBOL and FORTRAN—without the very exacting format requirements of those two languages. In its early incarnations it wasn't as "powerful"—that is, didn't allow as wide a range of instructional options—as either; but it has since been enlarged and expanded until it rivals any other programming language.

As with most human languages, there's no single "standard" version of BASIC; just as Jimmy Carter's English differs substantially from that spoken by Queen Elizabeth, so do BASIC versions employ different syntaxes. In general, however, it takes relatively few changes to convert from one version to another (although there are exceptions).

BASIC was the first easy-to-learn language for the non-expert programmer, and remains, probably because of longevity more than any other factor, the most popular. In addition, it comes "bundled" with some microcomputers. Probably about half the specialized transportation/distribution software I've seen was originally programmed in one version of BASIC or another.

The second favorite language used in transportation/

distribution programming seems to be COBOL (Common Ordinary Business Operating Language). It antedates BASIC by a few years, and was, as its name implies, developed for business-type applications. COBOL is, however, considerably more difficult than BASIC to learn and use; moreover, in my experience COBOL programs tend to run fairly slowly, especially when large data bases are involved.

FORTRAN (FORmula TRANslation), the other longest-lived language in any common use, was intended principally for scientific applications, and so is inappropriate for most transportation/distribution uses; I've seen very little specialized industry software programmed in it. Like COBOL, it's appreciably harder to learn and use than BASIC, although its use doesn't seem to negatively affect operating speeds in most cases.

More recently developed languages include Pascal (and a fairly new streamlined variant, Turbo Pascal); C language (and its own variant, Modula C, which requires a specialized operating system); Logo; and others. Some general-purpose software packages, such as d Base II and III and some other data-base managers, also offer such elaborate instruction options that they too can be used as limited programming languages. I've seen a smattering of transportation/distribution software written in all of these.

There is also the venerable Assembly Language, which predates even COBOL and FORTRAN. Assembly Language programs, however, are generally machine-specific (that is, a program written for one type or model computer has to be completely revamped to run on another), and require a fair amount of technical knowledge about the particular machine on which you're working.

And finally, there's Machine Language, in which instructions are delivered to the computer using its own lexicon of hexidecimal ("Hex") numeric coding. Indeed, even today Machine Language is the only instructional coding your computer actually understands; all other languages are basically translators that act as a buffer between the computer and the user. But Machine Language is exceedingly difficult to learn, and is comfortable only to the most dedicated of professionals or "hackers."

Any computer can be instructed in Machine Language; to use any other programming language, you must first acquire a version of the language itself. For the most part language software is inexpensive—as little as $50, and seldom more than $150-200. But then you can only run the programs you write if the language in which they are written is first "loaded" into your computer's memory to act as a translator; and since the act of translation itself occupies computer processing time, this tends to considerably slow down operation of your programs.

To get around this you must use a "compiler" so that, instead of needing to be translated afresh during every program run, your software is permanently translated into machine-readable format and stored on disk in that form. The compiler places a new suffix after the program's name (".COM", for "compiled," in some operating systems, ".EXE", for "executable," in others), and it will now run directly from your computer's operating system. Some languages and language variants are "self-compiling"; that is, the compilation function is an integral part of the language software. Otherwise, compilers must be purchased separately, for another $200-300; but they're worth the price (because of the increase in operating speed of compiled programs) if you do any serious programming.

Which language is "best?" Every programmer will have his or her favorite, which seem to be largely a matter of personal taste. But any programmer worth his salt will tell you, too, that there is no single "best" language; the optimum language for any particular programming task depends on the nature of the task. Each has its strengths, each its weaknesses, and each will accordingly do some particular types of jobs more or less efficiently than alternatives.

If you decide to learn programming, the best place to start is certainly with BASIC; it's fairly straightforward, comports more or less with normal English usage, and—most important—is in widespread use. And unless you're going to get into some pretty heavy programming, you can probably stop there, too. BASIC is the only programming language in which I'm at all conversant, for example, and I find it entirely adequate for my limited purposes. But if you do decide to go on from there, try Pascal next; it's growing tremendously in popularity, and also isn't terribly difficult. Beyond there, COBOL (more difficult) and "C" (perhaps the most difficult of all) would probably be most useful, although there are things to be said for virtually every other language, including Machine Language.

19

WORD-PROCESSING

It was when she was in seventh grade that Alexandra, my daughter, brought home an atrocious grade on a report she'd done for her science class at school.

The problem wasn't that she didn't know her subject matter; she didn't do badly in that area. But this particular teacher was a stickler for neatness, correct spelling and grammar, etc., and in those areas she'd scored just 22 of a possible 50 points.

"From now on," I decreed with the familiar authoritarian sternness of parenthood that children so detest, "you'll do all school reports on a word processor." She'd been working a bit with one, knew pretty well how to use it, but disliked it and so had been avoiding it. Now, however, with wheedling and two very eloquent eyes failing her, she finally sat down at my old Osborne and—painfully at first, keystroke by keystroke—began pecking away.

She wasn't marked lower than a B on any report she turned in for the rest of the year. And even with her snail's-pace typing, she got them done faster.

Neatness Counts. . .

I sought, and received, Alexandra's permission to recount this tale for a reason: What I said to her I would heartily like to repeat to quite a lot of people many years her senior. What seems to pass in many quarters for acceptable business correspondence, reports, memoranda, etc., frankly appalls me—and with the technology of word processing available to anyone who can find his or her way around a typewriter keyboard, at less cost than a month's salary for a (not very good) typist, there's just no reason or excuse for it.

Consider what showed up in my mail not long before I sat down at my own word processor to write this chapter. It was a letter from an individual who was seeking to "sell" me on his company's professionalism and expertise in a particular area so I'd give him a little publicity. We'd spoken on the phone, he was offering a useful answer to a problem I'd previously discussed in print, and I'd asked him to write.

The letter I got was of approximately the same quality as my then-11-year-old daughter's fateful report. Spelling and grammatical mistakes by the carload, obvious erasures, strikeovers . . . I could go on, but you get the idea. Far from persuading me of my correspondent's (or his company's) capabilities, the letter served only to convince me that either (a) he'd slept through every English class he ever took after about the sixth grade, or (b) he was unbelievably careless and disorganized. Either way, he made a very bad impression where he'd clearly been hoping to make a good one.

And the truly astonishing thing is that the letter was *typed!* It's not, in other words, that my correspondent (or whoever typed it for him—I refuse to dignify the producer of such an atrocity with the designation "secretary") lacked the mechanical skills necessary to use a word processor. It's just that one *wasn't* used—as the results made painfully obvious.

Nor are letters of this calibre especially unusual in my experience. I receive a fair volume of correspondence through the various magazine columns I write, my consulting practice, etc., and a sizeable proportion of it looks like something the cat dragged in, and reads just as poorly.

Now, I'm not expecting every businessman to produce the translucent prose of a Hemingway, or present me with illuminated manuscripts worthy of inclusion in the *Book of Kells.* But neither do I think I should have to struggle to divine the meaning behind ill-chosen words that wander aimlessly through thickets of strikeovers, erasures and misspellings.

And *why* are so many businesspeople seemingly content with presenting themselves and their companies in the light such slovenly workmanship sheds, when the answer is so readily and inexpensively at hand?

A Key Office Tool

If you ask me what's the single most important value of a computer in a business office—or even if you don't—I'll tell you instantly it's word processing. All by itself this one application is more than enough to justify the cost of acquiring, and learning to operate, a microcomputer.

Note that I'm *not* talking about so-called "dedicated" word (or text) processors. These machines have their adherents and, one supposes, their uses; but most of them are shockingly expensive, difficult to learn and use (one I've used has over 120 keys on its keyboard, each with its own special function) and, above all, useless for any task other than word processing—they're computers that won't compute.

By contrast, a microcomputer with a good word-processing software package can be had cheaply (in a pinch you can keep the total cost under $500, though I don't recommend quite this much frugality), can be operated by anyone who knows how to type, and has an almost unlimited array of other uses as well. And first and foremost, it will let anybody who isn't functionally illiterate make his or her paperwork look and read like a really professional job.

What word processing does is free you from the tyranny of pieces of paper. Make a mistake when you're using a pen or a typewriter and it sits there staring at you. You can try to erase it, gouging a visible little valley in the paper. You can "white it out" in various ways, building up an equally visible mound *à la* the barrows of ancient tombs archaeologists so love to excavate. You can XXX it out, or type or write over it, which is even more obvious (and ugly). Or you can just live with it. All unsatisfactory choices.

Make a mistake with a word processer and a keystroke or two will whisk it away electronically without a trace. You're free to consider and reconsider your words as often as you like, making as many changes as you want; a good software package will even help you in choosing your words and finding your mistakes. And best of all, you type in only your changes and corrections; there's no need to redo a whole page (or more than one) to fix a single error.

The reason, of course, is that a word processor doesn't generate any pages until you're ready for it to do so. Your deathless prose becomes a sequence of electronic pulses in your computer's memory banks and data-storage devices, which are reflected onto the display screen where you can see and review what you've written. When you see something you don't like you simply use a couple of keystrokes to direct the "cursor" (the little blinking light on the screen) to the offending passage; you can then add to, delete from or change your document to your heart's content while leaving everything else intact.

Even after *you're* satisfied with your document, you can ask the computer whether *it* is. Spelling checkers can look quickly for misspelled words you might have missed (mine has a built-in dictionary of 45,000 words, to which I've added several hundred more, and can review this whole chapter in less than a minute). A few keystrokes allow you to search out other types of mistakes that experience tells you may have been made, and correct them—either in wholesale lots or one at a time. And there are various other helping tools that can help you improve your document.

When it's finally time to print things out on paper, the computer continues to help. In response to parameters you can set, it fixes your margins, divides your text into pages, puts in page headings and/or footings, and so on, so that whatever it is you're writing—a letter, a memo, a report, etc.—comes out looking as neat and clean as it (presumably) reads. You get, in sum, a finished document that presents you and your company in the best possible light to those who read it.

I find it hard to believe the individuals who write to me are as illiterate and muddle-minded as their letters often portray them. I think rather that, like my daughter, they simply have difficulty keeping full track of what they want to say and writing it down clearly when the indelibility of ink and paper gives them no second chances.

Alexandra was a good speller even in seventh grade, and knew her grammar; she routinely got A's and B's on tests in these areas. Her problem was that, like every schoolchild studying several different subjects at once, she had trouble walking and chewing gum at the same time; when she was concentrating on science she tended to lose track of what she'd learned in English, and *vice versa.* The word processor let her give attention to the two things one at a time, rather than demanding that she do both at once.

Another factor was her penmanship, which unfortunately resembled my own uncoordinated scrawl much more than her mother's flowing strokes (it's improved significantly since). Not only did she have a tough time producing a neat piece of handwritten work that was legible to others, she couldn't very easily read her own writing; so it was harder for her to pick up the mistakes she made.

Neither problem is peculiar to adolescence; many adults, too, share them. I've been writing professionally for nearly a quarter of a century and am pretty much a whiz on the keyboard; but before I started using a word processor (and still on those occasions when I have to go back to a typewriter for some reason) I sometimes found myself staring unhappily at mistakes I'd committed to paper. And when it comes to handwriting . . . well, if it's more than a line or two I just wait till I can get at a keyboard of some sort.

To those who read it, a written document says much more than its ostensible contents. It offers a view of the writer—often the only view (especially as to correspondence) the reader has. Moreover, the manner in which the document presents its ideas inevitably colors the reception those ideas will receive; after all, you can't ask questions or seek clarification of a piece of paper. The neater that piece of paper can be made to look, the more smoothly and clearly it can be made to read, the better the writer will have presented both himself and what he wants to say.

And a word processor, as I told Alexandra, is the tool that best lets any writer, of anything, achieve that result.

What Word Processor?

It's for these reasons that word processing packages are most popular, best-selling of all computer software. Indeed, back a decade ago when microcomputers were just coming into existence one of the first and best-known programs written for them was the now-legendary Electric Pencil for word processing.

Electric Pencil, with a number of subsequent improvements, is still to be found in libraries of public-domain (*i.e.,* free) software. But it's been joined by a host of other word processors which, taking advantage of improved microcomputer memories and speeds, offer many more features—and which, while not free, are universally low-cost (none more than $500, and most discounted to far less).

You can spot most of them by their names. A number have names built around the word "Word"—one called only that, and others like WordStar, Word Juggler, Word Perfect, NewWord. Other names use variants on "write"—WRITE, Applewriter, pfs:Write, MacWrite, Volkswriter, XYWrite, Perfect Writer, Easywriter. There are PeachText and MultiMate, and others besides.

The only one with which I'm closely familiar is WordStar, which, because of its popularity, has become something of an industry standard. It's one of the most powerful word processors available, with a vast array of options that let you interleave several documents into a single text, shuffle columns of tabular material, vary margins, specify all manner of variations in formatting, etc., etc. A new version even adds a "windowing" feature (so you can look at two separate documents at once) and math functions.

WordStar's drawback is that it's also one of the toughest word processors to learn and use; keeping all the command keystrokes straight takes a little study and a *lot* of practice. I don't want to over-stress this problem; my daughter, for example, uses its basic structure without great difficulty. But users who don't need its more sophisticated features may prefer to avoid its complexities and opt instead for a less powerful, and simpler, package.

I have no particular recommendations beyond WordStar. I've heard some fairly negative things about MacWrite (the built-in program that comes with Apple's Macintosh and is available only for that machine), especially where longer documents are involved. A computer columnist I read and respect prefers WRITE, although he admits his version is highly customized. I've also heard and/or read some good things about Volkswriter, XYWrite, pfs:Write and Word Perfect, among others. But you should make your own choice, based on the specific features you want included and the degree of complexity you're willing to endure to get it.

Important Features

But I do have some recommendations as to features on which you should insist.

First and foremost, make sure the software displays on the screen exactly as it will print out on paper (usually referred to as "what you see is what you get"). You shouldn't have to guess at where lines, pages, etc., will begin or end, what tables will look like, and so forth.

Look for an "undo" feature—one that will let you rescind your last command if, for example, you've inadvertently wiped out a large block of copy you wanted to keep. (My version of WordStar doesn't have this, although it offers a clumsy substitute; but the new PC version does.)

Make sure you have freedom to format documents as you choose, in terms of margins, headings, footings, page length, etc. A few especially low-power programs lock you into one or a few preselected formats, which may not fit all your needs.

Also important is a "search" function—the software's ability to locate, anywhere in the text, words or phrases you want to find. All the good ones have this; you don't want to have to page through an entire document, display screen by display screen, hunting manually for a particular passage when the computer can let you jump directly to it.

Compatibility with other software—especially ancillary packages that will index, footnote, check spelling, etc.—is a big plus. All word processing files contain embedded command characters which, if they're not more or less standard according to industry practice, can confuse other programs that make use of those files.

If you're planning to exchange data prepared using a word processor with other computers via phone lines and modems, make sure the same or basically similar packages are used. The WordStar format (also used by several other programs with only minor variations) is the *de facto* standard in this regard.

Finally, make certain whatever word processor you choose has enough power and options to do the job you want done. If you only want to write letters, memos and the like, just about anything will do; but if you're doing longer or more complicated documents, which may perhaps require tabular material, preparation of form letters for multiple addressees and such, you'll find some that won't be adequate.

In addition to the word processor itself, you should also have a spelling checker, most of which will also help you check other types of errors that you tell it to look for. I use one called The Word Plus, by Oasis Systems, which is widely accounted one of the best (although it's unfortunately not, as of mid-1986, available except for 8-bit computers); but there are one or two other good ones.

It's important that your spelling checker give you the ability to add to its basic dictionary. You may not think your vocabulary is all that large; but remember, you're using the terminology of your own industry, company, etc., which the software doesn't know. It's awfully annoying to have such terms as piggyback, ICC, FIFO, LTL, microbridge and the like reported to you as spelling errors every time you use them; you ought to be able to educate the software that these are, for your application, correct.

You can also, if you need it, get software to "merge" word-processing files (so that, for instance, you can keep an address list in one file, a form letter in another, and combine the two when you want to send the letter out); to index reports (taking key words that you identify, noting the pages on which they appear, and alphabetizing at the end); to position footnotes properly at the bottom of the page where they belong; to allow "micro-justification" of printed output (proportionally spaced characters such as used in typesetting—though your printer must be able to accommodate this); and for other special-purpose applications.

No matter how fancy you get with your word processing system, however, you'll be hard-pressed to spend more than a few hundred dollars on it. And it should pay you back manyfold in terms of the power it gives you to "clean up" your written work.

A Curious Addendum

After the foregoing appeared in the *Traffic World* column I had what I can only describe as a curious letter in response.

This particular writer told me he wants no part of such the cleaned-up documentation word processing makes possible. He said he'd much rather see his own correspondents' work as they've prepared it unaided—"warts and all," as it were—the better, as he put it, to evaluate the worth of what they're saying.

Aw, come on. Next thing you know he'll be trying to ban cosmetics for women, toupees for men, even hair dye for Presidents. So far as I'm concerned, anything that lets people put their best foot forward—be it in their personal appearance or that of their correspondence—is much to be desired.

Indeed, this writer's comments serve to underscore what I said before: If people are going to judge you on the superficialities of your written communications, all the more reason to use every aid available to make those communications look good and read well; and the word processor is the best tool I know of for that purpose.

20

SPREADSHEETS

A "spreadsheet" program is, in effect, an electronic version of a blank accounting form which the user can tailor to his or her own taste and needs. But the spreadsheet offers more than accounting functions and capabilities; it's as complete a basic-math program (all the way up to calculus) as you could ask for.

The spreadsheet creates a matrix of "cells," which may be likened to blocks on a sheet of graph paper. The matrix will be at least 256 cells deep (in the vertical direction), and at least 64 wide (in the horizontal direction); many are significantly larger. Each cell may be filled with just about any information the user desires—brief text messages, numbers or, most significantly, mathematical equations or "algorithms."

Each cell is designated by a unique name, based on its coordinates in the spreadsheet matrix. That is, each vertical column is given a unique alphabetic designation (A, B, C and so on through Z, then AA, AB, etc., and so on), and each horizontal line likewise has a numeric designation (1-256, or whatever higher number of lines the spreadsheet offers). So a cell may be called, for example, A1, or Z20, or AD244, and so forth. Everything in the program is built around these cell designations.

For example, let's say you want to do a simple thing like add two numbers. You enter one of them in cell A1 and the other in cell A2. Then, in, say, cell A3 you write a brief equation to add them up and display the result; in SuperCalc (with which I'm most familiar), you could write either "A1 + A2" or

"SUM(A1,A2)." Cell A3 now always shows you the sum of what you've written in cells A1 and A2; change either of those, and the sum changes.

(Of course, you don't have to use adjoining cells, as I've done in this illustration; you can equally well add (or subtract, multiply, divide, etc.) any two (or more) numbers from any cells anywhere, no matter how widely scattered. But there are significant advantages to using adjacent cells, since a number of math functions allow you simply to specify a range of cells—to define the entire block merely by identifying its beginning and ending cell designations—which makes writing your equation a lot easier and shorter.)

Obviously it's possible to get a lot more complex than this simplistic illustration; and in that potential lies the real power of the spreadsheet programs. You can develop whole series of algorithms that depend on just a few simple numeric inputs; change any one of those inputs and the program automatically recalculates everything. Or, if you prefer, you can tell the program not to redo its calculations until instructed—to save time, since even at computer speeds extensive calculations cause appreciable delays. Then you can make all your input changes, and do the recalculation just once.

Most good spreadsheets also offer various other options. You can input words instead of numbers, so that, for example, cell A1 contains a brief phrase describing what the numeric input represents, while the number itself is placed beside it in B1. Then, in your screen display and on print-outs, you'll see both your description and the numeric input—as, say, "Assets $2000.00".

Although each cell can be only one line deep, it can be as wide (or as narrow) as you like; most spreadsheets let you adjust the width of your columns to suit your fancy. Most also allow for "header" lines atop the entire spreadsheet, or at the head of each column, or even in the middle of the spreadsheet. They also allow a variety of ways of expressing numbers; you can have them rounded to the nearest integer, or as dollars-and-cents (two decimal places only), or with full decimal extension, or in scientific notation (integer-plus-decimal times 10 to some exponential power).

In addition, a good spreadsheet will let you copy or move the contents of individual cells or blocks of cells around the spreadsheet anywhere you want. There's a global-change command to let you replace all iterations of a particular word, number, algorithm, etc., in every cell in which it appears. There are automatic functions to let you square or take the square root of any number, find its logarithm, extract trigonometric values (sine, cosine, tangent, etc.), compare numbers (greater than, less than or equal to), perform such basic financial calculations as determining the cost at different levels of compound interest, etc. You can even make algorithms conditional—for example, if the number in cell A1 is greater than the one in B1, then subtract B1 from A1, but if B1 is bigger, don't.

Here's an illustration from my own consulting business. I prepare and file tariffs for a few motor carriers. For the most part, especially when rates are published in tabular form, I keep the information stored in a SuperCalc data file. For example, for a table of point-to-point rates from Succotash Corners to 111 different points, cells A1 through A111 list the names of the points in alphabetical order and cells B1 through B111 list the rates.

Now, let's say my client wants me to (1) eliminate three points; (2) add four others; (3) increase all rates under 150 cents per cwt. by 5%, and (4) increase all other rates by 3%. By hand it would take hours, and involve retyping everything. On the spreadsheet I simply (1) erase the lines on which the three eliminated points appear, and (2) insert new lines at appropriate locations to input the new points and rates (keeping, in the process, strict alphabetical order). Then I (3) write in cell C1 an equation to take care of the increases—if you're interested, in SuperCalc it's "IF(B>150,B1*1.05,B1*1.03)"—and (4) replicate that equation to cells C2 through C112, which automatically makes the necessary adjustments to deal with cells *B*2 through

*B*112. I tell the program to do the calculations, erase column B (containing the old rates), and I'm done; the whole job's finished in just a few minutes.

And that gives you an idea of the real power that's available from spreadsheets.

Indeed, the better spreadsheets offer an even greater range of power through so-called "macros." A macro is, in effect, a small program written in the command language of the spreadsheet, which permits you to aggregate an entire sequence of commands for unattended execution. Using macros, for example, you can make the spreadsheet go through multiple iterations with changed data, algorithms, etc., to simulate different "what-if" scenarios for modeling or other purposes.

It's quite apparent that the entire 256-line-by-64-column (or larger) spreadsheet won't fit into the 25-line-by-80-character area of your display screen. So the program is set up to let you shift the display around to different parts of the spreadsheet at your command—much as you'd move your eyes if you were looking at a paper version. If you were dealing with paper, of course, you could fold it so as to bring together two widely separated areas; and you can do much the same thing with your electronic equivalent by means of a "window" command that lets you split the screen into independent sub-displays.

Similarly, when it comes to making a print-out, you can get a copy of your entire spreadsheet or any portion or portions of it.

Finally, many spreadsheets come with built-in graphics packages. That is, at your command the computer will make a graphic representation—bar graph, pie chart, line graph, etc.—of the numeric information you've input, or any portion of it you select. You can either look at the graph on your display screen or use a plotter to get it down on paper.

For business applications, spreadsheet programs are among the most popular, and the most valuable, because of their ability to handle just about any type of "number-crunching" the business manager could possibly need done. And you can use a single spreadsheet for as many applications, and as many purposes, as you might want, since each application can be saved (including format, data, algorithms and all) as an independent data file, and re-loaded whenever it's needed.

The spreadsheet had its origins with VisiCalc, one of the earliest programs for the original Apple computer. Subsequently Lotus 1-2-3, which was written for the IBM-PC and added graphic functions and some rudimentary data-handling capability, became the best-selling business software package in history. SuperCalc is likewise a popular program; others include CalcStar, MultiPlan, Enable, and such integrated packages as Symphony, Framework, etc. For the Apple Macintosh only there are also Excel (reputed to be one of the best spreadsheets available, perhaps *the* best) and Jazz.

Finally, for most of these spreadsheets you can get, both commercially and through public-domain sources, "templates" that considerably facilitate your work. A template is a structure and set of algorithms pre-set into appropriate cells to handle a particular task; all you need do is input the raw numbers into the proper cells. For example, an income-tax template would require only that you input your gross income, deductions, investment credits, etc., etc., and would then do all the arithmetic, including calculating how much tax you owe, on its own. Or you might get a statistical template that would automatically do, say, regression analysis on the numbers you fed into it. A financial template might set up a depreciation schedule for newly purchased capital equipment. And so forth.

Obviously, in most cases such templates will only deal with fairly standard, routine activities; and of course you're stuck with the format and algorithms built into it. (Yes, you can change them, but the difficulty of doing so properly is not much less than building your own template from scratch; a basic rule of computer programming is that it's easier to do the whole job yourself than to "debug" someone else's programming.) Even so, there will be times when templates can save you considerable time and effort, especially as a new spreadsheet user.

21

DATA-BASE MANAGERS

One of the computer's greatest strengths lies in its eidetic electronic memory; it has perfect recall of every input it's been asked to retain in its memory storage.

Psychologists say that's true of the human brain, too; under deep hypnosis, for instance, individuals can recall an astonishing wealth of detail about past observations and experiences. (Some individuals exhibit this capacity without hypnotic assistance, but such abilities are usually accompanied by offsetting mental deficiencies in other areas; for that reason individuals with such freakish abilities are generally known as *idiots savants*—"wise fools"—in recognition of the unbalanced powers of their minds.)

But such memories are useless, of course, if they can't be recalled to conscious awareness at will. This is accomplished in the human mind by means a type of mental structuring that psychologists call "relational associations"—mental "handles," as it were, that enable us to grasp particular memories when we want them. Without such relational associations, the memories, although still present, are forever inaccessible; they're "forgotten." Indeed, modern psychological theory is that the difference between a good learner and a poor one—between the "A" student and the one who's barely passing—lies almost entirely in this ability to structure what's been learned so that it's consciously "remembered" and not buried in the disorganized, and unusable, subconscious.

The computer, although vastly different from (and more

limited than) the human mind in most regards, shares this particular characteristic; its useful memory is limited to what can be structured for on-demand retrieval. The function of data-base management software is to provide the requisite structuring.

To switch to another metaphor, the data-base manager is the equivalent of the neat housekeeper—"a place for everything, and everything in its place." It stashes input data away into predetermined electronic cubbyholes, identified by one or more of those "relational associations," for ready retrieval when the user issues the proper commands. (It's for that reason that the information files created by data-base managers are known as "relational" data bases.)

Using a data-base manager effectively requires, first, careful advance planning and, second, the expenditure of considerable time and effort to learn the extensive commands and options needed to "drive" the software. For that reason, of the three main types of general-purpose computer software the data-base manager is, by a considerable margin, the least-popular. One can begin to generate at least rudimentary output from a word processor or a spreadsheet relatively quickly, and without mastering more than a fraction of its intricacies; but a data-base manager, even at its most elementary level, requires appreciably more mental exertion.

Nevertheless, for the computer user who needs to manipulate significant masses of information, the results will prove worth the effort; for the data-base manager is the only realistic way of accessing the computer's full capabilities in this area.

Generally speaking, you create a separate data file for each grouping of related data. For example, one file might deal with transportation rates, another with personnel records, a third with market data, and so forth. And, of course, in some instances it might be desirable to break these broad categories down into subdivisions where they're intended for different purposes, involve different types of data, etc.

For each such data file, the initial step is to create a structure, identifying each separate "data element" to be included. You must specify a name for the element, the amount of space to be set aside for each entry (maximum length, in characters), whether entries are to be numeric or not, and so forth. Only after you've done this—and you must do it for each separate data file you intend to create—are you ready to actually start storing away data. If you decide to change the structure later on you may, copying old data into the revised structure; but you must have a structure in place at all times.

The next step is the actual input process. The machine asks you, in turn, to input each separate element of an individual "data record" before going on to the next such record. You can skip over any data element you don't actually need for a particular record, but you must stay within the basic parameters you've established where you do make inputs. That is, you can't exceed the character length you've specified as maximum, you can't enter non-numeric characters where you've told the software to expect numbers, etc.

It's after you're finished with this basic input process that the data-base manager really shows its power. You can edit entries to your heart's content. You can sort them on any one criterion, or even multiple criteria, to change their order in your data file. You can, with most data-base managers, perform certain fairly elementary math functions on them—adding them up, multiplying or dividing by a fixed constant, subtracting one from another, etc. There are numerous other ways, too, in which you can manipulate them.

Then there are reports. You design your own report form, using the built-in utilities intended for that purpose, and tell the computer just how to display your data. You can get selective reports that only pick up certain data elements, entries, etc., according to criteria you establish. You can generate item-by-item or summary reports or combinations of the two.

If you're dealing with fairly large volumes of data, you may also want to make use of the software's "pointer" or "indexing" features to speed up data searches and recovery procedures. It's even possible to build multiple pointers/indexes if necessary. If you think of your data as the leaves on a tree, the pointer/index system lets you avoid having to examine each leaf until you find the particular one you're after. Instead you tell the software, in effect, go to *this* limb, and then *this* branch on the limb, and then *this* twig on the branch, and then look over only the few leaves that are there—obviously a much faster procedure.

Some of the more sophisticated data-base managers also incorporate modest graphics capabilities. Obviously there are practical limits to how much data you can usefully depict in any graphic representation; but on occasion you can use such software effectively for such things as frequency-distribution charting and the like. You can also get graphs based on summary information which may be of value.

I've touched here on only a few of the capabilities of a good data-base manager; to describe them in full detail would require a separate book in itself (and a good many such have been written). If you don't need to handle large volumes of data, you can and certain should spare yourself the time and trouble of learning your way around a data-base manager. But if you *do* have such a need, nothing else will do nearly so well; it's an extremely powerful tool.

Data-base managers come in two basic types. There are the more-or-less "simplified" versions intended for relatively small-scale applications. These are the packages that are often "bundled" with microcomputer hardware, and/or are sold at low cost (often less than $100) at storefront dealerships which cater primarily to home users. They vary somewhat in capabilities, but are usually perfectly suited to keeping files of your cooking recipes, phone numbers, Christmas card address lists, etc. They will also often work well for your children's schoolwork.

As a general rule, however, such packages are at best marginal for serious business use, and in some cases simply aren't up to doing the job that needs doing. Major rate storage/retrieval applications, for example, quickly outstrip the realistic limits of these lower-powered systems. Even if your initial uses *can* be handled by the smaller packages, the likelihood is that your needs will soon outgrow them; so you're probably better off acquiring and learning one of the big, high-powered managers from the very beginning.

Of these, the best-known and most popular is Ashton-Tate's dBase—dBase II for eight-bit computers, dBase III for 16-bit machines. Another well-regarded system is R:Base 5000. Other packages of which I've heard good things reported include Knowledge Man and pfs: File; and there are, of course, a number of others on the market as well.

22

FREE SOFTWARE—HOW TO GET IT AND USE IT

Not every software developer works with the profit motive uppermost in mind. Some (a surprising number) are simply hobbyists who do programming for their own pleasure and are happy to give the results away; indeed, some such hackers refuse as a matter of principle to seek or accept remuneration for their work. A lot of this programming isn't very good; and much of it (both good and bad) involves computer games and other programs not of any real value to the business user.

But if you look for it you can find some of this software that's both well designed and does jobs useful to the business user of computers. Here are a few examples:

• Communications software. The best and most widely available was developed by a Chicago hobbyist named Ward Christensen, whose name is revered among hackers. It started out under the name of XMODEM, and now has numerous variants (most of which have recognizably derivative names, such as XMDM7, XMODEMK, etc.). In its revised incarnations it works at least as well as commercial software than costs $100 or more, and better than most. One drawback, though: XMODEM won't let your computer communicate with mini's or main-frames, only with other micros using either XMODEM-type software or commercial software that will (and most will) support the so-called Christensen protocol.

• Print spoolers. A print spooler lets your computer split

its time between using a printer and performing other tasks, so you can do both at once. It takes advantage of the fact that you'll rarely be using the full power of your machine; it gives your on-line application first priority, and uses only its spare time to send information to the printer. The printing process may proceed marginally slower than usual, but your on-line use suffers not at all; for long print-outs it can be a Godsend. Such programs (there are many) are usually named SPOOL or UNSPOOL or something similar (SPL101, UNSPLK, etc.).

• Unerase utilities. Sometimes a user will carelessly erase from disk storage a program or file he or she really wanted to keep. Actually, the program/file was never touched; the ERA or DELETE command (depending on your operating system) merely wiped out the directory entry that reserved disk space for it and told your computer where on the disk it was located. If you subsequently save new programs or files on the same disk you probably can't get it back; but if you catch your mistake immediately, an unerase utility will let you restore the directory entry and recover the inadvertently erased program/file intact. Look for programs with names such as UNERA, UNDEL, and the like.

• Keyboard customization. The IBM-PC keyboard is a real loser for the touch-typist because of the awkward location of a couple of keys; unfortunately, many IBM imitators have copied that keyboard as is. Or you may have other reasons why you aren't satisfied with your keyboard layout. These programs let you redesignate keys to perform different functions than the manufacturer intended; you can, for example, make your backslash key (which on an IBM-PC board is located where your finger expects to find the SHIFT key) serve as a SHIFT, etc.

• RAM disk programs. Usually they'll have designations that identify them by their purpose, such as RAMDISK or the like. They set aside a portion of your computer's active memory, or RAM, to imitate a disk drive, the effect of which is to allow *much* faster storage to and retrieval from this phantom drive. *(See the discussion of RAM disk operations in Chapter 31.)*

• Templates for such popular programs as Lotus 1-2-3,

dBase II and III, SuperCalc, etc. Using these saves you the tedium of having to design your own formats for data-handling, computations, reports, print-outs, etc., for more-or-less standardized applications.

I could go on at some length; there's a *lot* of public domain software out there. You can even find free word processors, spreadsheets, data-base managers, graphics packages, etc. (although for the most part these are considerably inferior to the better commercial ones).

You don't, of course, get the detailed, slickly produced user manuals to which you may be accustomed; user instructions come in text files that are sometimes inaccurate and often sketchy and riddled with typographical errors. And if things go awry (as there's a better-than-average chance they may), you have no-one to hear your complaints that the software gave wrong answers or bollixed up your disks.

But if you're careful in selecting and using public domain software, you really *can* get something for nothing—thanks to the recreations of a coterie of computer hobbyists who are willing to share the fruits of their labors without recompense.

There are two ways of getting your hands on these programs. Many user groups, dealers, etc., maintain libraries of them; tell them what you want and they'll give it to you on disk, charging you only the cost of the disk and perhaps a modest copying fee (the total is usually no more than $5-10 per disk). Or you can use your modem to dial up such as CompuServe or The Source (both of which assess charges to their users) or various computer bulletin boards (which don't involve any cost at all), and then download the software directly to your own machine—although this requires some know-how you'll have to acquire if you haven't done this before.

If you're interested in pursuing this, I'd suggest you buy one of the several books published on the subject, which you can find at either computer dealerships or bookstores. One of the best and most comprehensive is *How to Get Free Software,* by Alfred Glossbrenner, published (copyright 1984) by St. Martin's Press in New York.

But here's an *important* word of warning about free software: Some of it's booby-trapped. For the same twisted reasons, I suppose, that vandals will deface building walls with spray-paint, demolish public telephones, etc. (or sometimes considerably worse), a few hackers seem to get a perverted joy out of doing damage to your stored data files and programs with destructive programs. They disguise their software as something else which they hope you'll find useful and desirable, but the main purpose of their programming is to put a "worm" or "bomb" into your computer where it can do wanton damage.

There are practical limits to the amount and type of harm such booby-trapped programs can do; and it's not difficult to protect yourself from such problems. The only injury you need fear is to your operating system and any program or data files that are on-line at the same time as is the vandal software; so you need only take steps to protect them.

If you're running an all-floppy-disk computer, it's quite easy to do so; just store the new program on an otherwise blank disk, copy your operating system onto that disk (so you can operate the machine with no other disk on line), and try the program out. If it works OK, copy some other program or data file onto that same disk and try again. If it *still* works fine, put some sort of dummy disk in the other drive (or drives, if you have more than two) and try yet again. If everything's still working fine, you're almost certainly safe.

If you're using a system with a hard-disk drive, disconnect it physically (if that's possible) while you try out the new program. If you can't do that, make sure you have current copies of *everything* stored on the hard disk before you run your tryout.

You'll normally know immediately if you encounter such a booby-trap; most vandals can't resist bragging about what they have done. Just about every such program I've encountered displays some kind of on-screen message such as "Gotcha!" or "Now trashing your data files." You can then get rid of the offending program, re-copy your operating system, programs and/or files to the extent necessary, and the damage is repaired.

You won't run into this kind of thing very frequently; indeed, the odds are you'll never encounter such a program at all. But I'd be remiss in not warning you that such problems do on occasion crop up.

Should you have this experience, by the way, you should of course report it immediately to the source from which you obtained the program. System operators (of bulletin boards, etc.) are seriously troubled by this sort of electronic vandalism, and will want to immediately strip the troublesome program out of their system as well as try to trace it back to its originator.

Part 7

SPECIALIZED-APPLICATIONS SOFTWARE

23

SOME RULES FOR BUYING SOFTWARE

You have a computer.

You've already mastered (or at least made a start on) the fundamentals of using it. You're ready to start putting the machine to work.

Now what?

A computer is the most versatile management tool ever devised. It can serve with equal facility (as your sales representative no doubt told you when you got it) to balance your books, process your words, keep your records and files, and zip through the most complex of math calculations. To get specific about its potential transportation/distribution uses, it can dispatch and route your trucks, consolidate your shipments, rate bills of lading and audit freight bills, perform the most complicated costing operations, etc., etc.

But to do any of these things it must have a set of instructions more detailed than you can probably imagine. Unless someone tells it *exactly* what to do, step by nit-picking step, it can't even add two and two; and it will respond to your commands with a persistent and maddening question mark or some other electronic equivalent of "what you talkin' about?"

What makes the computer hardware you have do the work you want it to do is "software"—the computerese name for the programming, or operating instructions, that you feed into it. In the early days of computers you generally had to develop your own software for your own needs (which pretty much was the situation when I first started using computers back in the very early 1970's). That entailed either learning one or another of the computer programming languages yourself and spending tedious hours doing the requisite work, or finding an individual already versed in programming and spending nearly as many hours explaining to *him* (or her) how you wanted the machine to work.

Neither of these things is, of course, very productive use of managerial time; it's roughly the equivalent of personally training your file clerks or dock handlers in every detail of their jobs. Unless you're one of those individuals who has fallen in love with computers and actively enjoys spending evenings and weekends writing programs as your hobby, you're probably better off with the option of so-called "off the shelf" software, which today (unlike in earlier eras of computerization) is quite widely available for a multitude of tasks and functions.

As the term implies, this is standardized programming predeveloped for your use by individuals and organizations specializing in that activity. Today there are an astonishing number of such software suppliers who offer an equally astonishing array or programming, much of it designed to serve the particular needs of particular economic sectors, including the transportation industry. Unless you have a virtually unique job you want your computer to do, chances are you can find an off-the-shelf program to do it—and probably more than one.

But it's critically important to be a smart shopper in selecting that software. Not only will the wrong software fail to do the job you want done, but (because the computer's internal manipulations aren't exposed to your view) that failure won't necessarily be an obvious one. So if you make the wrong choice you can not only waste the hundreds or thousands of dollars you've spent, you can cost yourself or your company countless more dollars by relying, and making decisions based, on information that has unrecognized computer-generated glitches in it.

To help you avoid this problem, here are eight rules I've developed to guide you through the software-buying process:

Rule No. 1: Define your objective(s). As a good manager, you wouldn't hire an employee without a predefined job description.

You need to give the same attention to your computer—probably more, because computer software isn't nearly so flexible as are human beings when it comes to shifting gears.

You may have had a picture of what you wanted when you bought your hardware; if so, you're a step ahead. On the other hand, you (or your corporate higher-ups) may simply have been beguiled by the promise of the equipment without clearly defining what specific jobs you would assign it; or you may, as you familiarize yourself with your computer's potential, see other and unplanned-for uses. This is where you need to spell things out in your own mind before you go shopping for software.

By "spelling things out" I mean, specifically, identifying what information you want to feed into the machine (the input) and what results you want it to feed out to you (the output). Since you're buying your software off the shelf, rather than having it custom-made, you need to maintain some flexibility; but without some solid input and output parameters you won't have any way of evaluating which software offering is best for you.

As you go through this process, be sure you're taking into account the inherent limitations of a computer. Computers can remember and calculate better and faster than anything else known to man; they can*not,* however, exercise judgment. Thus, the computer is superlative at difficult or repetitive analytical functions and/or storing and manipulating large volumes of data, but it's totally incapable of subjective decision-making or handling inconsistent problems.

Rule No. 2: Identify Potential Suppliers. If you can locate one company that makes software more or less along the lines of what you want, chances are there are a dozen or more others that compete with it. You need to see what the marketplace has to offer before you commit yourself.

Don't limit your search to just the "big names" in the field. First, in a market as volatile as that of computer software the big names come and go with uncanny frequency; Apples were, after all, nothing but fruit not very many years ago, and you may find an obscure supplier on the rise. Second, the entrepreneurial nature of a new and burgeoning industry such as computers means the "best and the brightest" may have preferred to create their own small outfits rather than work as employees for large, established firms. Third, the big names are often big because they deal in broad-spectrum products that are generalized enough to appeal to a fairly wide market; you may be better off with more closely focused software that's aimed more directly at your own specific application.

At the same time, however, you want to be careful about dealing with individuals or small, relatively newly established organizations. To begin with, their software and/or documentation may not be as complete, dependable and "bug-free" as the products of larger, more reputable organizations. Furthermore, it's important that the software developer be available later on for training, aftermarket support, etc., and you have to remember that the volatility of the software industry is a two-way street; just as companies are getting into the industry daily, so are others getting (or being pushed) out with equal frequency. You should vet out any potential suppliers thoroughly before you decide to buy their products; don't rely on future services from somebody who may not be available in the future.

Locating potential suppliers isn't always easy, unfortunately; there's no comprehensive directory on which you can rely. Some transportation/distribution organizations and publications maintain software developer listings, which may be a good place to start. Advertising materials, both in publications and direct-mail, are also valuable. There are a number of trade shows at which computer software and other services are exhibited (of particular value, since you can actually see the product in action at such events). And the supplier from whom you bought your hardware may also be of help (although be careful if the firm is also a software supplier). I recommend that you spend a little time and effort on this; it's a big marketplace, with a wide range of variety in both cost and quality.

Rule No. 3: Be sure the software is compatible with your hardware. No, all computers are not alike; and no matter how good it may be, a program is of no value to you if it won't run on the machine you have (or plan to buy).

Start with your operating system. There are several in use for microcomputers. The two most popular are CP/M and PC-DOS, which are fairly widespread. But both come in different variants (CP/M-80 and CP/M-86, and MS-DOS and PC-DOS and Concurrent DOS), all of which have, furthermore, a multiplicity of versions testifying to their evolution over time. Then there are UNIX and XENIX and Pick and Apple-DOS and TRS-DOS and Toolworks and so on, again in multiple variants and versions. And each is different; as a general rule (there are occasional limited exceptions), software readable by one system is gobbledegook to any other, so you must check to make sure the software you're considering works with your operating system (or else, as is sometimes—though not always—possible, purchase a copy of the operating system you need).

Then there's the matter of hardware compatibility. Most program commands are filtered through the operating system's interpreter, which automatically routes them to the proper hardware "addresses"; but this double-handling of instructions tends to slow operations down. To get around this problem, many software packages include some routines that bypass the operating system and pass instructions directly through to the hardware—especially commonplace for such things as updating display screens and other such "user-interface" activities.

But not all computers assign the same memory addresses to the same functions. Thus, a command that works fine on one computer may not function at all on another. This is so even of the so-called "clone" machines, which are intended to ape the performance of more popular units and represent themselves as totally "compatible" with those units. No matter how compatible the manufacturer *says* its machine is with some other one, it's still important to check out each package on the machine on which you're planning to use it if that machine isn't *exactly* the one specified by the software developer.

Two other factors, too, warrant mention in this context. First, some software is purposefully designed so it will run *only* on one particular manufacturer's equipment (usually IBM's, in deference to that company's dominance of the microcomputer market). Such programming incorporates a subroutine, periodically invoked, which does nothing but check the ROM (Read-Only Memory) address where the manufacturer's copyright data is permanently stored. If the copyright information is there, the software goes happily about its business and the user doesn't even notice the tiny interruption; but if the copyright information isn't in place, everything comes to an abrupt halt and no amount of cajoling can get the software to run. Since manufacturers are prohibited, under copyright law, from storing somebody else's copyright data in their own units' ROM, this makes the software strictly "machine-specific"—sometimes even specific to particular *models* in that manufacturer's line.

Second, some programming requires add-on hardware features—usually special "boards" or plug-in chips or crystals that aren't standard equipment for most microcomputers. Typical are extra memory (Random-Access Memory, or RAM) chips, color-display boards, math co-processors, crystals to increase the machine's "clock speed" and the like. Most microcomputers have "expansion slots" and other capabilities to let you retrofit them with these features, but some don't; and if you can't arrange for the proper add-ons, you can't run the software.

Then there's the matter of disk configuration. Your microcomputer probably doesn't use eight-inch floppy disks, which is a pity; in terms of format, they're standardized virtually industrywide. But they're a cumbersome size, and require bulky drives, and aren't very popular at the micro level.

More probably you use either 5¼-inch floppies or 3½-inch "minidisks"—and these *aren't* standardized as to format; by and large (with some exceptions for the "clone"-type machines), each machine insists on its own particular disk format. There's software that lets your machine read disks formatted for other systems, but it doesn't always work effectively when program, rather than data, files are involved. Once again, you should check this out for each separate software package.

And there are a number of other hardware considerations you must also take into account. Some software, for example, requires additional (non-standard) RAM, or you may need hard-disk storage, and so forth. Suffice it to say that *all* software should be checked out fully on your own system before you buy.

A word of warning, however: Look *very* critically at software where the developer insists that you have off-the-beaten-track hardware to run it. The IBM line (PC, XT and AT) has become the *de facto* standard for business-oriented microcomputer applications—which means that, if you have hardware that isn't IBM-compatible, you're effectively closed off from the primary market in both general-purpose and specific transportation/distribution business software. If the developer of the particular package you're considering says you must acquire a non-IBM unit (and *especially* if he's so helpful as to offer to sell or lease you the hardware, too), you should give the purchase decision some extra consideration.

Rule No. 4: Consider ease of operation. The term of art in the computer industry is "user-friendliness," denoting software that can be used with reasonably facility by persons who have little or no computer expertise. But it's a term very much overworked; just about every supplier touts his, her or its programs as being user-friendly, and many are anything but.

The surest way to find out is simply to sit down at the machine and try to run the program. *Don't* study the user manual first, no matter how greatly you're urged to do so by the developer's people; just try to get the software to *do* something. A truly user-friendly program will pretty well guide you along, giving you step-by-step directions as you go; you obviously won't be able to get maximum performance out of the program without experience and some later scrutiny of the user manual, but you should be able to at least get started this way if the program is *truly* user-friendly.

And don't be dissuaded from your quest for user-friendliness by the developer's promises to train you and/or your employees in the operation of the software. First, such training can eat up man-hours; and second, what happens if and when you have employee turnover and/or take on new people? Obviously, there will have to be *more* productivity-destroying training—and this time you'll probably have to pay for it separately besides (since the developer certainly won't go on giving you this kind of support indefinitely as a "throw-in" with your purchase).

Furthermore, you don't know either how good the supplier's training will be or how capable your operating employees may be of absorbing its complexities. The old principle of KISS—Keep It Simple, Stupid—is a far better protection for you than any amount of promised training where that principle's been cast aside.

Another test of user-friendliness is to look over the user manual itself. Ideally it will be fairly brief; the developer who boasts of his several-hundred-page user manual is really saying you'll have to do a good deal of study and memorization before you can use his software. The book should also be well-indexed, to let you turn directly to the proper section when you need particular help rather than forcing you to mount a page-by-page search. And it should be clearly written for the non-computer professional, in more or less "plain English"; computer jargon is going to be no more helpful to you than the specialized terminology of transportation would be to a computer specialist.

As you consider the above discussion on user-friendliness, of course, you must bear in mind that all things are relative. As in most things, the complexity of computer software tends to vary proportionately with its power; a program that can do a lot of fairly complicated things must almost inevitably be more difficult to operate than one that does only a few simple jobs. But no matter how much power a given software package may potentially offer, it will be pragmatically valueless if it's so hard to use that all this power is realistically inaccessible to those who will use it.

Finally, inquire as to whether, and to what extent, the developer offers aftermarket customer support. If you have a question after you get the system up and running, will the developer help you find an answer? Some firms offer toll-free phone numbers and assign employees whose sole duty is to answer user questions; at the other (and, unfortunately, more usual) extreme, you won't even be able to get your developer's key people to return your calls or respond to your letters. If there's a charge for this after-purchase support, find out what it is *before* you buy.

And *never* overlook this question, even if the particular software involved seems so simple and user-friendly that a child could seemingly operate it. I've found hidden "bugs" and undocumented features in even some of the most popular, best-regarded programs, which often don't surface until well after purchase time. The developer should be willing to help you cope with such things; if not, you can expect problems.

Rule No. 5: Try out the software. Do it *before* you buy it, preferably in your own office on your own hardware (see Rule No. 3 above). If the program is there to take over a function you're already handling manually or with other systems, do some comparison checks. Make sure your results match—and if they don't, find out why, and what that means.

If you're buying mail-order (and a great deal of software, especially in the lower end of the price spectrum, is sold that way), this can be something of a problem. The simple way for the developer to deal with this situation is to offer you a brief trial period, during which you may try out the software without obligation and, if you don't like it, return it for full credit. But few developers are willing to do this.

The reason, of course, is the ease of copying computer software. In any machine with two disk drives (the minimum configuration for virtually any business system), it's as simple as putting the program disk in one drive, a blank in the other, and using system commands to copy the contents of one onto the other. The process takes no more than a minute or two, and then the original can be returned (for credit or a refund) while the user retains a fully operational copy. Developers understandably don't want this happening, and are consequently loath to offer unchaperoned pre-purchase trials.

Some software is "copy-protected," meaning that either standard copy programs won't work on it or, more often, that the copies, although seemingly perfect, won't run properly. This more or less resolves the developer's problem (although a reasonably adept programmer can defeat most copy-protection schemes quickly; there are even programs designed expressly for that purpose). But it gives the user other problems that make the software a less desirable buy (see Rule No. 8 below).

In a few cases developers have worked out some inventive answers to this dilemma. One offers a copy-protected version of its software at one price and a version without the copy-protection at another, higher price. Others provide "crippled" versions of their software for try-out purposes—programs modified in some way that certain key functions won't work (disabling the features that allow print-outs of program output is a common approach). And in some cases developers feel that such caution is unneeded, relying on the integrity of buyers not to copy software they don't pay for.

For the most part, however, you won't usually be able to try out mail-purchase software before paying for it—and if you then find you don't like it, it doesn't work to your satisfaction, etc., you can expect considerable difficulty in getting a refund. The obvious corollary to this is that you should avoid such purchases unless you've either had the opportunity to check out the program elsewhere (using an acquaintance's copy, visiting the developer's or a dealer's facilities, etc.), or have, by virtue of past experience and/or reputation, a *great* deal of faith in the developer.

And even then, under *no* circumstances should you put software in full service, and start relying on it for your decision-making, without checking it out *very* carefully. Do test runs that cover just about every conceivable set of circumstances, and compare the results with manual or tried-and-true software processing. Programmers are human; they can make mistakes. And you need to uncover such mistakes, if they exist, *before* they have the opportunity to cost you or your company money through erroneous decisions.

Rule No. 6: Run some "hard-use" tests. Once you have the program operating, make, on purpose, as many mistakes as you can think of. Input words when the software asks for numbers; if it wants freight rates, give it shipment weights instead; use impossible classification ratings or shipment dates; and so forth.

No, I'm not suggesting this torture testing out of simple

perversity. These are just the kind of careless, brains-on-the-mantlepiece mistakes the average, untutored user is prone to make as he provides the software with the data input it demands. And you need to find out what's going to happen if such mistakes are made before you wind up being victimized by the consequences.

One of three things will happen when you do this:

(1) The whole program will "crash"—that is, will display some kind of error message on the screen and abort its running, in the process probably losing all the good data you input before the error was made, and perhaps even damaging existing data files in the process. (Or, worse, it'll accept the erroneous input initially, let you put in all the rest of your data, and *then* crash and lose your input when you try to make it run.) *Don't buy that software.* There's absolutely nothing more frustrating than having hours or even days of work electronically wiped out in an instant just because you made a single mistake. Most software these days isn't that unforgiving; and *none* needs to be.

(2) The computer will cheerfully accept the erroneous information and go on running—but of course the "garbage-in-garbage-out" syndrome will render meaningless any results it may generate. And since you won't know, in such circumstances, that your incorrect input has fouled up the results, you may wind up relying on them to your detriment. This is by no means a crippling defect; indeed, no program, no matter how attentive, can catch all possible errors. But be aware that you're going to have to double-check your input manually before relying on results generated from it, and institute appropriate procedures (to be followed rigorously) before you bring the software fully on-line in your operation.

(3) The computer will refuse to accept the wrong data, and insist that you correct it immediately. Even the best program in the world can't catch mistakes such as incorrect numbers, etc.; but it can, and should, pick up more obvious mistakes and refuse to let the user make them. Software that will double-check your input within realistic limits is obviously the most desirable; it both simplifies the input process and promotes accuracy of output.

At the same time, again, no software can be 100% error-proof. If you tell it a particular rate is 53¢ per hundredweight instead of 83, for example, there's no realistic way it can know you've made an error. So any package you buy should give you full opportunity to review your input and make any needed corrections. Ideally, you want to be able to do this both (a) during the input process itself (in case you discover your error as soon as you've made it), and (b) during an after-the-fact review of the input; and you want to be able to do it fairly readily, and without following excessively technical procedures, at either time. Virtually every package you'll encounter will afford you *some* capacity for error-correction; the good ones, though, will recognize the fallibility of human operators and make it easy for you.

Remember, to err is human; to forgive is the software's (and its developer's) job.

Rule No. 7: Look for customization potential. To what extent can the software be tailored to your own particular needs? When you buy a suit of clothes "off the rack" you normally figure that a tailor cancuff the pants, take the slack out of the coat, etc.; consider off-the-shelf computer software in the same light.

There are two basic approaches to such customization. The first is to have the developer do the job for you using his "source code" (the programming-language version of the program before it's "compiled" in operational form). You tell the developer what you want, and he/she/it does the requisite reprogramming. The value of this approach is that the developer, being of course intimately familiar with the program, can do the job both efficiently and effectively (altering someone else's programming can involve hours of drudgery in figuring out how things work, if it can be done at all). The drawbacks are that (1) you're vulnerable to communications failures between you and the developer in specifying the custom changes you want, and (2) developer-programmed customization almost always involves extra cost, sometimes a *lot* extra.

The alternative, increasingly common in modern software packages, is for the developer to provide you with utility-type program tools, as part of the package itself, to let you do your own customization to at least some degree. You need know nothing at all about programming to operate such tools; you simply invoke the appropriate subroutine or separate program which then presents you with a menu of pre-designed custom options. I've seen software that will let you alter numerous parameters with a few keystrokes, even design your own input and report formats if you don't like the ones provided. Obviously, your capabilities here will be limited to how well the developer has anticipated and allowed for your needs; you can't change the software except in the ways the built-in utility program allows. But within those limits you can make changes instantly (changing them again and again if you're still not satisfied), and with no more cost than the few moments it takes you to call up and use the utility.

It should be evident that this latter approach to customization is much to be preferred, especially since it allows you to accommodate changing needs—needs you may not even have anticipated when you made your purchase decision—on an ongoing basis. Consider, for example, the possibility that you may want to periodically add or eliminate stops from a truck-dispatching program, change your shipment-delay interval in a freight consolidation package, correct rate information as carrier tariffs or contracts change, etc. You should be able to do these things, and as many others besides, as you can reasonable expect you'll need.

You also want software that has a minimum of "built-in" command sequences and a maximum of user-programmable ones. Don't be overly concerned if the process of making such changes in somewhat cumbersome; you won't have to do it very often, and can live with a few problems here if you must. But if the changes can't be made at all, or require extensive computer expertise to accomplish, think twice before buying; the program's useful life will likely be a good deal shorter than if you could adapt it to changing circumstances and needs. Especially in the transportation/distribution industry of the 1980's, when a volatile marketplace is dictating frequent and often dramatic shifts in the real-world environment with which the software is supposed to help you cope, the capacity for user-directed changes in its operation is clearly beneficial.

Rule No. 8: Be sure you can copy the software—or, at worst, that additional copies will be made available to you quickly and without significant extra charge if something happens to your own disk(s).

Computer disks—especially the floppy disks on which the computer software you purchase is recorded—are pretty fragile as storage media. A tiny speck of grit, a child's horseshoe magnet, even the static electricity you generate when you walk across a carpet, can cause them to crash resoundingly. For that reason all computer professionals routinely make back-up copies of disks whose electronic contents they want to secure. (In some cases this is a technical infringement of copyright restrictions, but one routinely, necessarily overlooked.)

Moreover, floppy disks are a fairly inconvenient data storage medium. You have to find them and physically insert them in the disk drive in order to access their contents, which can be anything from a minor annoyance to (if you happen to misplace a key disk) a major problem. Most business computer applications these days use hard-disk drives that remain physically in place at all times, so that needed software is always available for use.

Copy-protection schemes prevent both the making of back-up copies and transfer to hard-disk storage, at least for the non-computer professional. The approaches to copy-protection vary; in some cases you can't copy any of the software at all, while in others you can copy the software but must have the original disk to "boot up" and/or use your copy. No matter what approach is taken, however, the user is invariably inconvenienced at best—and should his floppy choose an awkward moment to crash (as it most often will), he may suffer serious problems from his inability to use key software when he needs it.

My personal feeling is that copy-protected software should be avoided if at all possible. All of the off-the-shelf software I use in my consulting business is copyable (and I have multiple copies, including hard-disk versions). I follow the same philosophy in my role as a software publisher, too; the *Traffic World*'s Practical Software series of programs, with which I'm associated, is sold without copy protection.

Not all software developers and publishers take the same view, though; and you may find the software you want is copy-protected. If you decide to buy it anyway, at the least you should make absolutely certain you'll have no problem getting replacement disks if something goes awry with your copies, *without* having to pay full price for the new ones. Most suppliers do assess a small charge to cover disk costs, postage, etc., and also require you to return the defective original to them before they'll send you a replacement; this is annoying but, I suppose, not altogether unreasonable. But you most certainly shouldn't have to buy the program all over again just because the disk(s) on which it was originally recorded failed.

One last note on copy-protection: At one point a very few developers employed a particularly nefarious copy-protection scheme which involved imbedding a sub-routine known as a "worm" in their programs. Normally this sub-routine was inactive; if an attempt was made to use an unauthorized copy of the program, however, it served to activate the worm—which then, following its pre-programmed instructions, industriously set about finding and "trashing" any other programs and data files it could get at. Setting such a program loose in your computer could be disastrous; in seconds (or less) it could demolish the entire contents any disks, hard *or* floppy, currently being accessed by the machine.

No matter how honest you are, *don't buy a program with this type of copy protection* (or anything else even remotely resembling it). Data transfer between storage media and computer processors is by no means always perfect; random electric pulses from external sources (a minute power surge, static electricity, etc.) can cause unforeseen, unpredictable and unpreventable glitches. And it would only take one such glitch to persuade your machine that the proper, original disk you're using is actually an illicit copy, loosing that voracious worm to chomp away at your valuable data and other programs.

I haven't, however, encountered this type of copy protection in quite a while; and it was never much in use. Indeed, the most publicized report of it proved a false alarm. A few users of a certain version of a non-copy-protected general-application package were were understandably distraught when copies they thought they'd made legitimately flashed on the display screen the message, "The weed of crime bears bitter fruit; now trashing your disk!" It developed, however, that the only thing the program had *really* done was to display that message, which was the product of the overwrought sense of humor of one of the developer's programmers; there was actually no worm at all. The publicity given to this event, however, did much to discourage other developers from using this kind of copy-protection scheme.

Rule No. 9: Follow the other eight rules. If you approach your software-purchasing task with these eight rules firmly in mind, you'll have a lot better chance of picking, out of a very varied and diversified marketplace, the software that you need to do the jobs you want done. Remember that your computer is of value to you only to the extent that it's working for you; and it's the software that makes the machine work.

24

SHOPPING FOR SOFTWARE— A PERSONAL APPROACH

How do I go about getting the information I present when I write reviews of computer software? I've been asked this by a number of people in conjunction with my *Traffic World* column; and the answer may be of value in guiding computer users as they shop for their own software.

First, I won't review (and I believe no-one should buy) any program I haven't (he/she hasn't) seen in operation. In fact, with rare exceptions I won't review a product I haven't actually operated myself (even if briefly).

Mostly I see the products I write about at the various trade shows I attend. I'll usually start by observing the demonstrations being given other show attendees. Then, at a time when the exhibit booth isn't busy, I'll introduce myself, explain the purpose of my visit, and get a full demonstration. I'll ask questions about what I consider key features of the software, get in some hands-on time, and in general go a good bit beyond the standard presentation.

These sessions last for anywhere from half an hour to two hours or more, depending on the complexity of the software and other factors; except in one circumstance I'll mention in a moment, I never walk away until either (1) the demonstrator tells me I've seen everything major there is to see, or (2) the demonstration becomes hopelessly repetitive; and in either case I make sure I have a good working understanding of what I've seen.

I also try to get at least a look at user manuals and other product literature, and take as much away with me as the demonstrator will give me; but except for a few factual matters (price, name and address of vendor, etc.), I rely on my own personal impressions, not sales or other literature.

Less frequently, I'll use software packages that have been sent me on disk and put them through their paces by myself. This takes longer, since there's no demonstrator familiar with the program to steer me away from needless repetition or guide me to key features, but in the end I come away with about the same degree of information as I get from the trade-show demonstrations.

When I write up my results in *Traffic World,* my goal is to present, as fairly as possible, a summary of what I saw. Some of the things I particularly look for include:

- Does the software do what its vendor says it will?
- What other features, not offered by the particular package I'm considering, might its users want (if any)?
- Is the software reasonably user-friendly—easy to learn and operate, having clear and readable displays, supported by sound tutorials (user manuals and on-line help screens), etc.
- What hardware is required to run the programming?
- What's the price, and how does it compare to the cost of other, similar packages?
- Are there significant glitches that might interfere with smooth operation by the user?

It's this last consideration that gives rise to the exception I mentioned earlier. On occasion I've started to look over a package and encountered a defect I considered so major as to render the software unacceptable. Now, I get no pleasure in writing negative reviews; no matter how flawed a particular package may be, it represents a lot of time and effort by somebody, and it's no fun demolishing the product of that time and effort in print. If I can't say at least something good about a program, I'd rather not write about it.

In such circumstances I'll discuss the defect I've found with somebody in a decision-making capacity in the vendor's organization. I'll suggest that appropriate corrections be made, and that I look at the software again after that's done. Only if the vendor is absolutely insistent that no changes will be made, and that the software will continue to be offered to the public in its unaltered form, will I continue my examination and write about it as is.

Finally, no vendor gets a chance to edit, or even see, what I write before it's published; as anyone in the field will testify, such an opportunity for what amounts to pre-censorship is incompatible with journalistic integrity. Nor do my publishers impose any restrictions on what I write except for the legitimate standards of honest reporting, editorial style, etc. In particular, no-one gets special treatment because he or she does or doesn't buy ad space in the publication for which I'm writing.

I don't pretend to be either infallible or a thoroughgoing expert in computers. At best, I can be described as an experienced computer user. So what I write constitutes simply my own views, reflecting my honest impression of what I've seen in the circumstances I've been describing.

25

THE MEANING OF 'USER-FRIENDLINESS'

Not long before writing this chapter I spent about a week doing some serious programming.

A friend had developed an interesting piece of transportation-oriented software. But, as with so many transportation/distribution software packages I see, it wasn't very easy to work with. You had to bone up on the user's manual pretty thoroughly, and keep it right beside you for reference as you worked; and even then the wrong kind of mistake could "crash" everything.

I decided to see if I could build a "shell" around the software's central logic that would make it truly easy to use—"user-friendly" in a real-world, pragmatic sense, so that even if the user knew nothing at all about computers he or she could operate it readily.

Why put in all that effort? Well, first off, as I already mentioned, the developer's a friend. Second, I thought well of his concept; his software was in my experience both unique and of considerable potential value to transportation managers. Third and fourth, I enjoy occasional forays into programming (it's a kind of mental recreation to me) and, moreover, need to keep my hand in so I can do the programming I use to support my own consulting business.

And fifth, and most important in the context of this book, ever since I started writing about computers I've been inveighing about the need for greater user-friendliness of software. I wanted to see just how far it's realistically feasible to go down that path.

A 'Do-able' Job

I didn't, I have to confess, get the job completely done; I have a business to run, publication deadlines to meet, etc., and finally couldn't afford to devote any more working time to this. But I did get enough finished and working right to find out for sure that it's both possible and practicable to make programs really easy for the veriest tyro to use.

As with most special-applications software, my friend's package was divided into modules, each callable (at the user's option) from a "main menu" of options. Since I hadn't time to work on all the modules, I concentrated on the ones that involved the greatest amount of "user interface"—the ones that dealt with keying in, editing, etc., the data required by the package. These, after all, are the areas where where the user gives the computer its marching orders and the information it needs to carry out those orders, and where, accordingly, clear communication between user and computer is critical.

Operating a computer program shouldn't require any significant expertise on the part of the user—either in computers or in the software itself. The user shouldn't have to know anything more than how to turn his computer on and insert the program disk; everything else should be either automatic or self-explanatory, with the user given no opportunity to go wrong. My goal in working with my friend's program was to build in these elements without disturbing the logical core he had developed.

Screen Displays

OK, let's get down to specifics. What, in simple English, makes for a really user-friendly program?

Start with on-screen instructions—the computer's communication with the user. To be sure, every software package comes with a user manual. Some of these manuals are better, clearer and/or more complete than others, but most will, with sufficient study, guide you through the process of running the program. (And a few I've seen won't, or at least not adequately;

but the less said about such travesties the better, so far as I'm concerned.)

On the other hand, why should you have to dedicate hours poring over a book before you can even start work? And, in particular, why should you have to constantly ferret out references in that book while you work in order to know what to do next? Most user manuals I've seen for transportation/distribution packages run anywhere from 50 pages on up (*'way* up, in many cases), tend to be of fairly poor readability (in terms of both writing clarity and print quality), and are inadequately indexed; studying and referring to them is a wearisome task for both the mind and the eyes.

What's more, books and/or their pages can get misplaced, inadvertently discarded, etc. Why should you have to initiate a search of bookshelves, files, etc., every time you want to run the program (or at least until you've more or less memorized the user manual over a long period of using it)?

The better answer is as near and obvious as the display screen in front of the user's eyes. *That's* where the requisite instructions should be found—either in brief "prompts" that spell out the input parameters, command options, etc., or in more detailed "help screens" that can be called up with a keystroke or two. Virtually the entire user manual can and should be available on-screen while the program is in operation.

But the value of this approach will be impaired if it is not also coupled with good screen displays. By "good" I mean (1) clear and readable, and (2) simple. Note that I am *not* talking about fancy or "artistic" screen graphics. For some reason on-screen graphics hold a fascination for most programmers; they'll spend hours on end dressing up their software with complicated pictures and charts, swatches and patterns of color, even cartoon-like animation. Occasionally this will be helpful to the user; more often, though, it's either functionally useless or downright distracting.

Another failing I often encounter is screen clutter. Programmers fill their displays with line after line of densely packed text; you can get eyestrain just *looking* at such screenfuls, let alone trying to read them. Why oh why, I keep wondering, do so many programmers have such a fetish about filling every square inch of the display screen? It's very little harder to spread the same information, input prompts, etc., over two or three less crowded screens (carrying forward essential information, if need be), and give the user's eyes a rest.

My friend's software was pretty good on these two points—minimal graphics (only where really useful), and largely uncluttered, simple screens. But it fell down a lot in a third area: making sure each successive screen contained all key information the user would require.

As the program is run, each display should summarize, in just a line or two, the principal command and/or input options open to the user at that juncture. Some software I've seen does this in the "status line" at the bottom of the screen; others print out a line or two at the top; still others incorporate this information in the body of the screen display. The point is that the user shouldn't have to go paging through his user manual again and again just to find out what inputs/commands the software will accept at any given moment.

I added this feature to his displays, while shifting them around in many instances to make them read more clearly. But I stuck with the KISS principle (Keep It Simple, Stupid!) for all displays, which obviously limited the quantity of information I could put on-screen. To make available more detailed information about command sequences, input requirements, etc., I set up a series of help screens that the user could access at will.

If at any point the user touches the "?" key, the screen display is immediately replaced by a text passage telling him what he needs to know. The text stays on-screen as long as the user wants. The last line directs him to touch any key to return to the program where he left it; when he does, the help message vanishes from the screen and the display screen is restored to its original appearance.

The text of the help messages varies, of course, depending on where you are in the program. I made sure to word the messages simply, but also was careful to include all the information needed for the user to complete the particular operation he was performing *without* having to go back to the user manual.

Inputs and Errors

In sum, I went to considerable lengths to ensure that the computer would communicate clearly and effectively to the user. Now, how about communication in the opposite direction, from the user to the computer?

Most transportation/distribution software is geared principally to information processing—storing, manipulating, arraying and otherwise dealing with data keyed in by the user. And this, of course, is where the "garbage in, garbage out" syndrome comes into play; if the user fouls up his chore of inputting his data, no amount of skill on the programmer's part can make the software generate good results.

But although the programmer can't allow for the user's input mistakes, he can and should limit the opportunities for the user to make such mistakes. If the software is asking for a number to be input, for example, it can't be geared to know whether the user has entered the right number or not; but it should certainly be set up so that it won't accept any characters *except* numbers. Where whole numbers are wanted, decimals should be rejected; so should commas (such as 47,313 instead of 47313; although it's possible to program a computer to deal with such commas, it's cumbersome, and I've rarely seen it done). Lower-case letters should be rejected if capitals are wanted, and *vice versa.* Words, numbers, etc., longer than the program can accept shouldn't be allowed. And so forth.

I'm not being picky; I've seen cases where a single typographic error in the input process caused the entire program to crash, taking with it literally hours' worth of otherwise perfect data input. There's no taskmaster like a computer when it comes to perfectionism; it has no tolerance whatever for even the most understandable of human errors. In these circumstances it's only prudent to go to great lengths to minimize the potential for errors—and to allow ample opportunity for the user to easily and conveniently correct any that are made.

Again, my friend had made some fairly solid efforts in this direction—considerably more, I might note, than I've seen in many packages. His program insisted on numbers being input when numbers were expected, wouldn't accept words or numbers of excessive length, and both allowed corrections during the input process and gave the user an opportunity to review and edit the data after input was complete.

But it was still possible to flummox the software in some regards. For instance, if a numeric input was zero, "0" had to be entered; if the user took the not-unnatural action of simply touching the "RETURN" key instead, the software wouldn't reject the entry, but couldn't work with it, either. A few other types of unexpected keystrokes could give it other types of trouble. And the error-checking and correction routines were a bit cumbersome; for one example, during the review/edit procedure you were obliged to re-input a sequence of six separate data entries in order to change any one of them.

I reworked these areas to make things function a good deal more smoothly. To start with, I set up programming to ignore any undesired inputs—letters instead of numerals, overlength words or numbers, etc.—as each key is touched. Hit any key inconsistent with the parameters of a particular input and the machine simply ignores you; it won't even echo your keystroke on the display screen. You can still put in wrong information, of course; but you can no longer put anything in that will crash the program.

"RETURN" (or "ENTER"; different hardware manufacturers label this key differently) now equals zero where numeric inputs are required.

Corrections require nothing more than hitting the "BACKSPACE" key. To delete a data entry you hit the "DELETE" key. To escape out of a subroutine back to the main menu, you hit "ESCAPE." Easily remembered (and also highlighted in the on-screen instructions).

In the review/edit subroutine you now have to re-input only

the data you want to correct; to leave the rest of the input sequence unchanged you simply hit "RETURN" at the appropriate prompts. Meantime, the screen displays the data sequence both as it was before you started making changes and as it is with your changes.

And, of course, a "?" at any point invokes the ubiquitous help screens.

Other Features

There's one other significant feature I added, which again reflects the way I think good software should operate. My friend's user manual suggested that the user might want to adjust some numeric inputs in certain circumstances; but although they worked perfectly within the logical framework of the software, the adjustments *looked* illogical to the inexpert user. Moreover, they had to be done manually before the data was input.

I changed this sequence to allow the adjustments to be made by the computer during the input process itself, and added a detailed help screen explaining (1) when such adjustments might be desirable, and (2) what effect they would have on the data base. If the software suggests a particular type of operation, I think it should also ease the user's path as much as possible in performing that operation.

In this particular case the software also expected the user to arrange his data inputs in a particular sequence if certain detailed reports are wanted. This is one feature I didn't get around to changing; but it would be easy to program a sort subroutine that would let the user input in random order and turn over to the machine the task of putting the data in proper sequence.

No software should force the user to input large quantities of data at a single sitting; rather he should be able to add to his data files any time he wants. Here I didn't have to make any changes; my friend had already anticipated this need and allowed for it.

Another feature incorporated by my friend was the use of constants for data elements that tend to be repetitive. That is, the software presumes the new input will be the same as the last one in this particular field unless the user tells it otherwise. Why force the user to repetitively hit the same keystrokes over and over again when you, as the programmer, know in advance that the new input is likely to be the same as the one before it?

Finally, I eliminated the need for the user to constantly hit the "RETURN" key after certain types of inputs. Menu selections, for instance, are accomplished by simply touching the appropriate number; the "?" alone calls up help screens; and so forth. I don't regard this as especially critical; but it is a convenience, and makes the program look slicker. As a general rule, I think "RETURN" should be required for data entry and commands that will permanently alter data (in fact, in some cases it's a good idea to give the user a chance to reconsider irrevocable actions, such as erasing data files, etc.); but it's both inconvenient and an encouragement to make errors if the user has to confirm even the most routine commands with "RETURN."

How Feasible?

These, then, are roughly the parameters of what I consider to be a truly user-friendly program. Now: How feasible is it to incorporate these features into a given piece of software?

First, all the features I added didn't seem to slow the software down significantly or otherwise interfere with its operation. I purposely did the work using the Z-80 (lowest-power) processor of my Kaypro; and although the computer told me the programs were now taking up appreciably more memory, they continued to function just about as fast, and as smoothly, as they had before I touched them; any difference was too small to notice.

Second, the programming itself wasn't enormously difficult or burdensome. I don't pretend to be a real programming whiz; I do all right, but there are lots of folks much better at it than I. For the most part I was able to handle the job by taking the existing programming and simply adding on subroutines at appropriate points; no serious interference with the software's central logic was required.

To be sure, it did take me quite a while to get things done; as

I mentioned, I spent about 40 hours on it, and didn't complete everything I wanted to do. But I was operating under some handicaps. In particular, I wasn't familiar with the program's logic, it wasn't very well documented internally, and it was written in BASIC (a language in which, because of its structure, it's especially tough to reprogram someone else's work). Probably at least half my time was spent simply trying to sort my way through the labyrinth of the existing programming; if I'd been familiar with its internal workings (as would be anyone who was doing this job with his own software), I could have done it in *much* less time.

Putting the whole thing in perspective, if I'd been doing this job as a consultant I would have billed about $3,000 for the work I did, and another $2,000 or so to finish the job. Now, $5,000 isn't inexpensive; but when you consider that this software ought to sell for at least $500, it isn't prohibitive, either—it adds up to the gross from only 10 sales, and my own view is that the added user-friendliness should account for a lot more sales than that. And, as I noted, if my friend had done the job himself, already knowing his way around his programming's logic, it could have been done in a lot less time and at, consequently, a lot less cost.

In other words, user-friendliness is economically feasible, too.

If it's so feasible, then why hadn't my friend already taken care of this himself? His answer when I asked was a very human one, and probably explains why so much transportation/distribution software doesn't have the features I've been talking about.

"I just got tired," he told me. "When you spend as much time as I did working with the logic and getting it to work right, there's a point where you get sick of making changes."

I can certainly understand, and sympathize with, his feeling. I've been there myself; there comes a time when you want to stop working and have a finished product.

But that finished product ought to be *really* finished; and my opinion is that it isn't, in computer programming, if it makes the user work harder than necessary. Every job has its drudgery, and computer programming probably more than most; but if the programmer grits his teeth and does *all* the drudgery, he'll be saving his potential users—the ones he expects to pay him money for his product—a lot more drudgery of their own in learning and operating it.

26

USER MANUALS AND THEIR PROBLEMS

Why are software user manuals so often . . . well, to call a spade a blanking shovel, so often truly lousy?

I'm not just talking about confusing; I'm talking about downright incorrect, or woefully incomplete, or so badly written they're incomprehensible. And, of course, *abysmally* indexed (if, indeed, they're indexed at all).

If you must zero in on a single cause, lay it on our schools. The American educational system simply doesn't teach most people to express their thoughts adequately, either on paper or verbally. (If you doubt this, look at all the classified ads that want people with "communications skills" for managerial jobs. Think about it: If most people, even at the managerial level, didn't lack such skills, why would it be important to spell this out?)

Here's what happens with the typical user manual: First, somebody clever about computers writes the program. He or she may be terrific at writing code, but for the most part won't be as literate in English. So a professional writer—one who makes a living doing what we all *ought* to be able to do with reasonable facility—must be hired to write the manual.

Some developers either won't or can't spend that money; that accounts for the incomprehensible manuals. As for the others, they must wrestle with the difficulty of bridging the gap between the computer-ignorant writer and the inarticulate programmer—and *that* accounts for the wrong or incomplete manuals. Either way, it's the poor user, struggling to make heads or tails out of a manual that's already several steps removed from the actual programming process, who ultimately pays the price.

I've heard some real horror stories from software developers who have sincerely tried to produce good, usable manuals but whose efforts have been thwarted by this chronic inability to communicate in plain English. If you find a good user manual, treasure it; it's unfortunately a pretty rare bird.

27

AFTERMARKET SUPPORT FOR SOFTWARE

And why is technical support for most computer products—hardware and software alike—generally so abysmal?

The user manual you get with your new equipment, software, etc., almost always includes a little message from the vendor to the effect that, if you have any problems, you can always write or phone for help. And indeed you can; mostly they answer your letters or phone calls very courteously.

Then they give you either (1) the wrong answer, or (2) no answer at all. I never cease to be amazed about how *ignorant* most developers manage to be about the very products they produce and sell.

Now, maybe I'm not the usual customer; I don't pester hardware manufacturers and software developers unless I've already gone through the user manual pretty thoroughly, and maybe done a bit of experimentation on my own; so the questions I'm answering aren't easy ones. On the other hand, what's the point in offering support if your support people can't answer anything *except* the easy ones (and not even all of those)—can't tell you, in other words, anything a reasonably intelligent user can't read and/or dope out for himself or herself?

In what now must be a good dozen or so tries, I have yet to get a helpful answer from one of these support operations. What cross-wiring is necessary to hook up my printer to my computer? How can I fix my word-processor so it won't display its menus in glaring inverse video, or will merge two files in a fairly complicated way? How can I set my communications software to transmit or receive multiple files without my having to stay close by the keyboard? How to install a spreadsheet program to work with my co-processor? There *are* answers to these questions; I know because I ultimately found them myself (after extended and tedious trial-and-error experimentation). But the technical support people were unable to give them to me.

Now, that's ridiculous. It's bad enough that the user manual is wrong or incomplete, to the point where certain features don't work as described or are completely undocumented. But when the best the manufacturer's or developer's technical-support people can do is to read you passages from that selfsame wrong/incomplete user manual, you're not getting much real help.

I had an archtypal experience along this lines with two software packages—one new (to me) and another not so new—that were causing me various problems.

With regard to the new package, which ran under MS-DOS, admittedly I had some fairly unusual problems because I have an off-the-beaten-track system—one with an eight-bit basic processor, but enhanced by a special add-on board to let me run 16-bit MS-DOS programs. But it would seem that *somebody* ought to be able to help me make things work properly—particularly the producers of (a) my machine; (b) the add-on MS-DOS board; or (c) the software I wanted to get working.

As I've found is the rule in such situations, however, the correct answer is (d) none of the above. I phoned each in turn and got what amounted to no real help at all. The computer manufacturer told me to go talk to the company that manufactures the MS-DOS board. That company wouldn't even let me talk to anybody knowledgeable; the person who answered the phone said he "wasn't allowed to do that," and would have to pass my inquiry along, get the answer and call me back. He never called. And the developer of the program I wanted to get going just fobbed me off with some generalized literature that did help a little, but nowhere near enough.

As usual again, I had to ultimately work things out myself. Since I'm fairly inexpert about such matters, it was mostly a trial-and-error sort of process, which takes quite a while but is usually (if you have to patience to stick with it) successful. As it was in this case; two or three hours after I gave up on the phone calls and got down to serious work, I had the program doing just what it's supposed to do.

It was a few days later that I got the letter that drove home to me once again just how inexpert the "experts" really are. It was from the add-on board manufacturer, the folks who never called back. After checking with their top programmers, they said, they regretfully found it necessary to inform me that this particular software wouldn't work on my system. Oh, well; the "experts" used to tell us that bumblebees can't fly, too.

Experience No. 2 involved the word processor I'd been using for several years. One particular feature—the subroutines that let you mesh data from two separate files into a single text output—is real dogmeat, at least in the version I use. Oh, you can get it to work all right, but only by adding in a lot of commands that are nowhere documented in either the user manual nor the on-screen instructions.

Again, I had to dope this out for myself; again, the software developer was unwilling to discuss the problem with me. Only *after* I'd doped out my own fix, and was irritably describing it to a company representative over the phone (in hopes that he'd have a better and easier answer), was anybody even willing to admit there was anything wrong with the software.

"Oh, yeah," he said when I told him what I'd done. "You have to do that." I went on to tell him another problem I'd found and how I'd corrected for it. "Yes, that's right, you have to do that, too," he said sagely.

Thanks so much, friend; and where were you when I needed you? It seems awfully hard to find any dealer, distributor, developer—*anybody*—who'll really live up to their promises to "stand behind you" when you've got computer problems. If they actually do know what they're doing they seem to clutch onto their knowledge as if it were buried treasure I was trying to steal; and most of them show me little evidence that they know much about what they're doing in the first place.

28

THINGS TO WATCH OUT FOR WITH SOFTWARE

I have a few complaints about transportation/distribution software.

As the professionals will tell you, complaining is a psychologically satisfying thing to do (if it weren't, it wouldn't be such a popular human recreation). So to a certain extent it's self-indulgence on my part to write this—and perhaps on your part to read it, too, especially if you share some of my views.

More to the point, however, complaining isn't a bad way of achieving results. The squeaky wheel, it's said, gets the grease. So maybe some of these complaints will encourage those to whom they're directed to fix the problems I'm identifying, too.

Anyhow, for what it's worth, here are a few of my *un*favorite things about computer applications in our industry:

Operating Speed (or Lack Thereof)

Why do so many transportation/distribution programs work so *s-l-o-w-l-y?* Oh, sure, they go faster than they used to. I recall that the first rate-finding program I saw took a full minute or more to respond to each user inquiry; now most of them have got the lag down to 10-15 seconds. But that's still a pretty long time to sit and stare at that dreary message, "Please Wait" (or something of the sort) again and again. And you get the same thing with many packages designed for other types of applications.

You've probably had the experience of making a phone call and being answered with, "Smith Company, please hold," CLICK. It makes me want to bite the telephone. (Some people say their idea of hell is a place where sinners are kept on eternal "hold," phones glued to their ears as they wait for the voice that never comes.) I get the same sense of frustration from computer response delays; it seems to me both the system and its developer are showing me how little regard they have for the value of my time.

If these delays were truly necessary, forced by hardware or other limitations, I might be more tolerant of them; but they're *not.* I've seen a few specialized programs, and *quite* a few general-purpose ones, that go like greased lightning, even in dealing with enormous data bases and/or performing the most complicated of tasks. Computer operations are measurable in microseconds (a millionth of a second) or even nanoseconds (a billionth of a second), meaning you can cram an awful lot of them into a timespan too short to notice; and good programming is simply the art of trimming down to a reasonable number the operations the computer has to perform in response to each input.

I won't go into all the devices and methods used to accomplish this, nor do I even know all of them. Suffice it to say that it *can* be done, the proof being that it's *being* done by truly able programmers. So I think this is a legitimate beef.

Displays

Why are the screen displays offered by so many transportation/distribution software packages so coyote-ugly?

Not only does this offend my aesthetic sensibilities, it makes the displayed material plain hard to read. Since a program isn't much good if its output is prone to be misread or misinterpreted by the user, this is a complaint of more than casual significance.

The most common failing along these lines is trying to pack too much information into the 25-line-by-80-character space the computer makes available on the screen. In many cases all that information isn't even necessary to the purpose of the display;

much of it could be pruned away with no loss of *useful* display and considerable benefit in terms of increased display readability. Or, if all the information really *is* necessary, it could easily be spread across two or more screens, with the user given the capability of flipping back and forth between them with a keystroke (which isn't at all difficult to program).

I also dislike those displays that insist on using all-capital-letters format for text; it's *much* harder to read. To some extent, with on-line systems, this is a characteristic of the main-frame environment the developer is using. But it's a defect nevertheless, and can be cured either by (1) using another kind of main-frame system, or (2) recognizing that the microcomputer has a lot more power than a dumb terminal, and using a little of that power to translate all-caps into more readable caps-and-lower-case letters before they get to the display screen.

Finally, there are the programs that insist on using color for lengthy text and/or numeric displays. Now, it's possible to find color boards and monitors capable of displaying un-fuzzy alphanumeric characters; but most microcomputer users don't have such state-of-the-art equipment (which tends to be a bit pricey). Furthermore, some developers haven't paid adequate attention to their color choices. Anyone who's color-blind, for example, is going to have an awfully tough time with some of these screens. And in one program I saw recently, the developer got so carried away with varying color combinations that in a couple of cases even perfect vision wouldn't suffice to let you read the screen.

Coded Input/Output

I also get pretty tired of software that makes you memorize alphabetic or numeric codings in order to make your inputs and/or understand the outputs.

That is, to the program apples aren't apples and oranges aren't oranges; they're "01" or "ZQ" or something of that sort. And you either have to commit these codes to memory or make yourself a crib sheet that you keep near at hand; the software itself won't explain the codes to you.

I can understand the need for codes, especially where they take the place of very lengthy descriptions or nomenclature; not only do they allow the software to function more efficiently, but they considerably reduce the user's input problems. But few developers of transportation/distribution software take the trouble to make such codes mnemonic (such as "AP" for applies, "OR" for oranges, etc.), and fewer still offer you on-line capability to have a code reference displayed on the screen while you're working.

These things aren't impossible; general-purpose software developers manage both routinely. In the word-processing package I use (WordStar), for example, "P" is print, "S" is save, etc.—and there's a changing menu of such commands constantly in view at the top of the screen (which, moreover, you can turn off if and when you get to know the program well enough not to need it).

A related complaint concerns the failure of developers to use the display screen's "status line" to identify what the various function keys are supposed to do. Here, at least, I'm seeing some progress; but there are still quite a few transportation/distribution programs around that don't bother to give you this simple on-screen explanation.

User Manuals

One of the worst failings of specialized transportation/distribution software is with the user manuals and/or other documentation that you get with the program disks.

Remember those instruction guides that used to come with European or Japanese exports a few years back, before exporting got to be such an important part of the manufacturers' businesses—the ones that had been translated by people whose English came from language classes and textbooks? You'd get sentences like, "Next the plug into the wall inject, and the knob in clocklike wise on-turn." Compared to some of the user manuals I've seen, these were positive models of clarity.

If you can't figure out how a program works, how can you use it? I know it isn't always easy to find people who can put words down in paper clearly; unfortunately, written English isn't very well taught in our school systems. But I'm not looking for high literary art—just for documentation that effectively communicates its meaning. Software users shouldn't have to decode tutorials that seem to have been written in Sanskrit by Chinese-speaking Lithuanians.

Nor is this the only user-manual problem I've encountered. Any proper user manual ought to come with a *complete* index to let you find what you need quickly; you shouldn't have to thumb through it page by page for what you want. And it ought to clearly document all key features of the program, and do so correctly and thoroughly. A lot of the manuals I've seen fall down on one or both of these counts, too.

Normally I try to point out the failings of specialized transportation/distribution software by drawing comparisons with how developers of general-purpose software do the job. Here, however, even the general-purpose program developers tend to fall down. My WordStar manual, for instance, is woefully deficient in documenting some features of the program, and incorrectly documents others; the manual for my communications package (Crosstalk) leaves me in the dark about how to invoke certain functions; and so forth. Over the years I've had to dedicate long hours of study and trial-and-error experimentation to get the programs to do things they were designed to do, and the developer should have told me about in the first place.

But as every child's parents and teachers are forever saying, "Just because so-and-so did it, that doesn't mean you have to make the same mistake!" Good user manuals aren't impossible to produce, and they're *very* important.

Confusing Commands

How do you get the software to do what you want it to do? Too often the answer is confusingly inconsistent.

For example, there's a key on your keyboard that's clearly labeled "ENTER." That's how you enter your input into the program, right? Wrong, for one program I recently looked at; instead you have to hit one of the function keys to do that, while your "ENTER" key is programmed to do something else altogether.

What about making corrections to your data? I've seen one program that makes you enter a two-digit number to accomplish this which, moreover, varies depending on just where you are in the input process—sometimes you hit "07," other times you hit "12," etc. Another lets you use the arrow keys to move the cursor around the screen for some corrections, but you have to use the backspace for others. I've even encountered one program that won't let you quit using it by a built-in command; you have to hit a control-C, which kicks you back into your operating system while (if you aren't especially careful) wiping out the last couple of inputs you've made.

It's easy to understand how this state of affairs came about. Programs tend to be created in bits and pieces, which are then stacked together in the final version; and it's a nuisance to go back and change one of the early-written bits or pieces because its command structure doesn't agree with what's written later on. So if you've decided early to use a particular command for one function, and then realize later on you need it to do something else, it's a lot easier to either (a) leave the inconsistency, or (b) hunt up another key for the new activity (even though it's not really appropriate), than to go back and make the necessary programming changes. Easier for the programmer, that is; for the user it's a real annoyance (or worse).

'Vaporware'

Beware of "vaporware."

Vaporware is software that hasn't been written (at least in final, usable form) yet. It's just a twinkle in its would-be developer's eye, and, like a lot of such twinkles, you can't quite tell when, or even whether, it will actually come into being, or whether it'll be what you want if and when it does.

I've read about one sneaky program that gives considerable

aid and comfort to the purveyors of vaporware. It lets you design and save (for later retrieval) screen displays that can simulate what you expect your not-ready-for-prime-time software to look like. Used unethically, it can even make the unsuspecting believe the software *is* in existence and ready for use.

Thus, I urge you to try out any software product on which you propose to spend your money *thoroughly,* and to buy only what you see—not what the developer promises "soon." Ideas are a glut on the market; everybody has them, and they're easy to talk about. It's the implementation that's difficult, and that's the only thing worth real money. When you shop for software, make sure you're buying a real product, not just the idea of it.

Part 8

SOFTWARE COPYING

29

ABOUT PIRACY

Are you a thief? Are your friends and associates thieves? Do you knowingly do business with thieves?

As they say on the TV crime shows, you have the right to remain silent; and if you use computers very much, you may want to think twice before you give up that right. Because in several reputable surveys I've seen, anywhere from a third to more than half of all computer users have admitted to participating in a new form of thievery—stealing computer software.

Often it's not *knowing* theft; many people don't understand fully what's legal and what's not when it comes to copying software. But it's theft, nevertheless, ignorance of the law being (as traditional) no excuse. And whether out of ignorance or on purpose, whether for convenience or profit, it's happening with great frequency.

I confess I've been guilty of it (albeit in extenuating circumstances). The odds are that you have too.

What's Legal. . .

If you go by the complicated, fine-print "licenses" that accompany many software packages and which you're supposed to read, sign and return to the vendor (though not many people do), software theft is pretty tricky to define. Some of those licenses would give headaches to an experienced lawyer.

If you take a practical, real-world view, however, the definition is simplicity itself: At any given time, there should by in operation (or potential operation) no more copies of the software than have been legitimately purchased. Thus, if you give away or sell a copy, you've also given or sold your legal right to operate your own copy (although you can, of course, buy another). One copy of a program, in other words, equals one (and *only* one) right to use it.

Note that this doesn't mean you can't make copies, as many as you like. Indeed, recommended procedure is always to make at least one copy of each software package you buy, perhaps more (I make two), for safety's sake. The floppy disks on which the software resides can develop bugs that make the programming unusable, and backup copies are essential protection should such a thing happen. In addition, of course, copying is necessary if you want to transfer the software to hard disk storage so you don't have to hunt up the floppy each time you want to run the program.

Vendors' licenses sometimes purport to restrict your right to make such backup copies (limiting their number, or even supposedly allowing none at all). You can pretty safely ignore any such admonition; I doubt that the courts would uphold this limitation, and in any case I don't think any software developer would be silly enough to sue over mere backup copies. That even holds true where the software is copy-protected; if you can defeat the copy-protection scheme (usually not too difficult if you're adroit with computers), go ahead and make your backups.

. . . and What's Not

But that holds true only so long as your backup copies stay where they legally belong—on your shelves or in your files. It's when you start using them that you run afoul of the law.

Let's start with a simple illustration—an office with several compatible machines. Now, so long as you maintain just a single working copy of the software you can shift it from machine to machine at your convenience. (Some developers say you're supposed to use it on only one machine, but that's legal rubbish so long as you use it on only one *at a time.)*

But you probably won't do this; it's a nuisance, especially where machines are scattered around the office. This holds doubly true for managers who have one machine in the office and another at home; nobody lugs floppy disks back and forth. What you'll do is make a copy for each machine, with the result that you have multiple working copies even though you paid for only one. And now you've crossed the border into illegality; you've become a computer thief.

If you think I'm overstating the case, talk to Lotus Development Co., for one. Lotus has cracked down on several business users who've done exactly what I've described with its popular 1-2-3 spreadsheet, with a good deal of (mostly out-of-court) success.

Now, no reputable business concern is going to knowingly steal something it can readily buy for under $300 (the discounted price for Lotus 1-2-3 as of the time this was written). The companies I'm describing simply didn't know they were breaking the law; they had no idea that their few copies, made for convenience and efficiency rather than with any nefarious intent, were illegal. But if you multiply those "few copies" by all the many users of Lotus 1-2-3 who have acted similarly, you come up with a pretty sizeable amount of revenue from Lotus' standpoint, which it understandably wants to protect.

More obvious is the sort of software theft in which I got involved a while back. I needed a communications package for the computer I was then using, an Osborne I. By that time, however, Osborne Computer Corp. had gone bankrupt, and it had got awfully hard to find software for its orphaned machines. After trying for several days to get the programming from legitimate sources, I succumbed in frustration to a fellow Osborne owner's offer to let me have a copy of his. (He sanctimoniously told me he couldn't "sell" the program, but happily accepted the $40 I gave him "for his trouble.")

In the same circumstances I might well do the same thing

again; after all, if the developer isn't producing the software any more it's hard to see how it can be losing. Nevertheless, I technically violated the law; and a lot of people are doing the same thing with a lot less motivation than I had.

A situation described to me by a developer in the transportation/distribution arena goes a good deal further down this same pike. The developer's main product is a data-base, together with the software required to access it, which he sells rather inexpensively. Not long after making one such sale, he received a mass-mailed advertising flier from the buyer offering to sell him *his own programming*—at, moreover, nearly 10 times his (the developer's) asking price. A few cautious inquiries led to the further news that this buyer had *already* sold several such packages to others (who, needless to say, were no longer potential customers for the original developer).

I have to say that this type of really blatant, organized thievery is pretty unusual in my experience; more common is the kind of casual "sharing" between acquaintances, business associates, etc., that I described previously. But in law it's all equally thievery. You can't be a little bit illegal any more than you can be a little bit pregnant; either you are or you aren't.

An Easy Crime

Software theft is a popular crime not only because many people don't understand the law (although if you've read this far you can no longer make that claim), but because it's so *easy.*

If you want to make copies of printed matter—books, magazines, newspapers, etc., which are protected by the same copyright law that applies to software—you either have to have a pretty sophisticated (and expensive) copy machine or go to a fair amount of trouble. And your copies, no matter what you do, will look like copies, readily distinguishable from the original.

If you want to make copies of computer software, though, you can do so with only a few keystrokes, and then walk away while the machine does the work. Moreover, for all practical purposes your copy will be electronically identical to the original;

save for (perhaps) the physical appearance of the floppy disk on which they're stored, not even an expert could tell them apart.

It's the ease with which software copying is accomplished that lures many developers into spending a good deal of money, time and trouble developing copy-protection schemes. Unfortunately, in the process they also make life harder for the honest user.

Copy protection does work. To be sure, such schemes aren't crack-proof; I'm told an expert hacker can defeat the average copy-protection in about 10 minutes. But most users, especially of business software, aren't expert hackers, so the copy-protection scheme serves its purpose of discouraging the casual copying that (as I've already described) is the most frequent problem—just as a standard door lock, though far from burglar-proof, keeps casual intruders out of your home or office.

But for legitimate users it's a real pain in the . . . well, neck. You have just one copy on a delicate floppy disk; if that disk "crashes" (and it will invariably select the most inconvenient of times), you have to sit around waiting for the developer to send you a replacement for which, moreover, you'll usually have to pay at least a few dollars (some even charge full price!). If you have any data files stored on that disk they may be gone forever. And you can't, of course, run the software off your hard disk; you have to dig up the floppy and use it every time you want to run the program.

On the other hand, look at things from the developer's perspective. He's spent a lot of time and effort not only developing his program but documenting it, promoting it and marketing it; he doesn't want people stealing his "baby" (and source of income) without a second thought. In light of the fact that a pretty big proportion of computer users *admit* to having engaged in software theft at some point or another (and a lot more have probably done so but won't own up), you can understand the reasons underlying copy protection.

I think the best approach I've seen is that pioneered by Borland International, developers of such popular software as Turbo Pascal (a slick version of Pascal programming language),

Sidekick (a "pop-up" calendar/notepad/calculator), etc. You can get a copy-protected version of Sidekick for $60—or an unprotected version for $90. It's still illegal to make more than one working copy of the unprotected version; but Borland is willing to take a chance on your honesty if you're willing to fork over a 50% premium.

Another novel approach is the "Shareware" notion adopted by a company that bears that name. Shareware encourages you to distribute copies to your friends; if they like it, they're asked to send a modest payment to the company, out of which the company will give you a portion as your "commission" for helping it with marketing and in exchange for which your friend becomes eligible for (1) technical support from the developer and (2) commissions of his own when he gives copies to *his* friends and *they* pay to register them. The Shareware notion works, after a fashion, although I'm told the company is doing not much more than barely making ends meet.

And even Borland and Shareware (not to mention other developers) will have to abandon the notion of unprotected software unless computer users, as a group, start showing a bit more integrity than they have in the past. In our market economy nobody can afford to give away his revenue products; that's how people with otherwise viable businesses wind up *without* viable businesses in quick order.

When it comes to transportation/distribution software, the problem's particularly acute. Such specialized software has a small (relatively speaking) potential market to begin with; its developers need access to *all* of that market if they're to stand any chance of economic success and, thus, the ability to continue developing new products. In this kind of restricted market, even a small number of lost sales looms large; and thus even casual copying can be a crippling blow.

So before you make that extra working copy, remember how much you paid for the original—and ask yourself whether that's your price for branding yourself a thief.

30

THE IMPORTANCE OF BACKUPS

How often do you call up vendors, customers, government agencies, banks, insurance companies, etc., etc., for information, only to be told that "the computer is down?" I don't know about you, but it happens to me a *lot.*

Micro-computers both pose a problem and offer an opportunity in this area.

First the problem. Micro-computers are not especially prone to needing repair; as a class they're usually more problem-free than larger computers (mainframes in particular) which have, of course, a lot more things about them to go wrong. But when they *do* "go down," they can take several days to get fixed; and they can also wipe out any programs, data, etc., to which they happen to have access at the time.

The opportunity lies in the ease, and relatively low cost, of backups—backup hardware and backup copies of software and data files.

If a machine costs several hundred thousand dollars or more (as a mainframe or even a sophisticated mini-computer does) you don't buy more than you actually need. But if it costs only three or four thousand (as do micros), having a backup makes a lot better sense—especially when the likelihood is that you'll also find some additional work your backup can be doing to help pay for itself.

Backing up software and data files is even less costly—no more than the $2-apiece cost of floppy disks. Really careful managers insist on backups after each major session on the computer (and perhaps even more often if programs or files are especially valuable and/or hard to reproduce). It takes but a few moments and is essentially an unsupervised procedure (so the operator doesn't have to just sit there while the machine cranks away).

It's a straight cost/benefit calculation. If you're dependent on a computer, having it go down even once may cost you a lot more than the expense of backups. And despite the general reliability of micros, you can expect that sooner or later the law of averages will catch up with you. So why not be prepared?

A Personal Story

In connection with backups, here's a sad tale with a happy ending. Or maybe it's a happy one with a sad beginning. Either way, it illustrates the power of the computer to deal with problems that, in the pre-computer office environment, could have spelled major disaster.

There probably exist few individuals who haven't at one time or another, in a moment of inattention, discarded papers that were of utmost importance. Discovery of the mistake then leads to weary hours of sifting through trashbins, in the hope that the needed material can be rescued before the garbage collectors arrive. And then come more tedious hours of re-typing, re-copying, re-collating, etc., since papers that have once joined the used coffee cups and other detritus of the wastebasket rarely emerge in mint condition.

The same problem can arise with computer files, of course; computers aren't proof against carelessness any more than anything else in the office. But it can be easier to correct your blunder there, provided you take some time and effort to learn how.

The Lost Chapter

The events came at a time when I was spending long hours, often well into the evening, at work on a much-overdue book manuscript (no, not this one; my previous *Practical Handbook of*

Transportation Contracting and Rate Negotiations).* All went well until late one afternoon, at which point my mind took a coffee break while my fingers were telling the computer I use for writing to erase *both* copies of 40-page chapter 8.

Now, it would take me a good two days (or more) to re-create 40 pages of text—a dismaying prospect at best. What's more, I didn't have two days to spare; chapter 8, along with several others, was also to be used as text for my 1986 rate negotiation seminars, the first of which was less than a week away (and I still had a full slate of other work to complete first). I was, in sum, knee-deep in natural fertilizer.

As one does in such circumstances, I blew about the next 15 minutes alternately kicking myself (figuratively; I'm not physically that limber any more) and trying to wish the problem away. When it became evident that self-flagellation wouldn't help, and no fairy godmother showed up to wave a magic wand, I started to zero in on more practical answers.

To understand how there can *be* practical answers to such a problem, you have to know something about how computers work. When you "save" information to a disk, the system actually performs two separate operations: (1) it writes the data onto the disk, and (2) it jots down an entry into the disk's reserved "directory" area noting where on the disk the data has been written (so the machine won't try to write any *other* data in the same place).

But when you tell the system to *erase* a data file, it gets lazy; it just discards its directory note without wiping out the information itself. If you don't notice your error until you've saved additional files, the computer may "overwrite" your data (its place no longer being reserved in the directory) with new information, meaning it's lost forever. But if you *do* catch it promptly—and it took me only about five seconds to realize what I'd done—the data is still sitting on your disk in pristine splendor, just as it was before you "erased" it.

---

*Washington, DC: The Traffic Service Corp., 1986.

So my 40 pages were still there. But how to get at them? If I simply told the machine to call up that file it would look through its directory entries, find nothing, and respond with the electronic equivalent of "Say what?"

(There's an apocryphal story of a sailor who asked his skipper, "Captain, sir, is a thing lost if you know where it is?" "Why, no," said the captain. "Then, sir," quoth the seaman, "your chronometer is not lost, for it is at the bottom of the sea." I was faced with the same situation; I knew the general area where my missing file was to be found, but I couldn't pinpoint its location—and even if I could, without the directory entry I couldn't retrieve it.)

To get at the file, I needed the directory entry back in place. And to restore the directory entry I was going to have to dig around in the bowels of my machine's operating system.

'UNERASE' & Co.

The trouble is, computer operating systems aren't designed to let you do that. They'll let you write to, read from and otherwise manipulate data on about 95% of your disk space; but they set aside a few "tracks" for housekeeping purposes (including directory maintenance), which are inaccessible to the casual user.

What I needed was programming to bypass the operating system so I could get at the proscribed areas. For reasons I've never altogether understood—don't other people make mistakes too?—such software isn't terribly easy to find commercially; it exists, but it's not well-advertised and most computer dealers don't stock it, so you need to anticipate your emergencies well before they occur. I thought I had, but the version I had would deal only with floppy disks, and my erasure had been from my hard disk. No help there, then.

There are, however, a number of so-called "public domain" programs intended to "UNERASE" (the name of one of the better-known programs). Public domain programs have been written by "hackers" who didn't copyright them, but instead make them available to anyone who wants them through electronic bulletin boards, computer clubs and user groups, etc. *(see Chapter 22).*

Public domain programs have their drawbacks. First, they tend to be *very* machine-specific; you have to find one that works on your make, model, version, etc., and the usual standards of "compatibility" won't always apply. Second, they're not always (or even usually) fully de-bugged, so they can wind up doing some strange things and you have to be pretty careful with them. And third, it's more or less up to the user to figure out how they work; there are, of course, no user manuals, and the on-screen instructions are sketchy at best (if there are any instructions at all). But in my position it was either wrestle with the public-domain programs or nothing, so I set sail.

I won't bore you with all the details of the ensuing hours. First it took a couple dozen phone calls, plus an hour's fruitless search through the data banks of one of the major on-line service companies, before I could even find a usable program. Then I had to figure out how to "compile" it (most public domain software comes to you in "source code," which is fine if you want to read the programming instructions but not so fine if you want to use it). Then I had to dope out how it was supposed to work, *and* what were the undocumented bugs that gave me some woefully inconsistent results while I was experimenting. And so on, and on, and on.

Finally, about six hours later, I dug into my disk directory, changed a couple of data bytes here and there, and lo and behold! my missing 40 pages were back again, none the worse for wear.

Learning from Experience

If you don't have and/or regularly use a computer, all the foregoing is pretty academic for you. If you do, however, there are some lessons you can learn from my experience.

First and foremost, don't panic if you lose files. Whether it happens (as in my case) because of an inadvertent erasure, or because a disk has "crashed," most or all of the information will be recoverable if you act properly. (But stop using the disk the moment you discover the problem, to avoid any possibility of overwriting and thus forever losing your data.)

Second, don't wait (as I did) until you reach a crisis to try to find the software that will help you out; remember, you're apt to be under time pressure when files are erased, disks "crash," etc. (This is even more likely when you consider that time pressure tends to produce more mistakes in the first place.) So whether you seek out commercial software or use public domain material, make sure it's on-hand and available when you need it.

Third, be patient about the recovery process—and be careful. The "reserved" directory tracks weren't meant to be messed about with, and you can cause *more* damage if you're not careful. The best answer, if possible, is to copy your troubled disk "as is"—which will include erased files and/or damaged disk areas as well as everything else—and then work with the copy, so a mistake won't be irretrievable.

Fourth, try to avoid the problem in the first place by taking the time to make *frequent* backup copies. That won't protect you if your head isn't screwed on straight; in my case I carefully erased *both* the original *and* the backup of chapter 8 before I realized I was erasing the wrong file. But it will help if you aren't as thorough about your mistakes as I was.

And finally, bear in mind that it's no harder to make this kind of mistake with electronic than with paper files; it takes about the same effort to mistakenly throw away either one. But if you get the paper one back after scavenging through your trash, it's likely to look like something the cat dragged in. If you get the electronic one back, it'll still be fresh as a daisy. You may feel more comfortable trusting paper, since you can see it and hold it in your hand; but actually, you're probably better off relying on those invisible, untouchable electronic impulses when it comes to covering yourself against mistakes.

Care About Backups

Even the most conscientious of backup procedures won't

help you if you're not careful of the quality of your backups, as a friend of mine recently discovered.

A common practice is to use the same disk or tape for backups every time. But what that means is that, every time you make a new backup, you're writing your data, as well as your directory entry, right over the old file (erasing it irrecoverably in the process). And if your original data file has meantime gone sour, you're left with two (or more) copies of bad data and no copies at all of your prior, good data.

That's what happened to my friend. The day-to-day system operators were clerical personnel, who knew little about computers and did their work in by-the-numbers fashion. By-the-numbers called for daily backups, so they duly backed up the files each day, eradicating, as they did, the previous day's backup.

Unfortunately, they kept right on following that routine when a hardware malfunction began scrambling the data; they didn't know enough about the system to realize anything was wrong. By the time my friend discovered the glitch, every file copy, backups included, was full of garbles.

Moral: Browse through your files before you back them up; make sure they're in good shape throughout, not merely in the areas where you happened to be working lately. If you can't do this daily, keep archival backups intact until you can. That way you may lose a few days' work if things go wrong, but at least your entire data base isn't at risk.

(Indeed, I have another friend who insists on keeping *everything* in archives, and never erases or writes over old files. Floppy disks and tapes just aren't very expensive, he reasons, when you compare the possible cost of losing data you urgently need. You may think this much belt-and-suspenders caution is excessive; but his figurative pants are definitely going to stay in place.)

Part 9

SOME LESSONS FROM EXPERIENCE

31

USING A RAM DISK

I wrote this chapter this on my computer using something called a RAM disk.

What the term "RAM disk" means is that a portion of my machine's active memory ("Random Access Memory", or RAM) has been set aside to imitate, for all intents and purposes, a disk drive. I can save files to my RAM disk, retrieve them from it, etc., just as if it were a real disk drive. But actually the information isn't being stored on any permanent disk medium (hard disk or floppy); it's simply being shunted into the area of my RAM designated for that purpose.

Obviously you need a computer with a pretty sizable memory in order to be able to set some of that memory aside for your RAM disk; 256K is the rock-bottom minimum, and for most applications you'll need more than that. Or you may have, as I do, a machine with dual processors, in which case you can use one for a RAM disk while the other's doing the "thinking." If your system meets neither criterion, you'll have to either upgrade or forget about a RAM disk.

And you have to treat a RAM disk with a certain amount of care. In particular, it won't do for permanent storage; turning off your machine erases its contents completely. So you have to remember to copy your files over onto a real hard or floppy disk at the end of every session if you want to save them.

But a RAM disk works *fast*—unbelievably so, by comparison with the operations of those actual disks (hard or floppy).

That's why I use it; and that's why (provided you have a system big enough for it) it may be of considerable value to you in running transportation/distribution applications software.

Why a RAM Disk?

Why would you want to set aside a portion of your computer's memory to imitate a disk drive? Why not simply use all the memory for computational purposes? The answer is to be found in the way computer software is designed to function.

For technical reasons I don't want to delve into here, a great deal of programming—especially that which occupies many lines of code, and therefore takes up a lot of space in the computer's memory and/or storage—is written in segmented fashion. That is, instead of one large program you are actually using several shorter ones, which are interlocked to call one another into service on an as-needed basis. But only the currently active modules are "resident in RAM" as of any particular time; the remainder are sitting in disk storage patiently awaiting their call to action.

And there's nothing you can do to change that. Even if you have room in your computer's RAM for the whole package and in fact load all the programs into RAM, it won't help. The software isn't set up to look around in RAM for needed modules; its instructions tell it to get the additional modules from disk storage, and that's what it's going to do whether the modules are already in RAM or not. Which means your computer will be repeatedly swapping programs back and forth to disk storage, and there's nothing you can do to change it.

What's more, most software is geared to automatically "save to disk" any data you input during the course of using it. You can't, again, short-circuit this process without actually rewriting the programming (which, of course, you probably couldn't do even if you wanted). And it's likewise set up to retrieve data you may have input during a prior session from disk storage, another process you can't do anything about.

In sum, the average software package demands a good deal

of activity from your disk drive(s). Now, disk drives—hard or floppy—are mechanical devices; disks can whir around only so fast, and the electromagnetic "heads" that read them can travel only so rapidly. So while the rest of your computer is functioning at the nearly speed-of-light pace at which pulses of electricity course through its circuits, disk operations are limited by the much slower speed of the drives.

Which means the software slows down to a relative crawl every time it has to access a disk drive. This is the kind of delay you avoid with a RAM disk.

Eliminating the Mechanics

The RAM disk does away with all the mechanical activity involved in disk storage/retrieval. The computer still *thinks* it's working with a disk drive; but no disks actually spin, no heads actually move to read them, etc.

In other words, *everything* happens as fast as electricity can travel; nothing has to await the operational limitations of physical data-storage devices. If your computer were programmed for curiosity, it might wonder why things are happening so quickly; but since it's not, it goes merrily about its business just as if it were working with a regular disk drive, except a *lot* faster.

To give you an idea of just what this speed difference means, I timed my word processor in saving, and making a backup copy of, a data file the size of this chapter. Using a floppy disk, the process took 55 seconds. Using my hard disk speeded up things considerably; it worked out to 16 seconds. But on the RAM disk the entire procedure required less than eight seconds.

Even if you have a hard disk, in other words, use of a RAM disk can cut your disk-access time in half (or better). If you have nothing but floppies, you can cut that time by a whopping 85%! And you have to multiply this time saving by all the *many* occasions on which the software you may be using needs to store to or retrieve from disk storage.

And *that's* why it's worthwhile dedicating a portion of your RAM for use as a RAM disk. Especially if you have a "memory-enhanced" computer—one whose memory has been expanded beyond common limits—most of your software isn't making use of all the available RAM anyway, and you can't force it to do so. By setting aside the unused RAM as a RAM disk, you speed up the software's operation—you minimize, that is, the time you're required to just sit there while the machine flashes its dreary message "WAIT" on the display screen—to a phenomenal degree.

Indeed, with respect to a lot of transportation/distribution software I've seen, using a RAM disk makes the difference between the software's being marginal or even unusable, due to the chronic time delays involved, and its being *extremely* usable on a "real-time" basis.

How to Use the RAM Disk

It takes no special expertise to set up and use a RAM disk; anybody who knows enough to run any kind of software on a computer can do it. But it *does* require, as I noted at the beginning of the column, a moderate amount of care.

A special piece of software is required to create the RAM disk *(see below).* Since the computer incurs terminal amnesia every time you turn it off—its memory is wiped as clean as a newborn baby's behind—you'll have to run this software at the beginning of every session.

The software will ask you a few questions as you get started. First it wants to know what designation (letter of the alphabet) you want to give your RAM disk; it's customary to call it "drive M", but you can use any other letter not already in service as a designator for one of your actual disk drives. My program then asks if I want the "disk directory" wiped clean; since the RAM disk won't have any files in storage it wouldn't seem to matter what you answer to this, but I find that if I don't erase the directory the machine gets confused.

Finally, you have to specify how much memory space you want to dedicate to the RAM disk. Since RAM used for a RAM disk obviously isn't available for other purposes, you have to make sure to leave enough unused RAM to run any software you're planning to use (the software's user manual will tell you this). For example, if you have a machine with 640K of RAM and your software requires 256K in order to run properly, you don't want to dedicate more than 384K (640 less 256) to the RAM disk.

Unfortunately, all RAM disk programs I've seen don't make it quite this easy for you. Instead of simply asking you how many thousands of bytes of RAM you want to use for the RAM disk, they ask for starting and ending "memory addresses" as expressed in hexidecimal numbers. This will require a little research on your part before you use your RAM disk program.

First, what's meant by a memory address? Well, every time your computer puts a byte of data (equivalent to a letter of the alphabet, numeral, etc.) into memory it stashes that byte in a particular location. Each such location is identified by an address, much as you identify your friends' residences by *their* addresses. The difference is that in the phone book addresses are recorded by number and street name, such as 123 Main Street; in the computer's directory addresses are recorded using hexidecimal math notation *(see Appendix D)*. You want to use "high" memory for your RAM disk—that is, the memory addresses at the upper end of the scale. That's because most software automatically loads in the low end of the spectrum, so you need to keep that end in active service. So you should inquire—the easiest place to ask is probably the dealer from whom you bought the computer, or you can call your manufacturer's user-support phone number—(1) what's the final address for your RAM, and (2) what are appropriate addresses lower down that will let you dedicate the proper amounts of RAM to your RAM disk.

Say, for example, you have 640K of RAM, and want to use your RAM disk to run one program that requires 256K of RAM and another than needs 312K. For the first application you'll want to know the starting address that, when coupled with the final address, sets aside 384K; for the second you'll need the starting address that is 328K away from the final one. (It's actually a bit more complicated than this, due to differences in the "addressability" of your RAM; but in any event your dealer's or manufacturer's technical people will be able to set you straight quite readily without your having to learn any more than I've described.)

Now the software compartmentalizes your machine's RAM in accordance with the instructions you've given it. But the set-aside portion being used as a RAM disk is still empty. The next step is to use your copy utility (the program's called "PIP" in the CP/M operating system, "COPY" in MS-DOS) to copy your applications software from the hard or floppy disk on which it's stored onto the RAM disk. In most cases you're now ready to go.

The only glitch you might encounter from here on out is where the software stubbornly specifies the designation(s) of the drive(s) on which programs and/or data files are expected to be stored and won't allow you to change those designations during use. Most software I've seen isn't quite this rigid; but some is—and, of course, the designated drive will *not* be "drive M" (or whatever other letter you may have used to identify the RAM disk).

In such cases you have two options. The first and simplest is to use your operating system utilities to rename your various drives so their designations comport with what the software specifies. That may not be feasible, however, especially if the software expects programming to be on one drive and data files on another; you can only have one RAM disk, and it can only have one designation. The alternative is to get in touch with the developer and have him make the necessary programming changes so you can use your RAM disk. It's as simple and straightforward a programming change as you could ask for, and any developer who gives you a hard time about this, or tries to charge you large sums to do the job, is one with whom I, at least, would try to avoid doing business at all.

Getting a RAM Disk

You should be able to get a RAM disk program either at *very* modest cost ($50 would be about as much as I'd be willing to spend), or free.

Mine was free; it was "bundled" with my computer when I

bought it. This is often done when you buy a computer with upgraded memory or (as I did) with dual processors. Thus, you may have one already even if you're not aware of it; check your directory of utility programs for one called "RAMDISK" or something similar.

If you don't already have one, your dealer should either have one to sell you or be able to tell you where you can buy it. Alternatively, if you're enterprising enough to dig them out, there are several public domain (free) programs that will do the trick, which you can get through such as CompuServe, The Source, local electronic "bulletin boards," etc. *(see Chapter 22).* Either way, you shouldn't have any great difficulty getting hold of the requisite software.

Some Cautions

Remember, though, a RAM disk is *not*—I repeat, it's *not*—a real disk drive. This means you have to be a bit careful using it.

As I mentioned at the start of this discussion, turning off your machine completely erases both your on-line RAM and your RAM disk. So does a power interrupt, even if it's only momentary. If you're in an area where electric power problems are common, you'll have to watch out especially for this latter problem; and the same holds true about using a RAM disk when the weather's especially bad and power failures are accordingly more likely.

The situation's a bit more complicated if you simply reset your computer (using the hard-wired "reset" button or the triple-keystroke CTRL/ALT/DEL combination IBM and some of its imitators employ). Here it depends on how your reset circuitry is wired. On my machine the reset button affects only the on-line processor, not the one in use as a RAM disk; I have to re-run my RAM disk setup program, but if I'm careful *not* to erase the RAM disk directory the contents of the RAM disk remain intact. You should try out your own system, as one of the first things you do, to find out how it responds.

The reason this is so important is that you'll occasionally run into a software glitch that sends your computer haywire and requires a manual reset. If your machine won't preserve the RAM disk contents in such circumstances, you'll have to exercise particular care to avoid losing any hard-to-replace data or programs.

(This problem is particularly acute with machines that don't have a hard-wired reset button and use IBM's keystroke combination instead. Some software glitches that can normally be cured by a system reset serve to "lock up" your keyboard so thoroughly that even the CTRL/ALT/DEL command will be ignored; you'll be forced to cut the power and then turn it back on—erasing, of course, your RAM disk in the process.)

The key to avoiding these problems is simply to copy any critical files periodically (and, of course, at the end of any session) onto actual hard or floppy disks. Yes, that uses up some of the time you've saved using the RAM disk in the first place. But this way the copying process takes place at *your,* and not the computer's, convenience, and only as frequently as you feel caution may require. So you can do this at times when you're going to be momentarily occupied with other things—while you're on the phone, or taking a coffee break, etc., and the computer would otherwise be idle.

In sum, a RAM disk can do a *lot* to speed up the computer's operation and make your use of it more efficient. This is particularly true when you're using specialized transportation/distribution software, which in my experience (with, of course, some exceptions) generally tends to run a bit slow due to repetitive disk-access delays. Cutting even a few seconds off each access can make a big difference when you add up all the saved time. If you're having such problems, you might benefit a lot by checking into the possibility of a RAM disk.

32

'BUGS'

I have discovered why computer problems are always termed "bugs," and the story's worth repeating.

Back in the 1940's when electronic computers were first being developed there were no such things as the transistors or silicone chips that have made microcomputers so small and affordable these days. The innards of these early computers consisted of huge arrays—whole rooms full—of vacuum tubes and wiring. The tubes were prone to failure, and college students were paid to scurry about and change blown tubes as needed.

It seems that one day a prototype computer had a particularly bad glitch, and a student was sent back to see what had happened. A few moments later he emerged carrying a large dead moth that had zapped itself on some exposed wiring, short-circuiting the whole system. From that point on, of course, every problem became a bug.

Perhaps a revision is in order, though; with the miniaturization that's taken place since then, it might be more appropriate to refer to computer foul-ups as bacteria these days.

After the foregoing was published in my *Traffic World* column, a reader wrote in to ask how I could have fallen for such a palpably fictitious story. Everybody knows, he advised me, that "bug" is a computerese acronym for "Binary Unexplained Glitch."

Well, I suppose it's possible; computer people, like Washington politicians, have a propensity for dreaming up screwy names just so the acronym looks cute. I keep thinking of the debugging utility in the CP/M operating system, called Dynamic Debugging Tool, for example.

It all reminds me of my childhood in south Florida, when every family kept a spraygun loaded with the real DDT (formally, dichloro-diphenyl-trichloroethane) to defend itself against the humongous native population of mosquitoes. My contemporaries and I, having observed the instant and dramatic results when you nailed a bug with the spraygun, needed no chemical nomenclature to translate those initials; we knew perfectly well the stuff was making insects Drop Dead Twice.

33

MONOCHROME SCREENS AND THEIR ONE COLOR

After living for six months with my monochrome-display computer as it came, I finally broke down and spend $150 to have its display screen replaced. After I'd done it, I wished I'd done it sooner.

The computer's user manual boasted in big type about the machine's "big green screen." It was green, all right—green enough that with a little water and fertilizer you could probably start it growing.

It was also green enough to be, quite literally, an eyesore; if I sat in front of it long enough (and I sometimes put in some pretty long days), I could start to feel the strain. At the same time I'd been hearing cheery little nuggets on the TV news about how too much looking at green-phosphor computer displays can cause serious eye damage.

So I had the green screen replaced with an amber one, which I've always preferred anyway. The difference is remarkable; the more I use it, the more I'm convinced amber is definitely the color of choice for a monochrome monitor.

Green does have some advantages, especially for graphics; differences in shading show up *much* better on green-phosphor screens. And reflection of ambient lighting is less bothersome on a green screen; I also had to buy a non-reflective overlay for the screen after I shifted to amber.

But green, as one of the primary colors, principally excites just one set of the human eye's color receptors—and it works them pretty hard while the others take a nap. It's that overwork, with only some receptors trying to do the job that is normally shared more equitably by all of them, that can produce eye damage. (One early symptom of the strain is the red after-image you'll see after staring hard at something green; the green receptors are the same ones that perceive red. This also accounts for the relatively common ailment of red/green colorblindness; these receptors don't work in some people's eyes, so that both colors are seen as a dull gray.)

By contrast, amber is a mixture of primary colors and therefore engages a larger proportion of the eye's color receptors, reducing the risk of overload on any of them. Thus, for extended work sessions amber is much preferable, in my opinion.

What's more, I've found there's almost no "ghosting" on the amber screen; when an image leaves the screen it does so almost instantly. Because of the different natures of the phosphors involved (video screens work by electronically activating phosphors painted on the screen's surface), the images on green screens, by contrast, tend to fade away more slowly, with old and new images momentarily competing for your attention and further straining your eyes.

If you're having any eye problems with your green monitor, I strongly recommend you consider replacing it with an amber one. The cost isn't high, and your eyes will thank you.

34

MODEMS AND TELEPHONE LINES

If you're planning on making serious use of a modem for over-the-phone data transmission and receiving, expect some problems from time to time. Clicks, static and the like, which are merely annoying when you're talking, can garble computer transmissions beyond use or recognition.

The best safeguard is a dedicated data quality line, which your local phone company may or may not provide. (Traffic Service Corp., publisher of this book located in downtown Washington, DC, has one; I, just 25 miles away in suburban Virginia, couldn't get one as of when this was written.) Fewer users are permitted on these lines, and transmission quality checks are made frequently. But they tend to be fairly expensive ($200 and up per month); and they cover only the local end of the link-up (that is, from the phone company's exchange to your office).

Unless you have such a dedicated line at *both* ends of the transmission, it's probably a poor idea to transmit at anything faster than 1200 bps "bits per second," the equivalent of, say, 2,500-3,000 words per minute). The faster the transmission speed, the more opportunity there is for interference to mess up a transmission. Even at 1200 bps you may not get perfect results; when I transmit my various writings (such as the manuscript for this book) to Traffic Service, we encounter brief glitches with a fair degree of frequency. When long-distance phoning is involved, the likelihood of such glitches is, of course, appreciably greater.

I've also found particular problems in using certain of the low-cost long-distance services. Such services do save you money, and I've used them successfully for normal telephoning. But transmission quality tends to be more variable than by higher-cost carriers, which can play hob with data communications.

35

PLANNING FOR SYSTEM UPGRADES

A lot of communities seem to take a perverse pride in the changeability of their weather. "If you don't like it," residents announce boastfully, "just wait a minute."

Much the same can be said of the microcomputer industry. In the decade or so since the first low-priced micros came onto the market new developments have been virtually tumbling over one another, to the point where some vendors have found their hardware obsolete even before the first unit came off the production line. And we've by no means reached an end, or even a pause, in this rapid-fire technological progress.

This presents some problems for the microcomputer user. He's forever being impelled to upgrade his present equipment by the very real superiority of the newer generations of hardware, which he must normally do by buying a whole new unit (since in most cases, due to both marketing and technological imperatives, his present equipment can be equivalently retrofitted).

And every time he upgrades, he's probably going to have to replace at least some, if not all, of his software.

The Un-Adaptability of Software

Not every piece of software currently in use is "dedicated" to any specific model of computer. It's possible to design software that will run on a broad spectrum of equipment. Many programs, including most of the more popular general-applications packages, can be "installed" to many different hardware systems by using accompanying or built-in utility software. And it's not difficult to adapt the formats of both programs and data files to those used by many different machines.

But the different ways in which processors and operating systems function impose some fairly narrow limitations within which such transfers are possible. A program written for the IBM-PC family (as are virtually all specialized transportation/distribution packages) can normally (although not always) be used on one of the many "clones" made by other manufacturers; but it's not at all portable to any other type of machine, such as the older 8-bit computers, any of the Apple machines (including the Macintosh), etc.

What's more, even within IBM's own family of machines you'll occasionally encounter incompatibilities. The IBM-AT and its clones, for example, will run only some of the programs written for PC's and XT's. Indeed, in some cases even the production changes made in a given model can affect this; some software designed for AT models won't, for example, run properly on machines equipment with the redesigned keyboard the company introduced in 1986.*

So if you get a new microcomputer, you may well have to write off at least some of your old software. And since the aftermarket support services of most software vendors (if they offer any at all) don't normally run to letting you "trade in" older, now-outmoded versions, you'll have to buy the software you want all over again at regular prices—which, if you have very much or

*This was written as IBM was preparing for introduction of still a further generation of microcomputers, built around Intel's 32-bit 80386 processor. It was widely reported that both IBM itself and others working on similar designs were seeking to make the new hardware as compatible as possible with software packages designed for previous generations of computers. Yet even the most sanguine of experts acknowledged publicly that in at least some cases this wouldn't prove possible—that replacement of the hardware would also necessitate replacement of at least some, and perhaps a good deal, of the buyer's existing stock of software.

very complex programming, can easily cost you a lot more than the hardware itself.

Furthermore, if you lose the software you may well also lose the data files you've created with that software, and which can be read and used only by it—data files that may represent an investment of man-weeks of keyboard time, and require as much time again to re-create in the required new format.

New Hardware Developments

At the same time, the reality is that you are almost certainly going to have to replace any microcomputer you may now own within the foreseeable future. In the first 5½ years I used a microcomputer to run my consulting business, for example, I was compelled to upgrade twice—and I'm slower than most users to make such changes. But each new generation of microcomputer equipment, at least thus far, has offered too much technological superiority over previous models for any rational user to ignore it.

Developments—both historic and those which, as this was written, were in prospect—seem primarily concentrated in two areas. The first, and in my view the lesser in terms of importance, is "user-friendliness," an overworked term that simply means how easy the equipment is to use for someone who has little or no expertise in computers, doesn't care much about developing that expertise, and in fact doesn't even much like the machines.

Newer generations of hardware and operating systems offer significant benefits in this area over their predecessors. Many of them lead you gently by the hand through the required steps to get things done, and are far more forgiving of your mistakes. Special-function keys are coming into ever-heavier use, to let you accomplish even complicated, multi-step operations by touching a single key; and the Macintosh and some other equipment goes even a step further by letting you ignore the keyboard altogether in many cases and input instructions by using a desk-top "mouse."

All of these user conveniences, of course, eat up computer

power—and that leads me to the second, and I think the more important, of the two major areas of microcomputer development: the quantum leaps being made in raw computing power.

Back in 1977, the first generation of low-priced micros could deal with only about 4,000 "bytes" of information—programming and data together. (A byte is equivalent to a letter of the alphabet or numeric character; 4,000 of them represent perhaps two or three pages of the average popular novel.) At the leading edge of technology, this "RAM" (Random-Access Memory, the computer's basic "brain") has just about doubled in every year since then—from 4,000, or "4K," to 8K, 16K, 32K, 64K, etc. As of mid-1986 you could readily buy microcomputers with RAM capacity of one or two "megabytes" (1,000,000-2,000,000 bytes), and the promise of yet further increases was on the horizon.

Now, in simpler operations this increased power is fairly unimportant. A 1986-model computer can add two and two many, many times faster than can a 1977-generation model—but since the speed with which the 1977 model operated on such simple problems was already measured in microseconds, you scarcely notice the difference.

But you don't need a computer to add two and two; what you need it for is for *much* more complex operations, and/or to keep track of and manipulate increasingly large masses of data. Increased power means the computer can (1) do bigger and more complicated such jobs; (2) do them, once again, many times faster; and (3) save the data to and retrieve it from disks or other storage media (which are also undergoing rapid advances) both faster and more accurately.

Given the transportation/distribution industry's need to keep track of large equipment fleets and vast numbers of shipments, to model complex and multi-faceted distribution systems, to record voluminous and fast-changing rate information, etc., greater computer power is obviously of considerable importance in these applications. Moreover, as machines become easier to use more and more people, at lower echelons and with less training, are going to be able to deal with the time-consuming but essentially clerical function of feeding information into them and extracting it out of them.

Minimizing the Burden of Upgrading

Under these circumstances you'll have to face up to the need for periodic upgrades of your hardware, and all the problems and costs that entails. But here are some measures you can take to at least minimize the burden:

(1) Be patient about getting new equipment. "Generation-skipping" is probably a sound practice; wait for the second- or even third-level advance over your present equipment. If you change over every time a new hardware model or operating system version comes out, you'll be changing so often you won't even have time to get thoroughly used to one system before you move on to the next. And the model-to-model changes, although they quickly become cumulatively huge, are individually much less significant. The fewer transitions, the fewer problems you'll have.

(2) Give consideration to equipment and operating system compatibility. That doesn't necessarily mean you have to stay with one manufacturer, since there can often be a great deal of similarity between models carrying different brand names. But look for new equipment that's reasonably close to what you've been using. First, this will minimize the necessary learning process as you adapt to the new unit; and second, it'll cut back on the need to make new software purchases. If you have a Macintosh and upgrade to, say, a "Fat Mac," the changes this will entail will be relatively minor; if you shift from Macintosh to IBM, on the other hand, you'll have to virtually re-learn how to use your computer, and you might as well let your kids play frisbie with your old program disks.

(3) Be careful about straying too far from the beaten path when you buy equipment, operating systems, etc. Remember, the more popular a particular model or system is, the more people will be interested in writing software for it. I've run across

several machines that seem to me to represent truly significant advances over previous hardware but, because they deviated too sharply from what was on the market, couldn't run any software except that designed especially for them. There's not much point in having superior hardware or a state-of-the-art operating system if you can't get it to do anything useful for you without having to endure the tedium of doing your own programming.

(4) Similarly, look for software that's mainstream-oriented—that runs, in other words, on fairly commonplace types of equipment. A few vendors of transportation/distribution software have written programs "dedicated" to a particular piece of hardware, so that you have to buy the specified hardware if you want to use the software. Often the equipment in question is indeed high-tech; it may even be better in many respects than microcomputers in more common use. But, again, you'll cut yourself off from many other packages if you lock yourself into such hardware and software; moreover, unless that particular manufacturer elects to upgrade its own equipment and does so with compatibility in mind, you may cut yourself off from further advances as technology continues to leap forward. I'll make an exception here in the case of operating systems, since most systems have been adapted for use to most present-day micros and can be purchased as software for relatively small prices (a few hundred dollars or so); but make sure the operating system you have in mind is one that will work on the more common types of hardware. All things considered, the IBM-PC family (and, of course, the many clones of other manufacture) and the PC-DOS operating system should be considered the ones of choice; far and away the greatest proportion of specialized transportation/distribution software is written for these machines and that operating system.

(5) *Don't* plan ahead in your software purchases. If you don't need a particular piece of programming today, don't buy it today. By the time you *do* need it you may have a different computer to which what's on the market today can't be adapted. In fact, plans to buy a new computer soon are a good reason for deferring

software purchases even when you do see an immediate application, especially if the software runs fairly expensive. Moreover, a lot of software, too, goes through multiple generations; if you buy now, you may forego improvements that come about before you actually have a need for the package.

The need to upgrade your equipment is both foreseeable and inevitable, given the pace of technological developments today. If you bear that in mind, you can help minimize both the expense and the problems you confront when you do so.

Glossary

If you're familiar with computers and computer usage, you probably won't need this glossary. If you're *very* familiar with them, you may even find many of the definitions I've used here incomplete or inadequate. But then, I didn't do this compilation for you anyway.

I did it for those readers who *aren't* familiar with computer terminology. And for that reason I've tried to keep the definitions as simple and plain-English as I could. If the user doesn't need a lot of technical detail, I didn't provide it; why muddy up the waters unnecessarily? At that, I've had to use an awful lot of cross-referencing; if you look up one word you're apt to find yourself having to chase down two or three others as well. If you want more specifics, I'd suggest you consult one of the many technical computer texts on the market, where you can find all the detail you could ever want and, probably, then some.

Meantime, here, in as clear and non-technical terminology as I could make it, are the meanings of some of the words you'll run into in this book with which you may not be familiar, and some others you won't read here but are likely to encounter in discussions with computer dealers, software developers and others you'll come in contact with if and when you decide to go into computerization.

ASCII. Standardized coding for keystrokes (letters of the alphabet (capitals and lower-case), numerals, punctuation marks, etc.) to permit data interchange among computers.

Address. Designated memory location in the CPU.

Algorithm. Mathematical equation or formula, usu. expressed in the form of computer programming.

Alternate key. Special key on the keyboard of many computers which, when depressed while another key is struck, produces an alternate result (which varies from one key to another). The key is usually designated, on the keyboard and in user manuals, etc., as "ALT." *See also Control key.*

Arrow keys. Keys used to direct on-screen movement of the cursor in the direction indicated by the arrow.

Assembly language. Programming language.

BASIC. Beginners' All-purpose Symbolic Instruction Code; programming language.

BDOS. Basic Disk Operating System *(see DOS).*

BIOS. Basic Input-Output System; used to control communications between the CPU and the modem, printer, plotter, etc.

BPS. Bits Per Second; the rate by which computer data transmission is measured.

Backlit display. Form of LCD display in which contrast and readability are enhanced by low-level lighting emanating from behind the display itself.

Backup. Copy of computer program, data file, etc., used for archival purposes in the event the working copy incurs damage or otherwise becomes unusable.

Batch processing. Mode of computer operation in which data, etc., is submitted to the computer in a body, and computer processing then takes place while the user is off-line. Often used as an antonym to real time operations *(which see).*

Baud. Measure of the rate of computer data transmission; similar to (although not entirely identical with, in various technical ways) BPS.

Binary. Form of mathematical notation in which all numbers are expressed in terms of powers of two.

Bit. Binary digIT; one digit in a number expressed in binary code.

Blind prompt. Displayed prompt *(which see)* offering no indication as to what command/input options are currently available to the user.

Board. Circuitboard used in computers and other electronic equipment; consists of chips, crystals, etc., interlinked by printed circuits.

Boot. Start-up of a computer session.

Bubble memory. Computer storage memory not using mechanical contrivances; essentially a RAM-like segment of memory used solely for data storage. Must have independent power source (usually a small battery) to retain stored data while the computer is turned off.

Buffer. RAM area (usually quite small) used to temporarily store blocks of data during transmission procedures, so that the main RAM is freed for other purposes.

Bug. Fault or defect in any computer hardware, firmware or software.

Bundle. Term used in reference to software included ("bundled") with hardware purchase.

Bus. Circuit nexus used to direct input/output to proper channels.

Byte. Smallest standard grouping of bits (usually eight). For reasons having to do with the limitations of binary math notation, a byte may be regarded as equivalent to a single keystroke (letter of the alphabet, numeral, punctuation mark, etc.).

C. Programming language.

CCP. Console Command Program; used to control input/output between the CPU and the keyboard, mouse and other user-input devices.

COBOL. Common Ordinary Business Operating Language; programming language.

COPY. The basic copy utility in the MS-DOS (and PC-DOS) operating system *(which see).*

CP/M. Control Program for Microcomputers; most common operating system for eight-bit microcomputers. A version (CP/M-86) also exists for 16-bit computers.

CPU. Central Processing Unit.

CRT. Cathode Ray Tube; a type of display using a television-like monitor.

Cartridge Winchester. Winchester with removable data-storage medium.

Central Processing Unit. The computer's physical "brain," comprised of one or more integrated circuit boards.

Centronics. Standardized type of parallel port.

Chip. Strictly speaking, a silicon chip; but the term is also used to refer to a silicon chip and related circuitry encased in a plastic sheathing and having a multi-prong male plug, inserted into a female socket in a board.

Clock speed. The speed at which the computer's CPU operates.

Clone. Computer fundamentally identical, in terms of its electronics, operating system, etc., with another computer. Mostly used to describe microcomputers designed after IBM models, as in PC clone, AT clone, etc.

Cold boot. Initial start-up of a computer session accomplished by turning on the power switch.

Command-driven. Descriptive of software in which the user directs activities by keying in command sequences.

Communications software. Software used to mediate data transmission to and from other computers through a modem or by "hard-wire" connection (interlinkage of computers without a modem).

Compatibility. Degree of similarity of computer models. A computer that is compatible with another can run most or all of the same software.

Compile. To translate a program from source code to object code *(both of which see)* so it can be run independently through the medium of only the computer's operating system. This work is done by special "compilers," software intended solely for that purpose.

Control key. Special key on the keyboard of a computer which, when depressed while another key is struck, produces an alternate result (which varies from one key to another). Control keystrokes are always used for command purposes. The key is usually designated, on the keyboard and in user manuals, etc., as "CTRL." *See also Alternate key.*

Copy protection. Method of preventing the useful copying of software. Some types of control protection are built into the software itself, while others employ physical means.

Crash. Failure (as applied to software) or destruction (as applied to data storage). Used as a noun and a verb (both transitive and intransitive).

Crippled software. Software with one or more features disabled, used for demonstration purposes.

Crystal. Electronic device occasionally used for specific purposes on boards in lieu of chips.

Cursor. Display device used to identify on-screen location where the next keystroke of input will be echoed. Sometimes displayed as a solid square, sometimes as a flashing (blinking) square, sometimes as an underscore, etc.

DDT. The basic debugging utility in the CP/M operating system *(which see).*

DEBUG. The basic debugging utility in the MS-DOS (and PC-DOS) operating system *(which see).*

DOS. Disk Operating System; used to control data interchange between the CPU and disk drives or other storage media.

Daisy wheel. Specifically, the little plastic or metal wheel element of some typewriters and printers on which the characters are embossed. The term is also used to refer to printers that employ daisy wheels.

Data. Information, of any type, used and/or stored by the computer. A data file is distinct from a program file, in that the former contains information and the latter the instructions the computer is to follow in dealing with that information.

Data-base manager. A type of program whose primary purpose is to store and manipulate masses of data.

Daughterboard. A secondary board in the CPU that contains additional features and works in conjunction with the motherboard *(which see).*

Debugging. The process of correcting or eliminating bugs *(which see),* usually from software but sometimes applied to hardware and/or firmware as well.

Directory. Listing of all available files. A single computer may have multiple directories, its storage being subdivided in various ways for user convenience.

Disk drive. Computer storage medium using flat, electronically encoded disks (similar in appearance to phonograph records).

Display. The video-output device to which input keystrokes are echoed, and on which output is visible to the user. Also termed display screen. "Display" is also used as a verb, meaning to exhibit on a display screen.

Dot-matrix printer. Form of printer in which multiple tiny dots are arrayed in patterns to form print characters.

Dumb terminal. Keyboard/display combination not associated with a CPU; used to access other computers through telephone or hard-wire linkages *(see On-line).*

ELD. Electro-Luminescent Display

EPROM. Erasable, Programmable Read-Only Memory; a form of ROM that can be programmed by the user, then erased and re-programmed.

Electroluminescence. A form of display in which a sensitized screen is illuminated, often in color, using electrical current modulation.

Enter key. The key used to complete and finalize data entry during input procedures. Occupies the same keyboard position, and has in many applications much the same function, as the carriage-return key of a typewriter; on some keyboards it is even identified as the "return" key.

Escape. A special character in a computer keyboard used for special purposes—principally to abort the operation of a program, or to re-start operations after an error has been detected by the computer. Also used as a verb, meaning to employ or strike the escape key.

Expansion slot. Empty area inside the computer intended (and wired) to accommodate additional boards *(which see).*

FORTRAN. FORmula TRANslation; a programming language.

Fatal error. Any type of error that makes continuance of the operation in progress impossible. A fatal error often requires a reset and warm boot (or even, in some cases, turning off the machine and cold booting to restart); it may also destroy or damage data files and programs in use at the time it occurs.

File. Integral grouping of data or programming, accessed under a single identifier in the system directory.

Firmware. Programming stored in ROM.

Floppy disk. Flexible plastic disk with a coating capable of recording magnetically encoded information. Floppy disks are generally standardized to 8-inch and 5¼-inch diameters; most microcomputers use the smaller size.

Format. Used in many ways to describe various types of structuring. A disk or other storage medium, for example, must have a format readable by the DOS; a data file must have a format readable by the programming that makes use of the data; and so forth.

Function key. One of several (usually 10) special-purpose keys on a computer keyboard; used in various ways (according to the programming in use) for user commands.

GIGO. Stands for "Garbage In, Garbage Out"—a shorthand way of saying that the accuracy and validity of computer output is wholly dependent on the accuracy and validity of data and programming input to the computer.

Gas plasma. A form of display in which electrical current causes a layer of enclosed gas behind the screen itself to illuminate; similar to neon lighting. All gas plasma displays are monochrome.

Hack. As a verb, spur-of-the-moment programming (the word usually carries the connotation of a particularly creative or innovative type of programming). As a noun, a program or other computer activity that is the result of hacking.

Hacker. A computer hobbyist; one who hacks, usually for the simple pleasure of doing so.

Hard copy. A paper print-out of computer output.

Hard disk drive. A disk drive that employs an inflexible metal or plastic disk to store information electronically. Also known as a Winchester. Hard disks have considerably greater storage capacity than do floppy disks, and are usually encased so that the disk is not removable *(although see Cartridge Winchester).*

Hardware. The physical part of the computer, including chips, electronic circuitry, casing, etc. Also used to refer to peripherals.

Help screen. On-screen display of information intended as assistance for the user of the program in which it's incorporated, generally not displayed unless the user requests it by a special command.

Hex code. A form of mathematical notation using a base-16 numbering system (rather than the more common base-10). For technical reasons computers work with this numeric base.

Input. Any data, programming, commands, etc., provided by the user, usually (although not always) by means of the keyboard.

Install. To patch *(see Patch)* or otherwise adapt a program or group of programs to operate on a particular model of computer; accomplished by means of software provided by the developer of the software being installed.

Joystick. A hand-held device used to control cursor movement, or other on-screen activity in video games, by means of manipulating a lever capable of movement in all directions.

K. Abbreviation for kilo; a 64K-byte system, for example, has 64,000 bytes of available RAM.

Kilo-. Prefix meaning thousand. Actually, kilo is usually used as an approximation for 1,024, or 2^{10}; thus, a 64-kilobyte computer really has, not 64,000, but 65,536, bytes of available RAM.

LCD. Liquid Crystal Display; form of display used in most portable computers (as well as digital wristwatches, some hand-held electronic calculators, etc.). All LCD displays are monochrome, most often gray and white.

LED. Light-Emitting Diode; form of display rarely used for computers, although research is being done in this area. Most signal lights on computers (indicating power on, disk drive in use, capital-letter lock or number lock activated, etc.) are red or green LED's. LED displays are also used in some digital clocks, electronic calculators, automobile dashboard indicators, etc.)

Laser printer. Printer that operates by using laser (Light Amplification by Stimulated Emission of Radiation) beams to imprint characters on the paper.

Letter-quality printer. Printer capable of producing hard-copy output equivalent in appearance to typewriter output. The term is usually used in reference to daisy-wheel printers, sometimes in conjunction with laser printers.

Light pen. Pen-shaped device for inputting commands to a computer technologically equipped to receive such input. The device is pointed at the display area on which the desired command is shown in a menu *(which see),* and triggered to emit a flash of light which the computer detects by means of a sensitized screen.

Logo. Programming language.

MIS. Abbreviation for Management Information Systems, a common name for organizational computer operations.

MS-DOS. Operating system most commonly employed for 16-bit microcomputers.

Machine language. Aboriginal programming language; the language in which computers actually "think."

Main-frame. Extremely high-capacity, high-speed computer. The distinction between main-frame computers and minicomputers *(which see)* has been blurred in recent years, as the capacity of minis has reached levels previously attained only by main-frames (although the main-frames have grown in capacity as well). Price is often used as a practical distinction; a main-frame typically costs, in 1986 dollars, well over $100,000, often as much as $1 million or more.

Mega-. Prefix meaning million. Again for various technical reasons, "mega-" is most often used relative to computers as an approximation for 1,048,576 (2^{20}); thus, a computer with one megabyte of RAM actually has 1,048,576 bytes of available memory.

Megahertz. A measure of the clock speed of computers; often abbreviated as mHz. Typically, microcomputers operate in the range of 4-10 mHz.

Menu. On-screen display of operational options during the run of a program.

Menu-driven. A program that functions by displaying all available command-options in one or more menus, from which the user may make his selection.

Microcomputer. Desk-top or "personal" computer. Again, the distinction between microcomputers and mini-computers *(which see)* has been blurred as the power of microcomputers has increased dramatically. Price is often used as a rule-of-thumb dividing line; in 1986 dollars, microcomputers are those costing between a few hundred dollars and perhaps $8,000-10,000 or a trifle more.

Microsecond. Millionth of a second; used to measure to speed of computer operations.

Mini-computer. The middle range in computer capacity and operating speed, between main-frames and microcomputers *(both of which see).* Leapfrogging technological advances have tended to blur these three categories during recent years, as both micros and minis have increased in power to overlap the traditional boundary of the next-higher category. Price is often used as a rough guide to category; mini-computers typically cost, in 1986 dollars, between $10,000 or a bit more and perhaps $100,000-200,000.

Mini-disk. 3½-inch-diameter disk of rigid plastic with magnetically sensitized coating used for data storage in some microcomputers.

Modem. MOdulator-DEModulator; used to translate data into electrical pulses for transmission, most often over telephone lines but sometimes directly.

Modula C. Programming language; version of C language.

Monitor. The physical display device *(see Display).*

Monochrome. Single-color; used in reference to displays. Monochrome displays may employ various colors, and usually display illuminated characters on a black background (although some types use "inverted" displays, in which darkened letters are displayed on a pale background).

Motherboard. The main memory board in a CPU.

Mouse. Device that controls the movement of the cursor on the display by means of a ball-bearing-like device on the bottom; when it is moved across a desktop or other flat surface the ball turns opposite to the direction of movement, and the cursor is moved accordingly. The mouse also has one or more buttons on top that the user presses to indicate that the cursor is now in the position he wants.

NLQ. Near-Letter-Quality *(which see);* used in reference to printers.

Nanosecond. Billionth of a second; used to measure the speed of computer operations.

Near-letter-quality printer. Dot-matrix printer *(which see)* the produces very small dots so closely spaced as to blend together into characters almost as clearly defined as those of a daisy-wheel or laser printer *(both of which see).*

Network. An interlinkage of two or more computers in such a fashion that the CPU's can work together as a single computer with the full power of all interlinked units. Also often used as a verb, meaning to establish or create such an interlinkage.

Numeric keypad. Portion of a computer keyboard in which number and, often, arithmetical-function keys are arrayed much as on a calculator.

Object code. The coding in which the compiled version of a program is stated *(see Compile).*

Octal. Form of base-eight math notation employed in early computers. Octal codes are no longer in much use, having been supplanted by Hex codes *(which see).*

On-line. Connected, through keyboard and display, with a (usually physically remote) computer. An on-line service is one in which the user links up with a distant CPU and can give it commands and receive output as though it was his own computer; access may be either by a dumb terminal *(which see),* or by another computer which, in this application, emulates a dumb terminal.

Operating system. Firmware and/or software the comprises the primary set of instructions for the computer hardware. The operating system is made up of three separate components, the BIOS, BDOS and CCP *(all of which see).*

Output. The displayed, printed, etc., results of the computer's activities.

PC-DOS. A variant of the MS-DOS operating system *(which see)* modified for use by IBM personal computers and their clones.

PIP. Peripheral Interchange Program; the copy utility in the CP/M operating system.

PROM. Programmable Read-Only Memory; ROM that can be programmed by the user (although that programming cannot later be changed; *see also EPROM).*

Parallel port. Input/output link in which data is transmitted in multiple-bit groupings. Used principally to connect the CPU with a printer or plotter.

Pascal. Programming language.

Patch. To make a change in the object code *(see Object Code)* of a program so as to modify its operation in some way. Also used as a noun to describe the modification itself.

Peripheral. Any device physically external to the computer itself. Technically, even the keyboard and the display may be considered peripherals; but the term is most frequently used to identify disk drives (or other data-storage devices), printers, plotters, modems and the like.

Personal computer. Microcomputer. This term was devised, and is used, for marketing purposes.

Pick. A computer operating system. Pick is unusual in that versions of it exist for computers in all categories (main-frame, mini and micro).

Plotter. A device to make hard-copy printouts of graphs, line drawings, etc. Some plotters are monochrome, while others work with multiple colors.

Port. Physical connector allowing interchange of data between the CPU and peripherals *(both of which see).* Ports are usually female (occasionally male) plugs to which multi-wire cables are attached to complete the linkage.

Portable computer. A lightweight computer intended primarily for "in the field" (as distinct from fixed-site) use. A portable integrates CPU, keyboard and display in a single case, usually weighs but a few pounds (as little as three, as much as 10-12), and can be stowed in a briefcase. Most portables can be operated for a period of time off internal batteries, although a few require external battery packs or AC electrical power.

Printer. Device for generating hard-copy output using typewriter-style characters. Most printers are intended only to display computer output, although a few have independent keyboards so that they can double as typewriters.

Program. Set of instructions to the CPU that direct it to perform a particular operation or operations.

Program file. A single program held in the computer's storage. A program file is distinct from a data file, in that the former contains the instructions for dealing with data and the latter the data itself.

Prompt. On-screen output from the computer indicating that it is ready to accept commands and/or input.

Protocol. Standardized signaling system employed during computer information-interchange activities that defines when each machine is to transmit and when to receive. There are several protocols in use, each of which specifies that the computer will send a particular character sequence when it is done transmitting, and will not transmit until it receives that signal from the other computer. Much like the use of the word "Over" in radio transmissions.

RAM. Random-Access Memory.

RAM disk. Portion of RAM set aside for data storage, and treated by the CPU and operating system in the same way as a disk drive *(which see)*. The advantage of the RAM disk is that, being unconstrained by physical mechanisms (as are regular disk drives), it operates much faster; the disadvantage is that loss of power will erase its contents.

RGB. Red-Green-Blue, the three primary colors used in CRT displays such as color televisions. An RGB monitor is a color monitor.

ROM. Read-Only Memory.

RS-232. The standardized type of serial port employed in microcomputers. Although the physical port is standardized, wiring connections—that is, the purpose for which each connector pin and socket are employed—are not.

Random-Access Memory. The heart of the CPU; the computer's basic "mind." Each data element is assigned a particular memory address *(which see),* and can by accessed by the CPU in randomized fashion. Random-access memory can be erased (in part or in whole) and re-used as often as the user and/or the programming dictates.

Read-Only Memory. Pre-set memory in the CPU which can be read, but not written to, during operations; used to contain fixed instructional parameters that will not vary.

Real time. Used (as a noun or adjective) to describe mode of computer operation in which the computer does its programmed assignments while the user remains on line, and responds immediately to user inputs; akin to "while you wait" service in a retail establishment. Often used as an antonym to batch processing *(which see).*

Reset. To re-initialize a computer through a warm boot *(which see)* without turning off the power. Some computers have a manual reset button which, when pressed, accomplishes the reset; others use a combination of keystrokes (pressing the "Control," "Alternate" and "Delete" keys simultaneously is the most common).

Serial port. Input/output link in which data is transmitted one bit at a time. Used principally to connect the CPU with a modem, although can be used for a printer or plotter.

Shell. A portion of an operating system, program, etc., whose only function is to produce output display and/or simplify input procedures for the purpose of aiding the user.

Silicon chip. Wafer-like slice of silicon on which is engraved, usually using laser-photography techniques, extensive circuitry. The silicon chip, by allowing both extreme miniaturization of the circuitry and dramatically reduced production costs, is what has made the microcomputer a reality and reduced computer prices in general to affordable ranges. Silicon chips are also used in such other devices as calculators, digital timepieces, etc., etc.

Software. Computer programming recorded on disks or other storage media, and generally marketed independent of hardware.

Source code. The programming-language version of a program, before it has been compiled *(which see).*

Spreadsheet. A type of program intended primarily for accounting purposes; also in wide use in other mathematically oriented applications.

Status line. The 25th line of the display screen (at the bottom of the screen), which is generally inaccessible to the user and is employed to display brief messages concerning the status of the operating system or program.

Subroutine. A unitary portion of a program intended to perform a particular function.

Surge protector. An interrupt device between the power source (wall socket) and the computer to protect the machine's delicate electronics from damage in the event of power surges, electrical "brown-outs" and the like. The surge protector automatically shuts off all power to the machine in the event it detects a significant variance in the flow of electric current.

Tape backup. Data storage device used to make backup copies of data stored on large-capacity hard disks. High-speed tapes are also used as primary data-storage devices in some cases (especially for main-frame computers), but are far more expensive that disk drives *(which see);* lower-speed tapes, which are not so expensive, are too slow (by comparison with disk drives) for use as primary storage.

Touch-screen. Sensitized display screen employed on some computers capable of detecting the touch of a finger. Commands may then be input by touching the portion of the screen on which the desired command option is displayed in a menu *(which see).*

Trackball. Device for controlling cursor movement; essentially, an inverted mouse *(which see)* in which the user employs his hand to rotate the ball in the direction he chooses. The trackball is often used in video games, and is occasionally employed in computer keyboards as a more flexible, easier-to-use substitute for the arrow keys *(which see).*

Transportable computer. Physically integrated microcomputer which, although technically portable, is too bulky and heavy to carry about regularly. As with portables *(which see),* the CPU, keyboard and display, along with one or more disk drives, are contained in a single housing; but the machine is too big to fit in any reasonable-size briefcase (its housing serves also as its carrying case), and is not capable of battery-powered operation.

Turnkey. Used to describe packaged or bundled specialized-application computer systems, including all hardware (with requisite peripherals) and software. At least nominally, the system is ready for full operation from the mmoment it is activated.

UNIX. Computer operating system, primarily for microcomputers. UNIX permits multi-user access to the CPU, which is its chief advantage.

Uninterruptible power supply. A device that automatically interrupts the flow of power emanating from the wall socket in case of unexpected problems (power surges, electrical blackouts or "brown-outs") and switches seamlessly over to internally generated power sources. It acts as a surge protector *(which see)* except that it also allows the user a brief time—usually no more than a few minutes—to go through manual power-down procedures such as saving in-use files to disk, etc., before its internal power supply is exhausted. These provide more protection than do surge protectors, but tend to be quite expensive by comparison.

User manual. Instructional book or booklet that is provided with computer hardware or software.

Utility. Limited-purpose program subordinate to an operating system or software package, intended to perform housekeeping-type functions such as copying data files, making minor modifications in software, etc.

Vaporware. Sardonic name given to computer hardware or software that exists only on paper and/or in its (would-be) developer's mind and is not, in fact, actually ready to be delivered to purchasers.

Warm boot. Re-start of a computer session while the power remains on, accomplished by means of a reset *(which see).*

Winchester. Hard-disk drive *(which see).*

Word processor. Computer program whose primary purpose is to allow the user to input and/or manipulate long text passages.

Worm. A program or subroutine that, when invoked, damages existing data files and programs; intended solely for malicious purposes and (obviously) not documented to the user.

XENIX. Computer operating system; variant of UNIX *(which see).*

Appendix A

HOW COMPUTERS WORK (AND OTHER DETAILS)

A computer only knows two words—"yes" and "no." Or call them "true" and "false," or "on" and "off," or (as binary math does) "0" and "1." Everything a computer does, it does with these two words and nothing else.

When electricity enters a computer it flows through a vast number of electronic "switches," each of which has only two settings. If a switch is set to "yes" (or "true" or "on" or "0"), the electric current flows down one path; if it's "no" ("false," "off," "1"), another path is forced. By making a whole series of such yes/no choices for different switches the computer can use its two-word "vocabulary" to perform exceedingly complex tasks.

Each such switch setting is termed a "bit" of information (the word "bit" standing for Binary digIT). It takes eight bits to represent a standard letter of the alphabet, numeric integer, etc., which is also known as a "byte."

Bits are used to measure the capacity of particular processors. (A processor is the core of a computer—in effect, its "brain." Once upon a time the processor consisted of whole rooms full of vacuum tubes and wiring; today it is usually a thumbnail-size wafer, or "chip," of silicon material on which exceedingly complex circuitry can be etched ("printed") by means of high-precision processes.) An eight-bit machine can handle just that many—in transferring information from and to storage, screen display, etc., or in "thinking" about that information—at any given time; a 16-bit machine can handle twice as many; a 32-bit machine, twice as many again; and so forth.

It might seem, based on this, that a 16-bit machine would automatically work twice as fast as an eight-bit one, and so on; but that's only part of the story. Often more important is a computer's built-in "clock speed"—how fast it can process each group of bits. Clock speeds are measured in megahertz (mHz), and can vary widely; some older microcomputer equipment operates at 2-3 mHz, while technically advanced processors run as fast as 40-50 mHz.

(It's easy to overrate this question of computer speed, though. Even the slowest of modern-day computers performs each operation in such a tiny fraction of a second that new names ("microsecond," "nanosecond") have had to be invented to describe the time span. In most normal operations the difference between a "slow" and a "fast" computer tends to be the difference between instantaneous and *very* instantaneous.)

Computer memory, on the other hand, is measured in bytes—thousands of them. Computers built around eight-bit processors typically have working memories of "64K" bytes (64,000—actually 65,536, but it's customary to round to the nearest "power of 2" in thousands). Computers with 16-bit and 32-bit processors may have much larger memories—128K (131,072), 256K (262,144), 512K or "half-megabyte" (524,288), and one or more "megabytes" (1,048,576).

Although computers actually have two sorts of built-in memories, the usual memory-size nomenclature describes only one—"RAM," or "Random Access Memory," the area in which the computer actually processes information. The second memory type is "ROM"—"Read Only Memory"—which represents a set of pre-coded instructions built into the machine's hardware but which can't be altered by the casual user. A useful way to think about this difference is to regard RAM as the computer's conscious brain, while ROM may be compared to instinct. (Program instructions coded in ROM are also known as "firmware," as opposed to the "hardware" that's the actual circuitry, casing, displays, disk drives, printers, etc., and the "software" that's programming recorded on various types of data storage media.)

No matter how capacious its RAM, it would be silly to expect a computer to hold in it all the information it ever receives; what's more, even a brief power interruption (turning off the machine, resetting it, electrical blackouts and brownouts, etc.) will serve to wipe the RAM clean. Human beings have long supplemented their memories with written records, and the computer has its equivalent—the electronic data storage device.

Larger computers mostly use high-speed magnetic tape, much like "open-reel" audio tapes. A few smaller ones use cassette tapes (although these are agonizingly slow). But the most common type of data storage today is on disks, which look about like audio records but come largely encased in permanently sealed envelopes or casings.

"Floppy disks" are thin, flexible circles of coated plastic, and generally can store between 100K and a megabyte or so of information (depending on the make and model of computer); to use them you insert them in a "disk drive," which spins them and uses magnetic heads to write information onto them and/or read it back. "Hard disks" (also called "Winchesters," after an early manufacturer) come completely encased with their own drive mechanisms and can store *much* larger quantities of data—up to 100 megabytes and more.

There are also "minidisks," produced initially by Sony and popularized by Apple's Macintosh and a few other small computers, which work more or less like small-size floppies; and "cartridge Winchesters," which allow you to substitute hard-disk cartridges in the drive mechanism. And finally there's the rarely used "bubble memory," which stores information on RAM-type silicon chips; because of the requirement for a constant power supply (like RAM, bubble memory will be instantly wiped clean if deprived of electrical power), bubble memory needs tiny batteries to keep it "alive."

Reliability of the various data storage devices varies somewhat, but most experts deem only two of them seriously untrustworthy—floppy disks and cassette tapes. It is quite easy to "crash" either by exposing them to even tiny amounts of magnetism or atmospheric particles; even ambient tobacco smoke, for example, can foul a floppy. While it's always wise for users to keep "back-up" copies of all stored data, this need is particularly acute when either of these devices is being used.

To communicate with their human users, computers employ various types of visual display devices. The most common is the CRT (Cathode Ray Tube) screen, akin to your TV screen, which can come (like TV) in either monochrome (black-and-white, black-and-green or black-and-amber) or full color (also known as "RGB," for the red, green and blue "color guns" that are used to produce the color). Some machines, especially the new "lap-size" portables, use LCD (Liquid Crystal Display) screens, which produce dark-gray-on-light-gray displays (often used in digital watches and hand-held calculators); these tend to be a bit hard to read in any but the best light.

You'll also see a few gas-plasma displays, and the occasional ELD (Electro-Luminescent Display) screen. Both provide excellent display quality and readability, but tend to be more costly. And there's a budding technology in LED (Light-Emitting Diode) displays, the most common use of which is to make colored indicator lights, digital clock displays, etc.

More permanent forms of communications are provided by means of printers, which put the computer's output on paper. The common (and inexpensive) dot-matrix printer uses, as the name suggests, arrays of printed dots to form letters, numbers, pictures, etc. The "letter-quality printer" uses "daisy wheels" and similar devices, on which each individual character is etched in bas-relief, like modern electric typewriters. More recently there have come onto the market so-called "laser printers," which use laser beams to literally burn the characters into the paper; and there are also a few printers that work by producing their output on the equivalent of an internal (not visible to the user) display screen and then copying it onto paper *à la* a photocopy machine.

Another form of paper-copy (also called "hard-copy") output is produced using a "plotter." Plotters work by means of a tiny mechanical arm and hand; the hand holds one or more sharp pencil-like tools and the arm moves it around on the paper in accordance with the computer's dictates to produce line drawings.

Just as the computer needs to communicate with the user, so does the user need to communicate with the computer. Mostly he does so by means of a keyboard, similar in nature to a typewriter's keyboard and usually connected to the computer by wire or cable (although a few keyboards use infrared light to transmit their impulses to the computer, much in the fashion of a TV remote control).

There are three important ways in which the computer keyboard differs from its typewriter counterpart. First, most computers have a separate "numeric keypad," which looks about like the keypad of a simple calculator and is more efficient for typing in groups of numbers. Second, most have a separate bank of "function keys," which can be coded to send complex command sequences to the computer at the touch of a single key.

And third, most keyboards come with a set of four "arrow keys" pointing in the four compass directions. These are used to move a tiny blob of flashing light, called the "cursor," around on the display screen. The cursor is a positioning aid, indicating where on the display the computer will accept the next keystroke or command. In text or numeric applications the cursor tells you where on the screen it will print out the next letter or number you type; in graphics applications moving it around may inscribe (or erase) lines; and it is occasionally used to identify particular commands, from among a "menu" of them printed on-screen, that you may want to execute.

Some computers also make use of a "mouse," a cigarette-pack-size device with a little ball bearing on the bottom and a button on top, for cursor control. Rolling the mouse around on a desktop or other surface signals the computer to move the cursor around on the screen. When the cursor is positioned where the user wants it, he presses the button to confirm his choice and the computer takes whatever action may be indicated. Hewlett-Packard employs its "touch screen" much the same way; the surface of its CRT display is sensitized so that the touch of a finger to the proper spot activates the command or activity indicated. (A few systems use "light pens" to substitute for finger-touching.)

(Some home computers also use such devices as "joysticks," "trackballs" and "paddles" to let the user send signals to the computer. These devices are used mainly to control video games, and not for business applications, although Wico produces a keyboard that substitutes a trackball for the arrow keys.)

On occasion it's important for one computer to communicate directly with another (to exchange data which would otherwise have to be printed out from one machine and then manually keyboarded into the second). This is done principally by means of a device called a modem (MOdulator-DEModulator), which translates the information from one machine into a series of rapid audible beeps which can then be transmitted, usually over telephone lines (or, occasionally, microwave) to the other machine's modem, which then converts them back into electronic "yeses" and "noes" for the receiving computer to read.

Modems send and receive data at different speeds, measured by the "baud" rate. Modems can transmit anywhere between 60 baud and 19,200 baud, although the speeds in most common usage are 300 baud and 1200 baud, these being the optimum cross between the desirability of speed and the reality that electronic phone-line noise stands a better chance of fouling up accurate communications the faster the communication proceeds. Baud represents the number of bits being transmitted per second; divide by eight (remember the relationship between bits and bytes?) to roughly find the number of alphanumeric characters per second being transmitted or received. (Recently there has been a tendency to replace the term "baud" with the nomenclature "bits per second," or "bps.")

It's important to recognize that modems allow transmission between even computers of dissimilar make or model. There are a few exceptions; and communication between machines of especial disparity may require some fairly sophisticated translation programming. But a good rule of thumb is that any computer can talk to any other computer by use of a modem.

To keep from getting confused among all its various activities (user input, display output, printer/plotter output, data storage and retrieval and, of course, actual computing), the computer needs a "traffic cop"—its operating system. Actually, on most computers in widespread use the operating system is comprised of three interacting such traffic cops: the BIOS (Basic Input/Output System), which communicates with the display, the printer, the plotter, the modem, etc.; the BDOS (Basic Disk Operating System), which handles writing to and reading from storage devices; and the CCP (Console Command Program), which tends to user input from the keyboard, mouse, touch-screen, etc. Among them, these systems organize the computer's functioning so that the various devices and activities can be made to function as an integral unit rather than warring with one another.

Leaving aside the preternaturally capacious and fast multi-billion-dollar machines that do work for a few government agencies and scientific schools and institutes, computers come in three basic sizes. Biggest is the "main-frame," a large unit typified by IBM's 4300 series. Next down is the "mini," a scaled-down main-frame such as the IBM System 36. For the most part each make and model in these categories has its own proprietary operating system, incompatible with any other.

Finally there are the "micros"—desk-top units also known as "personal computers." The microcomputer market is far more heavily populated than those for the larger units; but, interestingly, relatively few of the manufacturers have seen fit to go it independently with respect to operating systems. Basically there are three microcomputer operating systems that have attained a significant amount of industry acceptance: CP/M, the "standard" system for older 8-bit machines but now in decline (although a 16-bit variant, CP/M-86, is in some use); MS-DOS and its IBM-popularized derivative, PC-DOS, the "standard" for 16-bit machines; and the AT&T-designed UNIX and *its* derivative, XENIX, which is fast becoming the standard for "networking" of two or more micros.

(In fact there do exist a number of other micro operating systems, but most are limited to one make or model line, and none have "caught on" for general application. Apple-DOS, for example, runs only on Apple, Apple II and Apple III series computers; TRS-DOS is used in older Radio Shack TRS-80 models; Toolworks is the operating system for Apple's Macintosh; PICK is a less-popular competitor for UNIX/XENIX; etc. It's noteworthy that virtually all machines using such off-the-beaten track operating systems can also be adapted to CP/M, PC-DOS, or both.)

The importance of standardization of operating systems for micro-computers lies in the fact that software is invariably specific to a particular operating system. As discussed, it is possible to interchange *data* between virtually any two computers; but *programming*—the sets of instructions that tell the computer what to do with the data—can only be interchanged between two computers that use the same operating system. (Even then, adaptations must sometimes be made to take into account variances between individual makes and models, especially among CP/M-using machines. But such adaptations are minor, even trivial, beside the major reprogramming task that confronts anyone seeking to translate software from one operating system to another.)

The relative universality of first the CP/M, then the PC-DOS, and (upcoming) the UNIX/XENIX operating systems have thus allowed the development of a mass-market software industry. Being able to sell to a diversity of computer users without (largely) make/model restrictions has encouraged programmers to write standardized off-the-shelf software for a wide range of applications, and has brought prices plummeting down to just a few hundreds or (at most) thousands of dollars for even the most intricate and complex programs.

As a result, the business user in almost any economic sector can find, with a little digging, dozens (or more) of programs that are geared specifically to his industry's needs, at readily affordable prices. And competition with the increasingly powerful micros has also exerted its impact on hardware and software pricing for mini-computers and even main-frames.

Appendix B

'PORTS' AND 'PERIPHERALS'

The heart of your computer—its central processing unit, or "CPU"—is an entirely self-contained unit; it does its work in splendid isolation.

But a CPU by itself is a magnificently useless piece of equipment; it's like a human being cut off from all of his or her senses, muscle control, etc. (if you can imagine such a horrible state of affairs). To perform any useful work, the CPU must be connected with devices for receiving input and generating output.

Some of these devices are so much an integral, and necessary, part of the modern computer that it's difficult to imagine a computer without them—the keyboard, for example, or the display screen. Yet early computers lacked even these basic accoutrements; you made your input not be typewriter-like keyboard but by toggling manual switches, each representing but a single bit of information, and your output was visible only in terms of electrical surges which were used to flash lights in particular patterns or to drive other electrical receptors.

Today, however, all computers come with standard hookups for attaching a keyboard and a display screen ("monitor"), which are now considered part of the basic computer system itself (even though they remain, with most machines, detachable and may be replaced with substitute units in all cases). Every computer comes with its own built-in routines (sets of instructions) for "addressing" the keyboard and monitor, which are unique to its basic electronic architecture.

Other input/output devices, however, are generically termed "peripherals," and must be connected to the CPU by means of "ports." The computer's hydra-headed operating system includes routines for sending signals to, and/or receiving them from, these ports; but to translate the signals into proper instructions each peripheral must also be equipped with its own microprocessor.

And unfortunately, the degree of standardization of microcomputer ports today is at best variable.

Ports used for storage media, such as disk drives, exhibit the greatest degree of standardization; most such drives, of whatever manufacture or model, can be connected to most computers. This is accomplished by use of an industry-standard "bus," or electronic connector; you can think of the bus as being, like its transportation namesake, a little electronic shuttle for ferrying bits of information back and forth between the CPU and a peripheral, with rigidly fixed "seat assignments" in its interior.

Many microcomputers come with built-in disk drives, with the connector ports inside the casing; those that don't have standardized connectors. But either way, you can only link so many disk drives (usually two or three) to the computer by its specialized ports for that purpose (although some have the capacity to add more such ports; see Appendix F); if you want to add more, you have to run through other ports such as are used for other types of peripherals.

There are basically two types of ports for such purposes: the "parallel" port (like that used for most disk drives), and the "serial" port. The parallel port allows transmission of multiple bits at a time, generally in powers of two beginning with 2^3 (8, 16, 32, etc.—it depends on the type of CPU employed). Serial ports, by contrast, require the bits to queue up like little soldiers and pass through one at a time (in, of course, pre-established sequence). Needless to say, a parallel port, by virtue of its wider "aperture," permits much more rapid information flow than does the serial port.

The type of parallel port in most common usage today is the "Centronics" port—a standardized port used to hook up many printers, plotters, add-on storage media, etc. Most modern microcomputers come with at least one, sometimes two, such ports. Again, because of standardization, most such peripherals will work effectively with most computers irrespective of make or model.

Serial ports, however, must be used for some applications; a modem, for example, must be connected through a serial port, since data bits can only be transmitted over phone lines one at a time. And here standardization effectively disappears, although in a deceptive way.

The deception lies in the fact that serial ports are generally (although not exclusively) standardized to the so-called RS-232 connector, a 25-prong male/female coupler. It would seem, therefore, that you could plug the male connector of any serial-linked peripheral into the corresponding female receptacle of your computer (all microcomputers have at least one RS-232 receptacle, some more than one) and get a valid link-up.

Unfortunately, although the *connectors* are broadly standardized, the *wiring* of those connectors isn't. Different manufacturers use the RS-232's 25 pins in different ways; and many of the pins are not used at all (and in some cases will actually be missing from the male part of the connector).

In some cases this can be corrected through programming changes in your computer's operating system, software, etc., telling it to rearrange the way it sends or receives through the serial port. In others, however, physical cross-wiring is necessary, by means of a "null-modem" interface that routes electric pulses from, say, pin 7 of the peripheral's male connector to pin 20 of the computer's female receptacle. This can make hooking up peripherals through a serial port a difficult and delicate undertaking.

Appendix C

A PRIMER ON BINARY MATH

Because of its technological reliance on the "yes/no," or "0/1," format, the computer has given currency to an arithmetic approach known as binary math.

In binary math all numbers are expressed as strings of "0" and "1," (such as 00100101), the significance of each digit being a function of its position in the string. Reading from right to left, each position represents an incremental "power of two"—2^0 (which, by mathematical convention, equals 1), 2^1 (2), 2^2 (4), etc.

It can readily be seen that every integral number can be represented by combinations of such powers of two; the sum of all previous powers of two invariably adds up to one less than the next-higher power of two (*i.e.,* $2^0 + 2^1 + 2^2$, or $1 + 2 + 4$, equals 7, or 1 less than the next power of two, 2^3, or 8). In binary notation, a "0" in any position indicates that the power of two represented by that position is not used; a "1" indicates that it *is* used. Add up all the powers of two whose positions are designated by a "1" and you have the number being represented.

Thus, the binary 00100101 specifies that you are to add 2^0, 2^2 and 2^5, or $1 + 4 + 32$; it therefore represents the number 37.

As noted, each digit, or position, in binary math notation represents a "bit" of information (a single yes/no decision); eight of them grouped together represent a "byte" (letter of the alphabet, number, punctuation mark, etc.). The range of numbers that can be represented by eight-position binary code is from 0 (binary 00000000) to 255 (binary 11111111). This, it develops, is an ample range to identify a full range of alphabetic letters, numbers, punctuation marks, graphics symbols, etc. (each of which must, of course, be represented by a unique number within the 0-255 spectrum).

You'll seldom have occasion in any computer application to make use of binary notation; even the "machine language" in which computers do their actual "thinking" is expressed in terms of Hex, rather than binary, notation (see Appendix D). But in the final analysis it's the basis for all computer functioning.

Appendix D

HEX CODES—AN EXPLANATION

If you spend much time around computers, you'll sooner or later run across references to "hex codes." You may even have some software that requires hex-coded inputs.

Hex in this context has nothing to do with witchcraft; it's the mathematical symbolism in which programming instructions are encrypted to be stored in, and read by, your computer's central processing unit (CPU). It's a symbolism in which such numbers as "eleventy-eleven" and "twelveteen," which you probably last encountered on the nursery-school playground, actually make perfect sense.

Instead of the normal base-ten numbers with which everyone is familiar, hex codes are numbers built on a base of 16 (the term "hex" being an abridgment of hexidecimal, the name applied to a 16-base numbering system). Thus, instead of the commonplace 10 numerical digits (0, 1, 2, 3, 4, 5, 6, 7, 8 and 9), hex numbers utilize 16 such digits. Since there aren't enough number digits to go around, hex coding employs the letters A through F (almost always written as capitals) as one-digit representations of what we usually designate as 10 through 15.

Thus, you can get some pretty odd-looking hex numbers, such as 1B, C8, ED, etc. (Hex codes for most microcomputers tend to be in two digits.) You can also get some that look deceptively like ordinary numbers—deceptive in that they (like their less ordinary brethren) stand for entirely different arithmetical quantities than you might expect.

In normal base-10 math, two-digit numbers are read by multiplying the first digit by 10 and adding the second digit; thus, $32 = (3 \times 10) + 2$; $79 = (7 \times 10) + 9$; and so forth. In 16-base hex notation, however, the first digit is instead multiplied by 16, and then the second added, so that 32 hex would be $(3 \times 16) + 2$ (or the number we know as 50 in normal math), 79 would be $(7 \times 16) + 9$ (or 123), etc.

By the same token, eleventy-eleven is how we might refer to hex BB ($(11 \times 16) + 11$, or 187); twelveteen might be hex CA ($(12 \times 16) + 10$, or 202).

Longer *(i.e.,* more than two-digit) hex codes are read the same way. In ordinary notation a three-digit number is 10^2 times the first digit plus 10 times the second digit plus the third digit; a four-digit number is 10^3 times the first digit plus 10^2 times the second digit plus 10 times the third digit plus the last digit; and so on. In hex, a three-digit code is 16^2 times the first digit plus 16 times the second plus the third; a four-digit code is 16^3 times digit No. 1 plus 16^2 times No. 2 plus 16 times No. 3 plus No. 4, etc.

Hex numbers are stored, two digits at a crack (each digit pair representing a data byte—that is, a letter of the alphabet, number, punctuation mark, etc.), in individual memory "addresses" in eight-bit computers. Since each address may contain no more than two hex digits, the largest number that can be stored in one address is hex FF, or 255. (That explains, by the way, one of the common limitations you'll find with eight-bit machines, where the largest allowable number of lines in a spreadsheet, the greatest number of characters in a line of BASIC programming, etc., is 255.)

Each such memory address is designated by a four-digit hex code. Thus, the total number of memory addresses is hex FFFF, or 65,536. (And *that* explains why eight-bit machines can have no more than 65,536 bytes—commonly (and not entirely accurately) referenced as "64K"—of random-access memory; there are no additional memory addresses to accommodate more.)

Sixteen- and 32-bit computers, of course, can handle larger numbers of hex digits, both in terms of memory addresses and the number of bits storable in each. Accordingly, they offer substantially greater capacity than do the eight-bit machines.

A couple of other minor points: First, hex codes are always written using all available digit "slots" for which the computer's memory has space. Thus, memory address No. 1 would be designated as hex 0001 (since four digits are allocated for addresses), even though the three prefatory zeroes are as arithmetically meaningless in hex as they are in standard math notation. Similarly, a data byte stored in that address might be identified as 02 or 0A, or even 00, again using prefatory zeroes to "flesh out" the code to the full two digits for which space is allocated.

Second, text references to hex numbers (such as in computer user manuals, etc.) often tag a capital letter "H" at the end of hex codes, such as 00H, 7BH, FFH, etc. The "H" merely identifies the preceding digits as being in hex notation (the same way "°", for example, is used to identify numbers as representing degrees of temperature), and is not itself any kind of numeric symbol.

Appendix E

ALL ABOUT ASCII

"What's Askey?"

I've been asked that question more than once after giving talks about computer uses in transportation/physical distribution. It's not a trivial question, and deserves an answer.

"Askey" is the way you pronounce the computerese acronym ASCII, which in turn stands for American Standard Code for Information Interchange. It's a coding structure that uses the numbers 0 through 255 to various computer keyboard inputs (see Appendix C for the reason why there are precisely 256 codings).

Only the first 128 (0 through 127) of these codings are entirely standardized throughout the industry; the remainder are sometimes used by different machines for different purposes. But 128 codings are quite sufficient to encompass all the normal typographic characters the machine is capable of producing, plus the "control" characters used for command purposes by your hardware and software.

Because of the way computers go about their business, there must be a separate coding for each "version" of any keystroke. Thus, control-A (where you hold down the control key while striking the letter, making it a command symbol) is represented by ASCII 001, capital A by ASCII 065 and lower-case A by ASCII 097. (Common usage is to express all ASCII numbers in three-digit format, adding prefatory zeroes where necessary.) The same holds true for all other letters, numbers, and typographic symbols (periods, commas, quote marks, etc.).

There are also special ASCII codes for the ESCAPE key, the RETURN (or ENTER) key, the space bar, etc. In other words, if you can do it with your keyboard there's a standardized ASCII code for it.

The importance of this standardization lies in its facilitation of inter-computer communications. Because of differences in operating systems, hardware configurations, etc. (see prior discussions), normal computer-language instructions or information is not transferable between different types of machines. A program or data file that works just dandy on one computer will be nothing but garbage if ported over to another.

But if the information in question is expressed in ordinary typographical symbols—letters of the alphabet, numbers, punctuation marks, etc.—ASCII coding will allow it to be transferred intact from any computer to any other. That normally won't help much when it comes to programming, since instructions must generally be machine-specific; but it *does* allow you to electronically swap data files (which don't contain program instructions) either by "hard-wiring" two computers together or through use of a modem (see Appendix A). Thus, you don't have to re-key the entire data file to move it from one machine to another.

An additional value of ASCII standardization is that it must occasionally be used for programming purposes. If you want to tell the program to output a RETURN/ENTER at some junction, for example, you can't just hit that key; the machine will construe it as part of your command sequence, not an output character. But if you tell it to output the character represented by ASCII coding 13, it'll dutifully feed back a RETURN/ENTER.

Appendix F

OPEN AND CLOSED

From time to time, in shopping for computer hardware, you'll hear references to the "box," the "architecture" and the "system architecture" being "open" or "closed." These are important terms, and will significantly affect your ability to use the hardware in the way you want to use it.

The "box" is the container (either metal or some form of hardened plastic) in which the processing unit of your computer is enclosed. It houses, in other words, the basic circuitry, silicon chips, etc., which constitutes the computer's physical brain.

An "open" box is not, of course, actually open; if it were, all that delicate electronic hardware would be exposed to dust, grit, careless spills of coffee and the like, and would soon begin to malfunction. But it's designed to *be* opened, by the removal of a few screws, by the user or anyone else who wants to inspect or fiddle with the contents.

The reason for opening the box is, of course, usually to change things around inside—to perform the electronic equivalent of brain surgery on the computer. With this in mind, manufacturers of open-box computers have left room for additional circuit boards ("expansion slots" into which the boards can be slipped), as well as, in some cases, empty sockets into which retrofit chips or crystals can be plugged, to enhance the computer's power and/or performance. Even a relatively ham-fisted user, lacking in both expertise and experience in dealing with the computer's innards, can with a little care accomplish these simple changes (I've done it myself, and I'm pretty clumsy about such things); usually there isn't even any soldering required.

An open box usually also means open architecture. That is, the manufacturer provides interested outside developers with diagrams and schematics of how its particular computer is designed, so that they can in turn design and produce the boards, chips and/or crystals that will work in the expansion slots and sockets. These "will-fit" add-ons are often as good as, or better than, similar products produced by the OEM ("Original Equipment Manufacturer"), and often sell for a lot less.

Even though an open box and architecture thus tends to detract from the OEM's aftermarket sales, by inviting outside competitors in, he also benefits from this approach—because the user benefits (and is thus more prone to purchase the basic unit from the OEM, even if he buys aftermarket products from other suppliers). It should be self-evident that no one company can hope to be all things to all customers; the outside suppliers often produce add-ons that the OEM either didn't think of or didn't feel would command a broad-based market (because a particular feature was needed only by a few customers). In addition, the competition tends to lead to improved quality in the retrofit boards, chips, crystals, etc., since there are multiple suppliers trying to woo buyers with additional features others don't offer.

Nevertheless, a few computer manufacturers have adopted, as a matter of policy, a closed box and closed architecture. They take the view that only their own trained people are qualified to perform any brain surgery, and they don't want you, the user—or anyone else—messing around inside.

You can fairly readily open a closed box, of course; things are still held together by just a few screws, in order to allow the manufacturer's own people ready access for service or other purposes (although sometimes the screws are of odd design, requiring special tools, in order to further discourage casual tampering). But there's generally some form of "tattletale" to show that you've done so—some kind of seal, such as those used to secure transportation cargoes. If you break the seal, you void the manufacturer's warranty on the machine.

That's not, alone, very much of a deterrent. Computer warranties tend to be short-term (90 days or so), and constrained by so many conditions and limitations as to render them not terribly important. Furthermore, once you have a computer past its initial "burn-in" period (the first few days or weeks of operation), the likelihood of electronic failures gets pretty small. In fact, conventional wisdom in the industry is that a used computer is likely to be more reliable than a new one, since most failures crop up during the very early stages of operation.

Trouble is, if you do open the box up you're not likely to find much room for any add-ons—few or no expansion slots and sockets. Manufacturers of closed-box computers sell their machines pretty much "as is," leaving little or no room for upgrades. If you want more features, they in effect advise, buy another computer that has them; as to any given machine, what you see when you first look at it is more or less what you get.

There's an exception to this rule where the manufacturer produces the machine in multiple models. For economy-of-scale reasons it's usually easier to produce all the models on the same production line, simply adding on to the basic unit, at the end of the line, the boards, chips, etc., that are required for upscale models. This means that if you open the box of your economy model you'll probably find the expansion slots and sockets in place to upgrade your machine to top-of-the-line—if you can get the boards, chips or crystals needed.

Manufacturers of closed-box computers try to keep this market strictly to themselves; that's the main reason they closed the box in the first place. They won't just sell you the parts; they insist on installing them for you (and charge you, of course, extra for doing so). And they keep their machines' architecture closed, too, so that competitors theoretically can't design will-fit parts.

Maintaining a closed-architecture policy; however, is one thing; *keeping* it closed is shoveling sand against the tide. With concentrated effort a good electronic engineer can "decode" the workings of any computer on the market simply by taking apart and studying a production model. And if the machine sells well enough to warrant it, the results of that analysis can easily be used to produce will-fit add-ons as readily as if the manufacturer had provided a full set of design specifications—and usually at considerably lower prices than offered by the OEM (because he's using monopoly pricing on *his* add-ons).

I adopted this route in upgrading the memory of the portable computer I carry on business trips. I'd purchased a machine with below-maximum RAM ("Random-Access Memory"), and found I needed more. The OEM wanted to charge me well over $100 for the upgrade, on top of which I'd have to let them have my machine for at least two weeks to get the job done. Instead I bought a will-fit chip for a quarter as much, broke the seal, opened the machine and stuck it into the waiting slot—a matter of only a few minutes. No fuss or service down-time, not much bother, a 75% saving, and everything works just as well as if I'd spent the extra and gone back to my OEM.

The open/closed system architecture matter is fairly similar, but involves principally software rather than hardware add-ons. Some hardware manufacturers want buyers of their machines to be reliant on them for software as well as hardware; they don't want others competing in that area, either. So they use proprietorial operating systems, the details of which they keep secret, and/or likewise won't disclose key "memory addresses" in the machines' built-in ROM ("Read-Only Memory").

It's still possible for anyone to write software for such machines, simply by using one or more of the programming languages the OEM makes available for the machine. But such software tends to run slowly and inefficiently, because it must perform *every* operation through the filter of the operating system. This particularly retards such processes as updating (or "re-painting") the display screen, disk storage input/output and the like; good software will normally bypass the operating system and issue instructions directly to the proper memory addresses to speed up such procedures, and that's what the closed system architecture discourages.

The OEM's own software, of course, operates under no such handicap; accordingly, it's very likely to be more efficient and, hence, more desirable to prospective purchasers—which is the whole idea.

Operating systems, memory addresses and so on can also be decoded by an experienced analyst, given enough time and (mostly trial-and-error) effort. But this is considerably more difficult than analyzing hard-wired circuitry, since there are no physical linkages (however microscopic) to trace, and manufacturers tend to be more successful at discouraging software competition than they are in the hardware market.

Open system architecture, on the other hand, encourages outside suppliers to develop software for the machines—an obvious benefit to the user, who does not become captive to a single software supplier. The marketing advantage this affords manufacturers of open-system machines is so great (since software availability is a key factor in the buying decision) that virtually all microcomputers on the market today are sold under this policy. A few OEM's still seek to reap at least some additional income by selling details of their system architecture at high prices, but since even this discourages software development it's a practice of dubious value.

Finally, even where the box and all the architecture is open, virtually all manufacturers try to build in safeguards against others copying their whole machine. As should be self-evident, designing and building a new computer "from scratch" entails a lot higher development costs than merely copying someone else's; so the copycat manufacturers tend to have substantially lower costs which they can exploit in pricing their machines *vis-à-vis* the original model; and manufacturers need to protect themselves against this copycat problem.

Mostly this is accomplished by building into the computer's ROM certain features which are protected under copyright law. Several lawsuits—most notably Apple's against Franklin Computer Co.—have confirmed the copyrightability of such information, even though it's in electronic form rather than on paper. Software marketed by the OEM, and sometimes by others, will then be designed to reference these copyrighted ROM addresses. If the addresses contain the OEM's proprietary data, all is well and the software continues to run (and the user won't notice the wasted nanoseconds while the check was made). But if the copyrighted information *isn't* present, everything freezes dead solid and you can't proceed. (A manual reset clears the machine, but the software will do the same thing again any time you try to run it.)

So there's no such thing as 100% compatibility between any two manufacturers' units; even the closest of "clones" won't run every program the original model can handle. Be aware of this if you elect to buy a "work-alike" rather than the machine it professes to imitate, and check out any software in which you have a particular interest before you make your purchase decision.

Appendix G

COMPUTERS AND NUMBERS AND ERRORS

Computers don't think about numbers quite the same way you or I do. Accordingly, they can, and do, come up with "wrong" answers from time to time if programming doesn't allow for, and correct, their errors.

Most of the time—just about all the time, in fact—it will add, subtract, multiply and divide absolutely perfectly, for all intents and purposes. You couldn't ask for greater accuracy.

But every once in a great while, for no apparent reason, it won't. It'll make . . . well, not exactly a mistake, but something that hovers at the fringes of being a mistake—and which, if not allowed for and corrected when it occurs, can ultimately become serious.

The computer, you see, has to go through quite a lot of separate, independent operations in order to do even a fairly simple math problem. First the decimal numbers you input must be translated into the binary 0/1 notation the computer employs. Then the resultant digitalized inputs must be cranked around in various ways within the machine, often at great length (although with such blinding speed that you're scarcely aware that any time has passed at all). Then everything gets translated back into decimal notation, and the result spews forth on the display screen.

And not every part of all that translation can be accomplished perfectly. It's like translating from one human language to another; there may be a perfect, precise word in one language for which there is no exact equivalent in another; so there's a slight, almost unnoticeable garbling when it's translated. Then, if you translate back again to the first language, you may get a little different result; and if you keep going back and forth often enough, you're going to have these tiny mistranslations multiplying until, in time, the original is scarcely recognizable in its re-re-re-re-(etc.)translated incarnation.

That's what can happen with computer math. And the effect is due in large part to the extraordinary precision with which computers work; they won't settle for anything less than the *exact* answer they've calculated.

I don't know enough about the operations of computers to predict when such things will happen. But I do know, from experience, that if you use it long enough sooner or later the computer is going to tell you, in effect, that two and two don't equal four; they equal, instead, 3.99999999999 (and as many 9's as the computer can display).

At this stage, of course, the difference is inconsequential. But keep on working with that 3.9999, etc., and the number of 9's on the tail end will start to shrink. Sooner or later it will become 3.98, then 3.97, and so on, until, if you go on long enough, what started out as the nearest thing the computer could print to a 4 has become closer to a 3. And if you *still* don't pick up the problem you can, obviously, get some off-beat results.

And from there on things can get *really* out of hand.

I once read a science-fiction story in which a computer kept dunning an individual for "$0.00" in money owed. (This has actually happened on a few documented occasions. If you've read what I've written so far carefully, you'll realize that the computer actually thinks, through the kind of math error I've described, that the individual it's dunning owes it something on the order of a billionth of a cent. It's only programmed to print out two decimal places, so the bill comes out as "$0.00"; but if it's also programmed to send out due bills to anyone who owes *anything,* this is the anomaly you can get if the programmer didn't allow for it.)

In any event, in the science fiction story, as in real life, the individual in question ignored the due bills. They mounted up, and time went along until, again automatically, the computer turned the bill over to the (fictitious) legal computer programmed to file lawsuits. As matters progressed the same sort of error led to an again seemingly inconsequential shift in the numeric coding assigned to the lawsuit, so that the judicial computers (in this story *everything* was computerized; I said it was science fiction) misread the charges and believed the accusation to be *much* more serious. Ultimately the individual in question was executed (by computer-driven equipment), notwithstanding that his only real-world "crime" was owing nothing.

The story ends with the computer sending out another balance-due of "$0.00" to someone else.

Obviously, this story was satire. But the occasional math error of this type, as I've already noted, isn't; it's real, and it happens. So if you find, occasionally, that you're getting a lot of unexpected decimal places in the answers your computer offers you, this is where they come from. And you'll also know you're working with a piece of software whose developer didn't make the necessary allowances to eliminate such problems.

Appendix H

EDI

If you want to say it properly, enunciate each letter separately: E-D-I. The trend of transforming acronyms into pronounceable "words" is generally reserved for those that run to more than three letters; thus, EDI is *not* "Eddie."

The letters stand for Electronic Data Transmission, an imposing term that at its root means merely the transfer of data, programming, etc., directly from the memory of one computer to the memory of the other without human mediation of or participation in the transfer process itself. This may be done either by use of modems (see Appendix B), which permit long-distance transfers by phone lines, or by "hard-wiring" the computers together (running physical wires or cables between them).

But EDI in the business world has come to mean considerably more than this. To understand just how and why the definition has evolved you have to understand a little of how computers deal with the information they have in their memories.

Computers are the archtypal tidy housekeeper—"a place for everything, and everything in its place." The slightest misalignment, the tiniest wrinkle in the bedlinens, and the computer gets bent severely out of shape; it can't deal with *anything* that's at all out of synch with the way it thinks things ought to be organized.

So in order to input data into a computer in a way the computer can do anything useful with it, you first have to tell it how you plan to organize your data. Sometimes these instructions are built into the firmware and/or software and require no user intervention; in other cases the user must take a more active role in this "structuring" process. But either way they must be given; and the data must be presented, during the input process, in a form consistent with the structure that's been specified.

It's obvious that any computer worthy of the name must be pretty flexible about data structuring. No one format can accommodate every type of data, and every use to which the user may wish to have the data put. So data structures are extremely "application-specific," and thus extremely variable.

Mere inter-computer transfer of the data alone, thus, is next to useless if the data isn't properly structured for use by the receiving machine. EDI has accordingly been broadened in meaning to encompass not only the actual *data* interchange, but also the appurtenant functions of making sure the participating computers are in accord about how the data is structured.

For that reason, EDI has required the developments of structural standards for the interchange of particular forms of data. If I want to transmit, say, the information on a bill of lading from my computer to yours, I must first put it in the standardized format so your machine (also instructed in the standard) can make productive use of it. Another standard would apply if the data involved were that of a freight bill, another for a loss-and-damage claim, and so on and so forth through a very wide range indeed of applications-based standards.

A number of organizations have developed such standards. In transportation, the most important are the general American National Standards Institute (ANSI) and the industry-specific Electronic Data Interchange Association (EDIA—formerly the Transportation Data Coordinating Committee, or TDCC). Access to, and a working knowledge of, the standards developed under the aegis of these and other organizations is a prerequisite to effective use of EDI.

Secondly, different types, makes and models of computers operate differently; in order to transmit data from one to another they must use various protocols and translators which range from simple to highly complex (depending on the particular computers involved). Again, various standards have been developed and are generally accepted, and knowledge of (and appropriate programming to implement) such standards are essential to DEI applications.

The value of EDI is obvious; a single input will suffice to make data available to as many machines as may be needed. In addition, although not entirely proof against error, EDI transmissions are likely to be much freer of mistakes than human input. As this is written, more and more companies are delving heavily into the potential of EDI to improve their efficiency and reduce labor costs in a wide range of commercial and other areas; and many foresee a day, not terribly far ahead, when the bulk of information interchange is conducted electronically, with human beings intervening only when necessary to interpret and apply the information in the real world.

Index

A

AT computer, 141, 189, 260
Accounting, 5
Algorithmic rates, 8, 49
Amber screen, 255
Analytical modeling, 10, 31
Apple, 62, 68, 75, 94, 145, 158, 167, 185
Apple, DOS, 187
Applewriter, 158
Artificial intelligence, 73
ASCII, 119
Ashton-Tate, 173
Assembly language, 150
Audits, 6, 183

B

Backups, 71, 230, 235, 252
Barrett Transportation Newsletter, 131
Barrett, Alexandra, 68, 153, 157
BASIC, 84, 138, 149, 211
Bible, 29
Bills of lading, 13, 27, 28, 183
"Bombs", 178
Booby-trapped software, 178
Book of Kells, 154
Borland International, 233
Bugs, 253
Bulletin boards, 177, 239, 251
Business Week magazine, 93

C

C programming language, 150
CalcStar, 167
Carrier rate systems, 7
Carter, Jimmy (President), 149
Christensen, Ward, 175
Civil Aeronautics Board, 38
Claims, 13, 27
COBOL, 149
Coleco, 67
Commerce, Department of, 145
Communications software, 25, 83, 175
Compilers, 151
CompuServe, 177, 251
Concurrent DOS, 187
Construction costs, 10
Copy-protection, 191, 196, 233
Costing, 9, 21, 37, 183
CP/M, 62, 116, 187, 250, 254
"Crippled" software, 192
Crosstalk, 223
Customs Service, 145

D

Data storage/retrieval, 25
Data-base managers, 83, 126, 169, 177
da Vinci, Leonardo, 19
dBase, 150, 173, 177
Defense, Department of, 140
Delivery receipts, 13
Delivery scheduling, 21

Depreciation schedules, 13
Directories, 71, 237, 251
Disk drives, 130, 176, 188, 245
Disk formatting, 71
Dispatching, 12, 183
Distribution modeling, 31
Dvorak keyboard, 97
Dynamic Debugging Tool, 254

E

Easywriter, 158
Electric Pencil, 158
Elizabeth (British Queen), 149
Enable, 167
Equipment maintenance, 104
Equipment management, 13
Equipment procurement, 13
Excel, 167

F

Fat Mac, 263
Federal Maritime Commission, 38
Fleet maintenance, 104
Fleet management, 13
FORTRAN, 149
Fortune magazine, 93
Framework, 167
Freight bill audits, 6, 183
Freight bills, 6, 13, 21, 28, 104
Freight consolidation, 12, 20, 28, 104, 183
Fuel taxes, 13

G

Generally Accepted Accounting Principles, 37
Glossbrenner, Alfred, 177
Graphics, 166, 172, 177
Green-phosphor screen, 255

H

Hackers, 46, 83, 119, 137, 175, 238
Hackers, 139
Help screens, 127, 200, 205
Hemingway, Ernest, 154
Hendren, Philip E., 51
Hewlett-Packard, 94
Hexidecimal notation, 150
Highway Form B, 9, 38
Hillary, Edmund (Sir), 102
Home computers, 68
Household Goods Mileage Guide, 12
How to Get Free Software, 177
Hunter, Stephen R., 132

I

IBM, 67, 69, 84, 145, 176, 187, 189, 260, 263, 264
Industrial site location, 9
Intel, 260fn
International Trade Commission, 145
Interstate Commerce Commission, 5, 6, 9, 24, 38, 53fn, 54
Inventory management, 11

J

Jazz, 167
Johnson, Sam. (Dr.), 114
"Just-in-time", 11

K

Kanban, 11
Kaypro, 210
Keyboard customization, 96, 176
"Keyboardphobia", 91
KnowledgeMan, 173

L

Labor costs, 10
Levy, Steven, 139
Light pen, 94
Lisa, 94
Lotus 1-2-3, 167, 176, 231
Lotus Development Co, 231

M

MacWrite, 158
Machine language, 150
Macintosh, 62, 63, 75, 94, 159, 167, 261, 263
Management Information Systems departments, 61, 108, 113
Manifests, 13
Market dominance, 9
Mathematical applications, 5
Matrix rates, 47
Modem, 25, 119, 124, 131, 257
Modula C, 150
Mouse, 94
MP/M, 116
MS-DOS, 62, 117, 125, 187, 216, 250
MultiMate, 158
MultiPlan, 167

N

NewWord, 158

O

Oasis Systems, 160
Official Directory of Industrial and Commercial Traffic Executives, 53fn
Operating licenses, 13
Operating systems, 71, 125, 187, 264
Order processing, 11
Osborne Computer Corp, 231

P

"Parasite" programs, 142
Pascal, 150, 233
Passwords, 137
PC, 69, 167, 176, 189, 260, 264
PC-DOS, 117, 125, 187, 264
PCjr, 68
PeachText, 158
Peddle-run service, 12
Penn Central Railroad, 102
Perfect Writer, 158
pfs:File, 173
pfs:Write, 158
Pick operating system, 62, 187
Pickup-and-delivery scheduling, 21
Portable computers, 24
Practical Handbook of Transportation Contracting and Rate Negotiations, 236
Print spoolers, 175
Printer, 124
ProKey, 96
Programming, 81, 117, 149, 203
Projection screen, 108, 111
Prompts, 71, 125
Public-domain software, 167, 175, 238, 251

Q

Qwerty keyboard, 98

R

R:Base, 173
Radio Shack, 68
Rail Form A, 9, 38
RAM disk, 176, 245
Rate bureaus, 7, 42, 51
Rate computerization, 45
Rate storage/retrieval, 6, 28, 45, 172
Real estate costs, 10
Regression analysis, 55
Rocky Mountain Motor Tariff Bureau, 51
Routing, 12, 183
RS-232, 132

S

Security, 6, 137
Serial port, 132
Shareware, 234
Shipment documentation, 13, 27
Sidekick, 234
SmartKey, 96
Software customization, 194
Software piracy, 191, 229
Source, The, 132, 177, 251
Spreadsheets, 25, 83, 117, 126, 163, 170, 177
Staggers Rail Act, 9
Standard Point Location Code, 52
Strategic planning, 28
Sulzberger, Arthur Hays, 19
SuperCalc, 163, 177
Symphony, 167

T

Tandy, 68
Tariff simplification, 45
Tariffs, 6, 21, 27, 45
Taxes, 10, 13
Telephone lines, 257
Templates, 167, 176
Texas Instruments, 67
Text processor, 155
Time magazine, 69
Time management, 23
Toolworks operating system, 187
Touch-screen, 94
Traffic Service Corp., 131, 257
Traffic World magazine, 42, 51, 101, 161, 199, 253
Traffic World's Practical Software, 197
TRS-DOS, 187
Turbo Pascal, 150, 233
Turnkey systems, 105, 124

U

Unerase utilities, 176, 238
Uniform Rail Costing System, 9, 39
UNIX, 62, 187
Upgrades, 259
User ID, 138
User groups, 177, 239
User manuals, 72, 129, 177, 189, 200, 203, 213, 215, 222
User support, 186, 190, 215
User-friendliness, 40, 62, 74, 105, 126, 189, 200, 203

V

"Vaporware", 224

VisiCalc, 167
Voice-recognition technology, 95
Volkswriter, 158

W

WarGames, 140
Waybills, 13
Wall Street Journal, 113
Word, 158
Word Juggler, 158
Word Perfect, 158
Word Plus, 160
Word processing, 5, 24, 26, 83, 126, 153, 170, 177, 217
WordStar, 158, 222, 223
"Worms", 178, 197
WRITE, 158

X

XENIX, 187
XMODEM, 175
XT computer, 108, 189, 260
XYWrite, 158

Z

Z-80 processor, 210
ZIP Codes, 46, 51, 54